R.E.M.

REVEAL
THE
STORY
OF
R.E.M.

R.E.M.

REVEAL
THE
STORY
OF
R.E.M.

JOHNNY BLACK

R.E.M. REVEAL THE STORY OF R.E.M.

Johnny Black

A BACKBEAT BOOK
First edition 2004
Published by Backbeat Books
600 Harrison Street,
San Francisco, CA94107, US
www.backbeatbooks.com

An imprint of The Music Player Network United
Entertainment Media Inc.

Published for Backbeat Books by Outline Press Ltd,
Unit 2a Union Court, 20-22 Union Road, London, SW4 6JP, England.
www.backbeatuk.com

ISBN 0-87930-776-5

ART DIRECTOR: Nigel Osborne
EDITOR: John Morrish
DESIGN: Paul Cooper Design
EDITORIAL DIRECTOR: Tony Bacon

Origination and Print by Colorprint Offset (Hong Kong)

03 04 05 06 07 5 4 3 2 1

CONTENTS

Chapter One

The End of The World As They Knew It

"When Bill Berry
was ill, our dominant
concern was his
health. But, when
you're faced with
mortality like that,
you have to consider
the future."
MIKE MILLS ■

Trouble ahead: Peter Buck on the Monster tour, 1995

The moment when R.E.M.'S world fell apart is etched unforgettably into the brain of guitarist Peter Buck. "Bill just kind of collapsed, pretty much into my arms," remembers Buck. "I was holding him, he was kind of shaking a little bit. He wasn't exactly convulsing, but his body was vibrating and there were tears in his eyes. He kept saying, 'My head. My head.'"

In 1995, R.E.M. were the most acclaimed band on the planet. Their Monster tour, in support of the worldwide chart-topping album of the same name, was conceived as a massive planet-wide campaign that would bulldoze its way across three continents.

When it had set off from the Entertainment Centre, Perth, Western Australia, on January 13th, it was probably the hottest ticket of the international rock calendar, and it looked to be unstoppable.Instead, it came screaming to a halt on the night of March 1st at the Patinoire De Malley Auditorium, Lausanne, Switzerland, when drummer Bill Berry unexpectedly lurched into Peter Buck's arms. The set had been proceeding smoothly until, towards the end of the song 'Tongue', Buck noticed that Berry's drum tempo had begun inexplicably speeding up and slowing down.

"I looked back and Bill looked to be kind of confused," he says. "The next song was to be an acoustic song where Bill would come out and play bass, and he came out from behind the drums, and he was holding his head."

"I was sitting at the keyboards," recalls Mike Mills, "and he just never made it to the bass. He sort of went down to one knee, and I could see that he was in some serious pain."

Berry was prone to severe migraines, so Buck's first reaction was to assume that this was another of those - painful, distracting, but not dangerous. Within seconds, though, Buck was beginning to realise that no migraine had ever affected Berry quite so seriously.

"I thought maybe something had fallen on his head. I was checking, looking for blood. I looked towards the side of the stage and everyone was standing there with their mouths open. It seemed like I spent an hour just holding him, and I motioned people to come on and said, 'There's something wrong. Get an ambulance right now. Get a doctor.'"

Despite the searing pain, Berry remained conscious throughout the whole unfolding drama. "It felt as if a bowling ball had hit me," he revealed later. "Just unbelievable pain. It was so bad that I fell over and they had to carry me off."

"Everyone was stunned, concerned and scared," is how Grant Lee Phillips, leader of support band Grant Lee Buffalo summed up the general mood, "while trying real hard to be optimistic."

Thinking on his feet, vocalist Michael Stipe sensibly relayed to the audience what he believed to be the likeliest cause of the problem – that Bill was suffering from a severe migraine. His words had the desired effect of calming the crowd, and the band carried on as professionally as they could under the circumstances.

Behind their relatively calm facade, the three remaining members of R.E.M. were already beginning to realise that they might soon have a terrifying decision to make. The man who had been their dear friend and rock-solid bandmate for more than 15 years was being led away into the darkness of the wings of the theatre with an unknown medical condition, potentially crippling or maybe even fatal, racking his brain. As Stipe, Buck and Mills watched him go, the immediate emotional response was to go with him, but a quarter turn of their heads reminded the trio that in front of them were 24,000 over-excited fans who had waited years to see R.E.M. play.

Looking back at it now, Buck reasons, "If it had happened before people were in the hall, we'd have probably cancelled the show. But I just felt that if we walked off

We did the acoustic set about four times longer than it should have been — because we had to

it could spark something really bad, you know? What if there's a riot, someone gets killed … You wouldn't want there to be a stampede, and people might die, or there might be a fire. So we decided to keep going."

The one small crumb of comfort was that, in one sense, Berry couldn't have chosen a much better moment in the set at which to collapse. The next song, 'Country Feedback', signalled the start of the acoustic portion of the show. "He was taken off and we did the acoustic set about four times longer than it should have been," says Buck, "because we didn't have anything else we could do. Then they said that Bill wouldn't be able to come back on, so we got Joey Peters, the drummer from Grant Lee Buffalo to get up and play the set with us."

Peters had seen and heard R.E.M. play often enough to be familiar with the songs, and he stepped into the breach admirably, but Buck still had to "stand in front of him and count him off, nodding at him, giving him hand signals. I'd love to hear a tape of it."

Running largely on nervous energy, and determined to satisfy the audience, R.E.M. played a set that was probably a little longer than normal but, as soon as they could leave the stage, all three hurried to the side of their stricken friend, who was still backstage. "There was a doctor taking care of him," says Buck. "They still didn't know what was going on, and they took him to the hospital after that. They couldn't do a full examination at first. They just had him sedated and stuff until the next morning." And then the waiting began.

According to Berry, even when he woke up in the University Hospital Centre of Vaud the next morning, the seriousness of his condition had still not been diagnosed. "It was, 'Oh, a rock star who's collapsed onstage last night and he still has a headache this morning.'"

"His neck hurt," remembers Mills, "which is a very, very bad sign. It's an indication that an aneurysm has burst."

It was early afternoon on March 3rd before the band was told that Berry's suffering was indeed being caused by the bursting of an aneurysm – a blood-filled sac that can form on the wall of a weakened blood vessel. "It's something you can have all your life and you never know anything about it," explains Buck, "until the moment when it bursts."

What can we do to make sure he doesn't die?

Stipe, Mills and Buck elected to remain in Lausanne with Berry, but the machinery of the tour was rolling relentlessly on, even without them. Grant Lee Phillips recalls how, "By the time we got the news, we were already in Zurich, the next date on the itinerary. Fortunately, Switzerland possesses the best when it comes to this type of surgery."

While it's true that, in terms of medical expertise, Berry could hardly have chosen a better country in which to suffer an aneurysm, it didn't swing into action with the clockwork efficiency for which is Switzerland is famed. "They couldn't do the operation that day, for some reason," notes Buck, "so we all gathered and it was obvious we were going to have to cancel shows."

"At a moment like that," points out Mills, "you don't think. You just hope he's going to be all right. It's just a case of 'What can we do to make sure he doesn't die?' The reality, though, is that all you can do is be there for him and try to make sure he gets the best care possible."

R.E.M.'s show-must-go-on pluck of the night before was rapidly evaporating as they began to grasp the full, frightening potential of Berry's condition. Even with the best possible treatment, no-one could rule out long-term brain damage, paralysis and even death.

"When Bill Berry was ill, our dominant concern was his health," said Mills later. "But, when you're faced with mortality like that, you have to consider the future. Would Bill still be able to play? Would he still want to play? But nobody ever said, 'Oh my God, let's quit the band.'"

Before the day was out, however, harder hearts than R.E.M.'s were already weighing up the financial implications of his collapse. "People from outside the band's organisation were saying, 'Let's get another drummer in …'" remembers Buck, with evident distaste. "But we weren't going to do that. That's not the way it works."

Warner Brothers Records was quick to issue an official statement: "Following overnight observation by Swiss doctors, an examination revealed that Berry, 36, had suffered a ruptured aneurysm (subarachnoid haemorrhage) on the right hand outside surface of his brain. There was no internal bleeding. On Friday, March 3 an operating team performed a craniotomy. This is a micro-surgical procedure in which the aneurysm is clipped, securing it against any further bleeding. The operation was uneventful and 100 per cent successful and the doctors are happy with Berry's recovery."

Although it appeared that neither his brain nor body had been impaired, all remaining European dates were cancelled on March 6th, because Bill was required to spend the next week to ten days recuperating in Switzerland. "So we just cancelled and sat around and waited," remembers Buck, "and it was not always good news. He had to go back and be operated on a second time: it was really scary. But we all felt we couldn't go home. We couldn't just leave him over in Switzerland. We got to know Lausanne, Switzerland, really well."

Berry's recovery, however, was more rapid than anyone had any right to expect. MTV news was able to report on March 12th that he was "up on his feet Friday at the Swiss hospital where he's recuperating", and that "his prognosis continues to look good, although he's still experiencing intense headaches and some swelling …"

His physical symptoms, however, were only half of the story. "There was a kind of spiritual ordeal I went through," he subsequently told *Mojo* magazine. "Lying in a hospital bed for three weeks made me look at things a little differently and shift priorities. I used to be so excited about going into the studio, I couldn't sleep the night before. But I was getting to the point where I couldn't sleep because I was worried about why I wasn't happy."

A news report of March 21st confirmed that Berry's condition had now improved to the point where he had been released from hospital in Switzerland. Berry himself has described the moment when the doctors told him he could be discharged. "They said, 'As long as your vision's not impaired and your memory's OK, you're fixed.' It's like a flat tyre. It goes flat, you put on a brand-new tyre, and there's no reason to think you're going to have any problems. I'm just trying to put it out of my mind and just go on."

Ahead of him lay a further three weeks of rest and recuperation at home in Georgia. On April 16, MTV news was able to report that he had been playing golf and tennis, attended the finals of the Masters tournament, and had even practiced with the band in anticipation of resuming the world tour on May 15th Although his health was now no longer a serious concern, the weeks he spent off the road had brought about a radical change in Bill Berry. The prospect of spending the rest of his life shuttling around the world as a member of R.E.M. no longer seemed to hold much glamour for him. As he explained in a 1997 interview, he had come to the realisation that he was "looking forward to maybe a simpler life". But he was uncertain of exactly how and when he should reveal that feeling to his bandmates.

The Monster tour did indeed resume on May 15th, at the Shoreline Amphitheater, Mountain

View, San Jose, California. Out front in the audience, it seemed as if half of the rock world had turned out to welcome Berry back to active duty. Neil Young, Sheryl Crow, Metallica's Kirk Hammett, Green Day's Billie Joe Armstrong and Mark Eitzel were all there, willing him on.

Scene magazine critic Lynne Thompson reported, "Drummer Bill Berry, fully recuperated from the brain aneurysm and subsequent surgery that halted the band's world tour last March, was behind his drum kit once again, to begin the group's jaunt across North America. Thankfully, he's now able to joke about the burst blood vessel that forced him off a stage in Switzerland. Throughout the show he hammed it up, feigning convulsions and collapsing each time lead singer Michael Stipe turned to inquire about his health."

In truth, all that Thompson and the audience were seeing was Bill Berry the trouper, the loyal friend and compatriot who was determined not to let his band down at such a vital time. But, as he told *SonicNet Music News* a couple of years later, "I just didn't have that same drive to go in and work like I used to. It's hard to describe, but I realized that there was something just very ghastly wrong. I wasn't enthused about it. I thought maybe this was a phase, maybe I don't want to bring this up right now. But months later, I felt the same way."

Meanwhile, though, the show had to go on. Although Stipe and Mills also suffered their share of illness during this second leg of the Monster tour, when it rolled to an end on November 21st, at The Omni, Atlanta, Georgia, the 69 US dates alone had grossed $45m. Financially and creatively it was a triumph. To the outside world, it appeared that, with Bill Berry restored to full health and good humour, all was well again within the ranks of R.E.M.

But the real fall out from Bill Berry's long weeks of staring death in the face would not hit the band until many months later, on the eve of starting work on the new album, eventually to be titled *Up*.

The sessions were to begin at John Keane Studios in Athens, so Peter Buck flew in from his home in Seattle and booked into a local hotel. Installed in his room, he answered the phone on the evening of Sunday, October 5th, and found himself listening to a clearly uncomfortable Mike Mills trying to prepare him for some sort of shock. Having been a close friend of Berry's since high school, Mills had got wind of the fact that the drummer was about to make an announcement that the others really wouldn't want to hear.

The following day, at rehearsal, he revealed that he had decided to quit the band. As Stipe recalled it, "Bill came in and said, 'I've got some news.' We did not accept it at face value that he wanted to leave the band. We kind of challenged him to stay."

For Buck, the notion of an R.E.M. without Berry came as a bolt from the blue. It was unthinkable. "He came and told us that he didn't want to do it any more, but he wanted us to continue, because he knew we were ready to do it. I just never foresaw that. I could see that he didn't want to do it, but I thought he would do it anyway. For me, it seems like it's a great job. Why would you want to give it up? He quit on the first day of the recording sessions, so it threw into question exactly what we were going to do. I think he'd talked to Mike about it, but I didn't know."

Mills confirms that he had known about Berry's change of heart. "There were certainly a lot of things about being in a band that he didn't like. I think he was given the time after the Monster tour to reflect on what he'd been though. It finished in 1995, and well, we'd spoken of it and I knew after that tour that he wasn't thrilled with it.

"I knew he was thinking about quitting at some point. I didn't think it would happen that fast, but I'm sure there's nothing like a brush with death to make you want to ensure that your life is as satisfying to you as it possibly can be."

Shortly after, the recording sessions were abandoned and Berry's departure became public knowledge when he told an R.E.M. website, *Remnants*, that "I pretty much presented to these guys the idea that I wasn't really as enthusiastic about doing this as I once was. It was [the rest of the band's] opinion that they were ready to keep doing this, which is great. I didn't want to be the schmuck that broke up R.E.M."

"Bill was embarrassed about it," said Stipe later. "He was afraid the band was going to break up because of it. He felt bad about it. Bill said if it was going to break up the band he would keep playing drums and be miserable."

In the official statement for the world's media, Berry declared, "I loved my 17 years with R.E.M. but I'm ready to reflect, assess, and move on to a different phase of my life. The four of us will continue our close friendship and I look forward to hearing their future efforts as the world's biggest R.E.M. fan."

In an MTV interview shortly afterwards, however,

I loved my 17 years with R.E.M. but I'm ready to reflect, assess and move on to a different phase

he was able to be more open about his feelings. "I feel horrible about it. But it's what I feel in my heart. And I feel like it's the fair thing to do … for these guys anyway. I just don't want to go in there and work at 50 per cent capacity, when everyone else is at 100 per cent."

It had long been an R.E.M. tenet that, if any member of the band was to leave, the band would cease to operate; so all four members of the band were now pitched into a battle between heart and head. Their hearts were saying, "Bill can't leave. An R.E.M without Bill Berry isn't R.E.M." Their heads were saying, "Bill has every right in the world to leave if it's what he needs to do."

That dilemma was soon being reflected in their statements to the media. Stipe, for example, was able to intellectually rationalize Berry's decision, saying, "It's kind of documented that people who have near death experiences tend to reprioritize. It definitely puts a different angle on your life."

Emotionally, however, the impact was shattering. "It really threw us for a loop and shocked us," he told Michael Goldberg of *Addicted To Noise*, "sent us into this spiraling, tumultuous, chaotic mindset."

Asked if he could understand what might have driven Berry to make such a decision, Buck now admits that he had been aware of changes coming over the drummer. "He had been unhappy with a lot of stuff. He didn't like meeting new people, he didn't like travelling, he'd got to the point where he didn't like being in recording studios, hated doing videos, hated having his picture taken, doing interviews … Basically he just didn't like anything that you have to do when you're in a band."

"If Bill had died in Switzerland when he was ill, we probably wouldn't have gone on," said Mills at the time. "Bill is an adult making a totally adult decision. And he's leaving because he's tired of it. And we accept that. There's no reason for us not to do it any more, because we're still excited about what we're doing."

Trying to put a brave face on it, Stipe declared, "I think it's a very courageous move for Bill

Bill is an adult making a totally adult decision . . . and we accept that

to make. We're backing him in his decision, as sad as it is. It's a positive, because he'll be a lot happier out of the band, and we'll be able to continue without him with his blessing." Beneath this outward appearance of calm acceptance and understanding, however, the remnants of R.E.M. were riven with confusion, frustration and repressed anger. Berry's departure pushed the most highly respected rock band in the world to the brink of tearing itself apart.

Stipe told the UK's *Radio Times* in June of 2003, "It took a lot out of us when Bill left. It's complicated but, basically, we rushed into being a trio. It didn't work, and the emotional landscape of the band was sad and po-faced."

Stipe's recollection is a masterpiece of understatement. The band was, in fact, fast becoming dysfunctional. And with Stipe plunged into an extended period of writer's block, the next album would be the hardest they'd ever make. If R.E.M. were to survive at all, they would effectively have to re-invent themselves and completely change the way they worked. And the only man who could make them do it wasn't even in the band.

R.E.M.

Chapter Two

Let's Go To Church

"I could stay up as late as I wanted to. I could wake up whenever I wanted to. I thought it was heaven on earth."
BILL BERRY

Home turf: back in Athens, 1986

As anyone with even a passing interest in R.E.M. knows, the university town of Athens, situated on the banks of the Oconee River in north east Georgia, is the band's spiritual home.

The area now known as Athens was previously Cedar Shoals, a small settlement at the foot of the North Georgia mountains, located on the intersection of a Cherokee trading trail and the Oconee. The days of Cedar Shoals, however, were clearly numbered by 1801, when work started on building the University of Georgia on the top of a nearby hill.

Athens was incorporated as a city on December 8th, 1806, on and around the site of the new university campus, and by 1860 it had become the seventh most populated city in the state, home to 3,486 people, of whom 1,955 were white and 1,890 were slaves. Do the arithmetic and you'll see there's one inhabitant missing – the one free black man living in Athens at the time.

Right from the start, as befits a centre of learning and culture, this was a town blessed with more than its fair share of free-thinking people. At the top of one steep cobblestone street, for example, a tree stands behind a fence that was erected in 1875 at the instigation of one William H. Jackson. He so loved this tree that he couldn't bear the thought of it ever being cut down. Jackson also arranged for a sign to be attached to the fence, reading, "For and in consideration of the great love I bear this tree and the great desire I have for its protection for all time, I convey entire possession of itself and all land within eight feet of the tree on all sides." In other words, the tree owns itself and the land around it. That's the kind of town Athens is.

Like many southern cities, however, it also has a past that is steeped in blood. On February 16th, 1921, John Lee Eberhart, a young black farm worker accused of murdering a white woman, was dragged from the county jail on Washington Street by a 3,000-strong mob. It proceeded to burn Eberhart at the stake before his guilt or innocence could be established. At that time in Georgia, a total of 40 such lynchings a year was not unusual. To Athens' credit, Eberhart's killers were, in the main, out-of-towners drawn from neighbouring boroughs by the scandal, and intent on devilment from the start.

Athens had grown to accommodate about 50,500 people when the future members of R.E.M. converged there in January 1979. The university remained the heart of the town, but the local economy now also benefited from poultry processing, and the manufacture of clocks, watches, radios and textiles.

It was a town still proud of its Colonial mansions, its welcoming and sociable campus quads, tree-lined streets, rocking chairs on front porches, friendly secondhand bookshops and mouth-watering fried chicken.

The only native-born Georgian in R.E.M. is John Michael Stipe, who arrived on Earth on

January 4th, 1960, in Decatur. A slightly younger settlement than Athens, Decatur was found-ed in 1823 and managed to retain some of its historic character by turning down an offer to become a major railroad stop in the 1830s. The railway terminus was thus moved seven miles west, and the city of Atlanta grew around it, rapidly outstripping Decatur to become the state capital in 1868.

Not that any of this mattered much to the young Stipe, because by the mid-1960s his family had relocated to Copperas Cove, near Dallas, Texas. Then, before he had time to get used to the Lone Star State, he and his sisters Lynda and Cyndi were moved again, spending the latter part of that decade in Germany. Then came another spell in Georgia, before moving to Collinsville, Illinois, in 1973. They weren't on the run from the law, just being shifted about the face of the planet at the whim of the US military. Michael's father was serving in the US Air Force.

Much has been made about the effects this had on Michael, allegedly making it difficult for him to maintain lasting friendships, turning him into an inward-looking personality, making him reliant on his family and, on the positive side, instilling him with a remarkable pragmatism which enables him to ride through dramatic changes in personal circumstances that might crip-ple a less self-sufficient per-sonality.

Although he has charac-terised his young life as "unbelievably happy" Michael has displayed a curi-ous reluctance to talk about his childhood, which means that only snapshots of his early development are available

Is he really of Cherokee descent? Did his great - grandad really die of falling on his axe?

from his perspective. What's more, his wickedly dry sense of humour (apparently inherited from his father) means that not everything he says comes with a guarantee of veracity. Is he really of Cherokee descent? Did his great-grandad really die of falling on his axe? Was his great-grand-mother an opera singer? Did he really write backwards until sixth grade?

It seems a reasonably well-founded fact that the family was a loving one, in which even Michael's hatred of war was something he could discuss with his father without descending into bitterness or rancour. "My father was gone at war in Vietnam and in Korea during my child-hood," he told me when I interviewed him for this book, "although that didn't affect our rela-tionship at all as father and son. It was always difficult when he came back and it was hard on him and hard on us, obviously, to have him gone for that long."

Michael is very close, too, to Lynda and Cyndi, to such an extent that when Peter Buck first encountered the trio, he assumed they were his girlfriends. He has described himself in childhood as "a little charmer" but by the time he hit his mid-teens, he had transformed into a "nebbish Woody Allen type" who was aware of – and comfortable with – his bisexuality.

His musical evolution is equally interesting. His parents displayed solid middle-American tastes, running from Gershwin to gospel to movie soundtracks, but with a smattering of popular classics thrown in. So it's not surprising that, asked to name the first song he ever heard, Michael plumped for Henry Mancini's middle-of-the-road classic 'Moon River', from the movie *Breakfast At Tiffany's*.

His spell in Texas saw him and his sisters benefiting from a friendship with a local record store owner, Mr Pemberton, who handed out freebies of Tammy Wynette, Roger Miller, The Beatles and Elvis Presley, thus exposing young Michael to rock'n'roll and country. He was struck too by bubblegum pop, 'Yummy Yummy Yummy' by the Ohio Express being cited as a particular favourite.

On February 2, 1976, *Horses*, the debut album by New York City's famed punk poetess Patti Smith, peaked at No 47 in the US album chart. Michael Stipe, now living in Illinois, had bought that album on the day it was released, and felt his world begin to open up. He has described it as "an epiphanal discovery. It was like the ground fell from under me - honestly. I can trace it back to 'Birdland', a song on that first album. It was like the ground didn't exist. At that moment I decided what I would do with my life, with all the arrogance of a 15-year-old who'd never written a song."

At that moment I decided what I would do with my life

New York City now became something of a musical focus for him. He was already a subscriber to the Greenwich Village-based bohemian newspaper *The Village Voice*, which was where he had first read about Patti, and the paper was feeding his vivid imagination with all sorts of other fuel. "As a teenager exploring my sexuality, trying to figure out who the fuck I was, to have people like Patti Smith, the New York Dolls, Iggy Pop and Marc Bolan – it meant the world, you know?"

On March 4th, 1977, another pioneering New York new wave outfit, Television, released their debut album, *Marquee Moon*, which Michael lapped up voraciously, finding it to be, "Just the most angular, the most brittle and brutal thing I'd ever heard. Then I picked up on the people who influenced them – The Velvets, Stooges and Dolls and so on."

Now he was off and running, emancipated from parental tastes, with a whole world of his own to explore. By the time he was 18 he had even joined a local Illinois band called Bad Habits, who performed punk covers, but this fell apart when the family moved again, this time to Watkinsville, a stone's throw from Athens. By the time he enrolled at the University of Georgia on January 4th, 1979, his long curly hair was bleached blond band and he was affecting the dark-glasses-all-day look so beloved of the Velvet Underground. He had, of course, no way of knowing that two other young men, Mike Mills and Bill Berry, had also enrolled on the same day, or that a certain Peter Buck was working as manager of Wuxtry Records, a second hand vinyl store at the intersection of College Avenue and Clayton Street.

All four members of R.E.M. were now in one place, and it was one hell of a place. Despite its small size, Athens had been making giant ripples on the national US rock scene since Valentine's Day in 1977. That was the night the B-52s played their first gig, at a party in a house on Milledge Avenue where, according to founder member Cindy Wilson, "People were dancing so hard the floor was like a trampoline."

The B-52s' raucous, surf-inflected party hits, 'Rock Lobster' and 'Loveshack', put Athens on the rock map, but it's fair to say that the scene was already there, waiting to happen. "It isn't like other southern towns," pointed out their drummer Keith Strickland, in a 2003 interview with the *Washington Post*. "It isn't now and it wasn't then. The university draws people here, and it's full of outrageous characters and all this creative energy. There were always eccentrics in Athens, but we took it out onto the streets."

Another significant development came on Halloween night in 1978, when Curtis Crowe and Bill Tabor, two tenants of an apartment block largely occupied by art students on College Square, charged admission to a party up on the top floor. The room was lit by a single light bulb, so they christened the establishment the 40 Watt Club.

Shortly thereafter, Crowe became drummer for a fledgeling band called Pylon, who played their first gig on March 9th, 1979, rapidly moving into the space vacated by the B-52s when they left town to go national. This was the start of the first great musical surge in Athens. "Everybody and his brother was forming a band," is how Bill Berry recalls it, and it wasn't long before, with dozens of bands in town, instead of playing records at parties, students would invite a band along to play.

For Peter Buck, this was a golden age. "You could go and see Pylon, one of the greatest bands in the world, and there'd be 100 people there." Not only this but, as with all golden ages, "Beer was 90¢ and it was $1 to get in."

By May of 1979, just five months after hitting town, Bill Berry was drumming for The WUOGerz, a garage band closely affiliated to the campus radio station, WUOG.

Within the year, R.E.M. would spring into existence, and in their wake came the second generation of Athens rockers, including Love Tractor, Side Effects, Method Actors, Dreams So Real, and Widespread Panic. And, from the surrounding area, bands like Guadalcanal Diary, Indigo Girls and Let's Active came to be considered as part of the Athens scene.

The history of geographically based rock scenes is littered with small towns that flourished for a couple of years and, almost invariably, withered and died. Athens, astonishingly, didn't. As recently as 2003, *Rolling Stone* magazine chose it as the best college music town in the USA. "It's not just alternative music either," notes Pete McCommons, editor of local entertainment weekly *The Flagpole*. "There's a pretty active jazz scene, there's country rock and bluegrass."

The little town that could still supports over 40 clubs, theatres, bars, cafes and other venues, from the large Georgia Theatre to the tiniest of coffee houses, and clubs as diverse as Tasty World, The Firehouse, The Globe and yes, The 40 Watt.

But back in the spring of 1979, the melting pot was just starting to bubble.

Peter Lawrence Buck, the oldest member of R.E.M., was born on December 6, 1956, in Oakland, on the east side of the San Francisco Bay in California. I won't go into detail on the history of Oakland, because Buck didn't stay long enough for its culture, society or geography to have much discernible influence on him, except perhaps that he was aware of the existence of hippies from an early age.

His earliest memory of music, however, does date back to those West Coast days. "When we lived in Richmond, which is near Berkeley, there used to be a show on K-FOG, the San Francisco channel. It was a Sunday afternoon big band show, where they'd do an hour-long show on one particular big band leader or singer. My dad liked that kind of stuff, so I remember hearing Glenn Miller and Tommy Dorsey. I remember the Frank Sinatra one very well. It was fairly conservative music, but I remember realising that, wow, these people have lives and they have stories, and they make music. This is pretty interesting."

An even more significant influence from those times is the fact that his parents set him on the road to rock'n'roll by giving him a transistor radio when he was five years old. "The thing that first blew my mind," he recalls, "was when I first heard The Beatles when I was about six. That was the first time I heard 'She Loves You'. I had this little radio. I was standing in the street and it came on, and I was like, 'Man, what is this?' I think that was the moment when I decided I'd like to make music."

Courtesy of his little radio, The Beatles, The Byrds and The Supremes filled his head late every night under the bedclothes and, in common with Stipe,

I used to see every show
that came through town

he wasn't averse to a little bit of bubblegum pop, The Monkees being his earliest introduction to the genre.

The Bucks moved to Indiana when Peter was nine, and they'd moved again to Atlanta by the time he was 13. Already in striking distance of Athens, he now took an interest in a peculiarly British phenomenon: glam rock.

In an early-1970s, when America was dominated by worthy singer-songwriters in denim, acts like T.Rex and Mott The Hoople seemed to him like "a message from another planet." And he liked the look of that planet.

Not that he was entirely averse to singer-songwriters. Around this time he was also intrigued by the likes of Neil Young and Van Morrison, exploring the Rolling Stones and, like his distant soul-mate, Michael Stipe, he was getting into the Velvet Underground.

Peter also took an early interest in avant-garde music, in particular the compositions of the weird and wonderful innovator Harry Partch, who not only built his own bizarre instruments, but also composed according to a 43-note tonal system entirely of his own devising.

It may be simplistic to suggest that this early exposure to tuneful pop and exotic modern composition has remained the key to everything Buck has done since, in and out of the context of R.E.M., but it's also hard to resist.

He dabbled with guitars, played in a high school band and went to gigs at every opportunity. "I used to see every show that came through town, you know, like, at the Municipal Auditorium. I saw things I'd never even heard of. I'd never listen to Johnny Winter, but I went to see him. " On October 4th, 1973, he went to the Auditorium to see Mott The Hoople, but was more taken by their support band, the New York Dolls. "Mott were horrible, and the Dolls were by any definition wretched, but I thought they were wonderful."

In a 1981 interview he went further, declaring that particular Dolls performance to have been "the No 1 experience in my life", adding, "The thing that was so important about them was that they weren't stars and didn't go through that whole solo trip. They staggered around and missed chords but the magic was there. They were the one band that influenced me the most."

Then, in December 1975, he did precisely the same thing as Michael Stipe – he bought the first Patti Smith album on the day it was released. Much as she had done with Stipe, Smith fanned the flames of Buck's interest in the New York New Wave, and that spilled over into a fascination with its transatlantic offspring, the British punk scene.

He made a point, for example, of checking out The Sex Pistols in Atlanta's Great Southeast Music Hall on January 5th, 1977, but recalls them as "kind of like The Angry Monkees. They were put together and they were – well, you know, it was a package, and we tended to like the stuff that was just a little bit more … out there. I mean, Wire were one of the first bands where we kind of played each other's records and said, you know, 'This is a really great record.'"

Academically, Peter Buck's career was undistinguished, and ended with him dropping out of Atlanta's Emory University in order to become a record shop assistant at an establishment known as Doo Dah's in Emory Village. He quit Doo Dah's for a brief spell with a record distribution company, but hated the work so much that he wangled his way back behind the counter, this time at Wuxtry Records in Athens. And it was at Wuxtry, in the early months of 1979, that Buck would encounter Michael Stipe.

Meanwhile, William Thomas Berry, the fifth child of Don and Anna Jane Berry, had let out his first scream in Duluth, Minnesota, on July 31st, 1958. Described by the satirical novelist Sinclair Lewis as a "radiant, sea-fronting, hillside city", Duluth is an industrial port on the Western end of Lake Superior, founded on logging and mining. The area's only other notable rock hero was Bob Dylan, but neither that fact nor the town itself had much impact on young Bill, as the family soon moved to Wauwatosa, a suburb of Milwaukee, Wisconsin.

Like Duluth, Milwaukee is a port, located on the western shore of Lake Michigan and, prior to Bill Berry, what made the place famous was beer. It was here that he first became interested in music, largely through listening to his siblings' collections of Motown hits, James Brown and The Beatles. "It never occurred to me to buy my own records," he has said, "because my brothers and sisters had records all over the place." In fact, in classic youngest child mode, he eventually inherited a whole record collection when his eldest sister went off to college.

Any early aptitude for picking out tunes on the ukulele might have led Bill to a career as a capable guitarist, except that he joined the school band as a drummer when he was ten, relegating stringed instruments to second place thereafter.

When Bill was 13, the Berrys moved to Macon, Georgia. Enrolled at Northeast High School, Bill found his introduction to the area far from encouraging. The bussing system – a means of racially integrating schools by driving busloads of kids from white areas to predominantly black schools, and vice versa – had lately come into effect. Bill, having grown up in the somewhat more integrated and liberal north, befriended a black girl, only to have the living daylights knocked out of him by a gang of her male friends.

And it was in Macon that, despite earlier grand dreams of becoming an architect or a psychologist, Bill developed into a fully-fledged, underage drinking and smoking juvenile delinquent. Since it was the home of Capricorn Records, the city's major rock format at that time was southern boogie, as exemplified by the label's flagship combo, The Allman Brothers. But Berry's first playing experience in Macon was as a member of the high school marching band, whose bassist was a nerdy, intellectual type named Mike Mills.

Michael Edward Mills, the son of Fred and Adora Mills, was born in Orange County, just south of Los Angeles, on December 17th, 1958.

With Fred being an operatic tenor and Adora accomplished on both piano and guitar, music was around him from the start. "I used to go to sleep hearing tenor arias and piano concertos," he has recalled. Like Brian Wilson of the Beach Boys, he also cites 1950s vocal harmony quartet The Four Freshmen as an influence, courtesy of Fred's record collection.

Like Peter Buck, who started life about 450 miles to the north, in San Francisco, the infant Mike had moved with his family before a California state of mind had taken hold. In the Berrys' case, though, the move took them to Georgia, Fred's birthplace. So Mike's early teens, like Bill Berry's, were spent in Macon.

Unsurprisingly, reared in such a music-rich background, Mike was encouraged to play instruments, taking lessons on piano, tuba and sousaphone. It was only a matter of time before this clean-living, hard-working lad found himself in the Northeast High School band, marching alongside the pot-smoking, class-cutting Mr Berry, who recalls Mike as virtually his polar opposite, "the class nerd, straight As … He was everything I despised; great student, got along with teachers…"

And, as Mills has explained, the feeling was mutual. "I didn't like him, because he was an asshole."

Their musical backgrounds too were strikingly different. While Bill had been soaking up soul, rootsy funk and pop, Mike's moves beyond the classical influence from his parents started when his mother gave him three records, 'Come Together' by The Beatles, Harry Nilsson's 'Theme From Midnight Cowboy' and, er, 'Hitchin' A Ride' by Vanity Fair. "It was those three that kick-started my interest in records," he says. "I didn't know much but what I did know I knew well."

Fired by those three 45s, Mike set out to find more. "My first record store," he recalls, "was a place in Macon called Moon And Star Records, run by an old hippie." Mike's choices were nothing if not eclectic, embracing the AOR country rock of Seals & Crofts, the white-boy soul of Three Dog Night, and heavier rock bands like Led Zeppelin and Queen.

"I was madly in love with this woman called Toni," he told Dorian Lynskey of Q magazine, "and our song was, don't ask me why, 'Killer Queen'. I think of her every time I hear those finger snaps."

Noble instruments though the tuba and sousaphone undoubtedly are, their applications in the field of rock'n'roll are somewhat limited. It was only to be expected that Mike would gravitate towards some other method of blasting out those deep sonorities, and it was a concert by the school jazz band that proved to be the decisive moment. "We were sitting in these pull-out bleachers," he has recalled, "and when the bass player hit certain notes, the bleachers would vibrate and everyone would go 'BZZZZZ'. And I thought, 'That's what I want to do - make people vibrate!'" Before long he was the keeper of the school's Fender Jazz bass, and ready to join his first real rock band.

The way Bill Berry tells it, "A friend of mine was a guitar player and he lined up a jam session. He said, 'Take your drums to this house.' So I did. I spent half an hour setting up my drums and we were all there, tuning up and waiting for the bass player."

Bill's heart sank when the hotly anticipated bassist eventually clumped down into the basement rehearsal space – and turned out to be his arch-nemesis Mike Mills. Despite their in-built antipathy, however, thundering through a bunch of southern boogie classics melted some of the ice. "Right after that, we made our peace. I said, 'Look, this is ridiculous,' and he said, 'Yeah,' and we've been best friends ever since that day.'

The other outcome of the session was the formation of a band called Shadowfax. "We weren't really writing songs," says Mills. "We would play these sock hops and dances where the kids would love to hear the Top 40 stuff – ZZ Top, Bad Company – but in Macon you could get away with having half your set be blues, because it was always a rootsy town."

As their experience grew and their tastes changed, Shadowfax mutated into the Back Door Band, which saw them begin to include their own compositions, and to move towards a bluesier sound.

The Back Door Band were well-enough received to play in Atlanta's Great Southeast Music Hall, an impressively respectable venue, but to Berry and Mills, by the time they graduated from Northeast High in 1976, it didn't seem as if the band was going anywhere. "After a couple of years we got sick of playing southern boogie," says Mills. "So we quit and sold our instruments."

Resigned to earning a living by some means other than rock stardom, Mills got a job at Sears department store, while Berry found himself employment in Macon's premier talent booking agency, Paragon, located conveniently next door to the pair's rented Arlington Street apartment. Fortunately, Paragon boss Alex Hodges had enough sense to know that southern boogie was on the wane. He took the innovative step of inviting Ian Copeland, a London booking agent, over to Macon with the aim of expanding Paragon's roster to include some up-and-coming punk acts.

When Ian flew into Macon in 1977, the driver who collected him at the airport was Bill Berry. "He was the office gofer and he'd all but hung up his drums," Copeland explains.

The record collection Copeland brought with him from London horrified some of the old guard management at Paragon, but the ears of Berry and Mills immediately perked up. "He started playing us all the punk stuff that hadn't filtered down to the hinterlands at that point," Mills remembers. "So by listening to The Ramones, The Damned and the Dead Boys, that revived our interest. Ian had a stereo, headphones and a bass rig at his house. So we would play along to The Ramones' first record and *Rocket To Russia*. And the first Police single, which was 'Fall Out' and 'Nothing Achieving': that was huge. That was the sort of stuff that got us playing again."

Although their love of playing live music was rekindled, their enthusiasm for Macon certainly wasn't. "By the end of 1978," says Mills, "Bill and I decided we were going nowhere in Macon. We had to leave, because if you don't get out of Macon early, you never get out. We figured the only way was to go to school, so we went to the University of Georgia (UGA) at Athens in January."

Officially Berry was studying to become an entertainment lawyer, and Mills was taking general courses with little more than a vague thought of becoming a journalist, or maybe a teacher. Immediately after enrolling, on January 4th, 1979, however, the pair found to their delight that Athens was Party Central. "I could stay up as late as I wanted to," Berry recalled, "I could wake up whenever I wanted to. I thought it was heaven on earth."

Michael Stipe, meanwhile, was charming his way through the first year of his art course. "I was a wretched student. I was able to convince my teachers that what I was doing was worthwhile, when I wasn't really doing anything."

Peter Buck, similarly, was whiling away the time at Wuxtry Records, doing as little as he possibly could in order to justify collecting a wage at the end of each week. "The only thing I ever remember Pete doing," says one of his old Wuxtry bosses, Dan Wall, "was sitting around playing guitar along with records."

In a community as small as Athens, with its even smaller student body, all four of them shared a number of friends and acquaintances without even knowing it. It was almost unthinkable that they wouldn't all meet up somewhere along the line.

Paul Butchart of the Side Effects has pointed out that "the scene in Athens at this time was a group of around 150 indi-

We had to leave Macon. If you don't leave Macon early, you never get out

viduals, who would meet at parties and go out to Atlanta clubs together, to see such acts as The Ramones, Talking Heads, and Devo. There was no club in Athens that would take a chance with the new music at that time. Bands mostly played at parties, or as an occasional opening act in Atlanta."

As previously mentioned, by May of that year Berry had staked his claim as part of that fraternity by drumming for the college-radio band WUOGerz. But although Mills and Berry were more actively involved in the music scene, Peter Buck recalls, "I met Michael first. He came in to Wuxtry, and he was just a really nice guy with interesting musical tastes. He also had a visual sense of things, good taste in art, he was interesting to talk to, kind of mysterious, but I guess that's 'cos he was a little shy. He told me was a singer, and I said I really didn't want to be in a band unless it had a real good singer. So we just sat with acoustic guitars and it was obvious he could really sing. We pretty soon started writing songs together. Then we said, 'Hey, we're gonna have a band together. Sure. OK.'"

The other members of that band might have been anybody, if not for Dan Wall of Wuxtry. "I had bought a disused church on Oconee Street," he explains. "I fixed up the pulpit area, which had broken floorboards … and rented the church to them."

"It was a real zoo," remembers Buck. "We lived with some girl who dealt drugs – all of these sickos coming over at four in the morning with the urge."

A drug-sodden zoo it may well have been, but this is the location that looms largest in R.E.M. lore: St Mary's Episcopal Church at 394 Oconee Street. It was here that the quartet would finally come together.

Chapter Three

The Most Phenomenal Party

"Everyone danced
around on the floor.
Until it broke. "
PETER BUCK

Local heroes: at Tyrone's club in 1980

Peter Buck moved into the five-bedroomed St Mary's Church some time in around July of 1979, with Michael Stipe not far behind. The church was already something of a local landmark, boasting an intriguing history.

Mill workers from the Athens Manufacturing Company had given their labour to build the place, between 1869 and 1871, but after a few busy and productive years, the building began to fall into disuse when the mill closed in 1892.

Despite a brief second flourishing under the aegis of the American Red Cross in the mid-1940s, it was in a serious state of disrepair by the 1960s, and Peter Buck recalls that in 1980 it was, "A monstrous old church with a huge back room, no ventilation and lots of strange foreign animals."

Ironically, though, its state of decay meant that the church fitted right in with the prevailing Athens landscape. Scott Bellville, who taught Stipe at UOG, told Martin Townshend of *Vox* magazine that: "There's a funny bleakness down here. It's a mixture of lush undergrowth with bits of old development underneath which have become overgrown. There are structures that have been started and left half-finished, and others that were good for ten years and then cast aside. There's no clean, manicured edge to the town."

Stipe, at this point, was still able to bamboozle the lecturers on his art course at UOG into believing he was making good progress. He had also begun to establish a small circle of friends, largely in the wake of being befriended by fellow student Linda Hopper. "He was new to town and I could tell by looking at him that he was interesting," she has said. "I sat down next to him and said, 'I've got some friends I think you'd like.'" It was the beginning of a lifelong camaraderie.

He had even found his way into a covers band called Gangster, for which he changed his name to Michael Valentine. "I did it for the money," he admitted years later. "They paid me well, but it's deeply embarrassing. It was a step back, just a reaching out for anything. I wore some elephant bells [extravagantly flared trousers] I had from high school and they all thought I was serious."

He was, by all appearances, starting to come out of his shell, but still counted himself among the outsiders. A fellow student, Armistead Wellford, remembers, "There were a few of us who sat at the same table – it was where the weirdos sat. At this table there were many discussions about modern art and modern music. Michael was very passionate about both topics."

He was also becoming passionate about Athens itself. "This place just grew on me," is how

Stipe has explained it. Given a childhood wandering the face of the earth, this was the first town he really considered home, the first place where just "seeing the pine trees and the red dirt" after a spell away could move him to tears. "It's like my blood is in the clay or something."

A key member of the set Stipe and Buck were now hanging with was another student, Kathleen O'Brien, who had her eye on one of those bedrooms at St Mary's. "I wanted to move in there because I thought it would be a really cool place to live." Kathleen was, more significantly, also a WUOG Radio DJ.

WUOG's importance to the development of the Athens music scene shouldn't be under-estimated. As Mike Mills has said, "We've got a big powerful radio station, WUOG, one of the most powerful college stations I've ever heard anywhere – 10,000 watts. And they support local bands really well. They supported us when we needed it."

In her WUOG DJ capacity, Kathleen knew The WUOGerz, and the manly charms of their drummer, Bill Berry, hadn't entirely escaped her notice. "I had known Bill Berry through the dorm the prior year and had a huge crush on him," she says. "Basically, I did whatever I could to throw us in the same situation." And, in pursuit of that objective, she would unwitting fit together the two major pieces of the R.E.M. jigsaw.

August in Athens is the quietest month of the year. "There's about 24,000 students," points out Mills. "The entire population is about 60,000. It's a small place. When summer school is over in August, and everyone's on vacation, you can lie down in the middle of Broad Street. They might as well turn the traffic lights off because it is dead with a capital D."

And it was in the dead calm of that autumnal Southern hush that Stipe and Buck started rehearsing. Stipe's involvement with Gangster hadn't lasted long once he had found a soul mate in Peter Buck, but despite Buck's assertions that they clicked immediately as a song-writing unit, Stipe has claimed that it was an uphill struggle to motivate Buck into seriously considering the idea of starting a band. "I had to coerce Peter into doing stuff. He had this feeling that everyone in rock bands was an egotistical asshole. Plus, he couldn't play guitar to save his life."

Peter couldn't play guitar to save his life

For all his love of music, it seemed, Buck was more than happy to let it remain a spectator sport, which consisted of building up a huge vinyl collection, going to every gig he could, watching every rock documentary on tv, drinking beer and talking trash.

With Stipe's encouragement, their first fumblings towards becoming a band took place, naturally, in the big back room at St Mary's, with Michael and Peter augmented by a couple of acquaintances. "Dan Wall, who lived in the church before we did, would come over and play bass and saxophone," remembers Stipe. "And some other guy played drums. We set up in the church and played a couple times, but that was about it."

The "some other guy" was called Tim, but his surname has been lost to history, and Dan Wall moved out of the picture when he transferred to Atlanta to work in his Wuxtry branch there.

So before long, it was back to being just Buck, Stipe and a bunch of half-formulated songs with incomprehensible lyrics. "We decided that the words didn't matter," explained Stipe later, "'cos nobody cared what we were saying. It was just a good sound they wanted."

For Buck, that attitude was one of the key elements in their relationship, and it remains important to him that he and Stipe didn't start creating music together as a commercial proposition. "We were friends before we were in a band. Some people try to put a band together and then try to figure out if they're friends or not. It's like getting married to a stranger. It's been done, and you can make it work, but I wouldn't like to do it."

The duo were already, as Roger Lyle Brown noted in his excellent book, *Party Out Of Bounds*, evolving a public image that, consciously or otherwise, aped that of Mick Jagger and Keith Richards of The Rolling Stones. Stipe was the slightly effete, sensitive, poetic Jagger type, while the knife-carrying Buck was the bad boy, the Keef-a-like, complete with skull-and-cross-bones earring.

Something else happened that August that would have a significant impact on their future careers. Up north in New York City, their friend from the Paragon days, booking agent Ian Copeland, started his own company, FBI, which would become one of the premier agencies in rock. When the time came for R.E.M. to move beyond Georgia, there would already be somebody who knew them, cared about them, and was in a position to give them a break.

Dedicated to her ongoing pursuit of Bill Berry, Kathleen O'Brien went with Stipe and Buck to a party in October. There she immediately spotted Berry, and made a point of introducing him to the others. Buck was instantly won over. "I really liked him and we talked about music, and he said he was looking for a band, so I told him about Michael and me."

Berry's response, naturally, was to tell Buck about Mills. "I said, 'A friend of mine up here plays bass. We've got bass and drums up here. Let's get together and see what happens.'"

At the same party, Berry was, of course, also introduced to Stipe. Rather than being impressed, as Buck had been, by his good taste in music, Stipe was struck by his looks. "Michael said he liked my eyebrows," says Berry. "He claims to this day that's the reason he wanted us to get together."

But before Berry could arrange the all-important meeting between Mills, Buck, Stipe and himself, another significant Athens event took place. On October 31st, Pylon, then the hottest band in town, initiated a new-wave night at Tyrone's O.C., which was, in the words of Mike Mills, "the best club Athens has ever seen".

Located in an old warehouse, Tyrone's had formerly been a club known as Chameleon, hence the O.C. suffix, standing for Old Chameleon. Supporting Pylon at this historic gig was a newly formed band called The Method Actors. The very existence of a new-wave night and the arrival of bands like The Method Actors was the surest indicator that the success of the B-52s and Pylon had transformed Athens. If ever the time was right to start a new band, this was it.

It was in Tyrone's in November that the members of R.E.M. first met under one roof. "Mike did not give the best first impression," recalls Buck. "Bill took us with him to this club to meet Mike, and he was as drunk as I've ever seen him, sitting on the floor in a leather jacket, trying to get to his feet, just out of his mind. I said, 'I'm not gonna be in a band with that guy.'"

Stipe felt exactly the same way. "He was really drunk, swaying on his feet and holding on to the bar and then this table so he wouldn't fall down. I said, 'No way. Ab-so-lute-ly no way!'"

Given that Stipe and Buck were no strangers to virtually every intoxicant known to mankind, and that Berry's familiarity with drink and drugs had all but landed him in jail on several occasions, it's curious that nice guy Mills had chosen this of all nights to go on a bender of mammoth proportions. Berry and Mills, however, were inseparable. They came as a job lot, and Bill wasn't going to let his best friend be passed over lightly. As Buck remembers it, "Bill said, 'Oh, he's not always like that. I don't know what's going on.' Then he showed up the next day and he was really nice. He didn't actually have any memory of having met us the night before."

Despite their poor first impressions, Buck and Stipe were now persuaded to give Mills a break and a rehearsal date was fixed, but fate was still not on Mills' side. "As it turns out, one of us didn't make it," says Berry, "so we bagged the idea. It never would have happened, but I saw Pete again three weeks later in a bar and we said, 'Let's just give it one more shot,' and we did."

It happened in the big back room at St Mary's, surrounded by pews, with the temperature so close to freezing that Mills played bass with his gloves on, and clearly remembers their breath turning to steam as it left their mouths.

Michael claimed he liked my eyebrows. He claims to this day that's why he wanted to get together

Watching from the sidelines was Kathleen O'Brien. "They were all real wary of each other," is how she remembers that first jam, pointing out that, as personalities, they were all remarkably different. "You've got Peter, Mr Atlanta, cool, rock'n'roll guy; Michael, this introverted, insecure, displaced-in-the-south artist-type; and these two from Macon – Bill the bad boy and Mike the good nerd kid."

But despite, or maybe because of, those differences, there was a chemistry between them that clearly combined into something significantly more than the sum of its parts. "Even though it was freezing," Mills has said, "I really enjoyed what Michael and Peter were doing with the songs Bill and I brought, and it was clearly working. We decided to play only for fun and free beer, but it grew from there."

This was the start of a six month period in which the foursome, which Buck has described as "pretty competent almost immediately", rehearsed regularly, slowly building up a live set. "When we first got together," Stipe remembers, "it was just, 'What song does everybody know?' We played old 1960s stuff, like 'Stepping Stone', Troggs' songs, stuff like that."

As well as developing a repertoire, however, they had a philosophy. "The idea was that if you sounded like another band, that was horrible," explains Buck. "Most bands in Athens tried not to sound like one another ... Like Pylon, where did they come from? Where did the B-52s come from? That was just something they pulled out of the air. The whole idea in Athens at that time was to express yourself individually."

To achieve that end, of course, it was necessary to write their own material, so they did. "We sat down and wrote a bunch of songs which probably took as long to play as they did to write," admits Stipe.

"Michael and I used to say how much we hated most rock'n'roll lyrics," recalls Buck. "We had this idea that what we'd do is take cliches, sayings, lines from old blues songs, phrases you hear all the time, and skew them and twist them and meld them together so that you'd be getting these things that have always been evocative, but that were skewed just enough to throw you off and make you think in a different way. It seemed like a really pretentious thing to do, but that concept does work its way in."

Even without playing gigs, the quartet began to attract attention. "There was a crowd of us that would just go and listen to them practise all of the time," says Kathleen. "We'd get in the back of the church and just dance and party. Somewhere around that time, Bill and I started going out and it became a more personal interest."

Once again, it was Kathleen who prodded the band gently but firmly towards the next step in their evolution. Her 20th birthday fell on April 5th, and she thought it would be a good idea for her boyfriend's band to play on the night. They didn't agree. She persisted. "She begged us to play," is how Berry puts it. "We didn't want to do it."

Kathleen's persistence paid off, though, and once she had one band lined up, she started to think bigger. Paul Butchart, of another recently formed combo, The Side Effects, recalls, "On February 29th, 1980, after John Cale played the last show for a long time at the Georgia Theater, Kathleen O'Brien asked if we could play at her birthday party on April 5th. She said her room-mates' band was also going to perform, if they could get a set together. Nervously we agreed, also hoping to have our set together, too."

It was around this time that Mills, who had been living on the outskirts of town, finally moved into the church with the other three, slyly managing to get out of paying rent by sleeping on a couch rather than taking a room.

Bill, meanwhile, had been asked to leave the university. That was hardly a surprise, given how rarely he attended, but it meant that he now had to find a way to keep himself in the manner to which he had become accustomed. Being qualified for nothing much else, he took a job at the local Holiday Inn. "I had to get up at four in the morning," he recalls ruefully. "There would be parties still going on at the church, and I would be dressed up in these brown polyester pants and Peter and Michael would be sitting there, wasted, drinking beer and laughing at me." Ah, the trials of youth.

With the big gig just days away, the band still had no name. A trawl for suggestions among the denizens of St Mary's resulted in some fairly obvious non-starters, including Can Of Piss and Negro Eyes, although Buck has pointed out that "We were thinking that since no-one is ever, you know, gonna like us, we should have some weirdly offensive name, 'cos we figured we'd do it just for fun, basically." There was also a clutch of just about possibles, including Slut Bank, Africans In Bondage, The Male Nurses and Third Wave. Nothing really took their fancy, not even Twisted Kites, but that's the one they settled on, as the best of a bad bunch.

Stipe and co had, by this time, mustered a set that consisted of about 60 per cent covers and 40 per cent newly written songs. Paul Butchart of the Side Effects was one of the first outsiders to hear how they sounded, and it made him nervous. He was convinced that they were already far more professional than his own band.

"The night before the gig," says Butchart, "we loaded our equipment into the sanctuary of the church, which had a two-storey apartment occupying half of the available space."

Once the gear was set up, Side Effects played their set in the gloomy darkness for the church's resident band. Showing an interest, Berry commented amiably on Butchart's drumming technique, which tended to accentuate downbeats as much as upbeats. Butchart was baffled. "I honestly had no idea what he was talking about, having never taken a lesson in my life."

No doubt it was through Kathleen's influence at the station that The Twisted Kites were interviewed live by presenter Kurt Wood at WUOG radio on the day of the party, April 5th, thus notching up their first media coup without having played a gig. As a result, although the location of the party was not announced, word spread quickly through the Athens hip community. Kathleen had invited 125 people but, on that cold and wet night, at least 300 showed up.

"It was a big deal at the time," noted Mike Green of The Fans, yet another of Athens' many bands, "not necessarily because we thought anybody was going to get famous, but because the party was huge. You couldn't breathe once you got in." Some recollections even tell of people hanging from the window ledges beside the stage, taking care not fall through gaping holes in the floor.

Despite Paul Butchart's anxiety, when the Side Effects climbed up on to the altar that was serving as a stage they pulled out all the stops and played a highly energized set that won a well-deserved encore. "They were great," remembers Pylon's Curtis Crowe. "Kind of real dumb surf music. They were a ragged three-piece outfit. You could really, definitely dance to it."

Seeing the size of the crowd and the rapturous reception for Side Effects, it was now The Twisted Kites' turn to feel the carnivorous butterflies gnawing at their innards. "We were scared shitless," Bill has admitted.

Recollections differ as to precisely which timeless rock classic The Twisted Kites chose to launch their live career, but The Troggs' 'I Can't Control Myself' seems the likeliest suspect. Berry is certain, however, that the second song was 'God Save The Queen' by The Sex Pistols, and that by that point their stage jitters were evaporating in the warm glow of adulation flowing from the party-goers.

From what I've heard, I spent half the night on the floor on my stomach

Stipe encouraged this rapport with the crowd by making a point of saying hello to his many friends in the audience, obviously already beginning to behave like an experienced, confident frontman.

According to Mike Green, "They sounded like a garage band and everything they played sounded like it could be a cover." Dan Wall noted that when they thundered through Paul Revere And The Raiders' '(I'm Not Your) Steppin' Stone', "People raved as if the original Yardbirds had come to play."

Other covers performed vigorously during their two hours on stage that night included 'Nervous Breakdown', 'Hippy Hippy Shake', 'Shakin' All Over', 'Roadrunner' (The Modern Lovers' song), 'California Sun', 'Honky Tonk Women' and 'Needles And Pins', but, as Curtis Crowe has pointed out, this was hardly likely to win them respect. "We were on the 'leading edge of a musical revolution' and we thought playing cover songs was taking two steps back, and everyone kind of put their nose in the air about that." Twisted Kites' saving grace, however, was that "they were really good and had a lot of energy".

Better yet, among all those party-friendly covers, their self-penned debuts that night included 'All The Right Friends', 'Dangerous Times', 'Different Girl', 'Mystery To Me', 'Narrator', 'Just A Touch', 'Permanent Vacation', 'Action' and 'Baby, I'. "We had 15 songs and a bunch of covers," is Stipe's estimation. "We ended up doing three sets that night. It was a real hootenanny."

Stipe's college acquaintance Armistead Wellford recalls that, "Michael was very energetic onstage, he moved a lot and was a good dancer. I guess he was closer to Iggy than J.J.Cale. He hung on to the microphone with the stand like he still does now."

As the evening wore on and the beer flowed copiously, the crowd became progressively more energized. "Everyone danced around on the floor," says Mike Mills, "until it broke."

The final jubilant set was essentially an extended encore, during which they played requests and had a stab at anything they thought they might reasonably stagger through, sometimes with assistance from members of the audience, standing in for Stipe who claims to have drunk so much that he can't remember anything about the last half of the evening. "From what I've heard, I spent half the night on the floor, on my stomach."

Curtis Crowe, however, remained sufficiently sober to recognize that this had been no ordinary night, and took the time to write a review of the performance. "It just felt like something had happened," he says. "It needed to be documented. It was the first and last review I tried to write in my life."

For Kathleen it was "the most phenomenal party ever", despite an unexpected bill for $200 to cover the cost of damage done by drunken revellers to the beer kegs she had rented for the night. But even this downer played its part in continuing the band's momentum. To help Kathleen out, they offered to pay a share of the bill by playing a fund-raising gig.

As luck would have it, Mike Hobbs of Tyrone's had been in the church that night and was sufficiently impressed to want to book them as support to Atlanta band The Brains on May 6th, with a $100 fee that would go some way towards helping Kathleen out of her difficulty.

It seemed that their first appearance had been a consummate success, opening doors for them all over town. As well as the Tyrone's gig, they were offered a slot at another new venue, the 11:11 Koffee Klub. The word around town was that The Twisted Kites were poised to become the best band in Athens. "We were real popular," remembers Buck, "right from the very first time we ever played, and we could draw real big crowds, only knowing 20 songs."

One thing that still wasn't quite right, though, was their name. Twisted Kites had served its purpose as a stopgap, but it wasn't something they felt they could live with. "All the good names were taken," jokes Buck. "I was heartbroken that Strawberry Alarm Clock had already been used. We had to settle for second best." Typically, it wasn't until April 18th, the night before the Koffee Klub gig, that they seriously attempted to think of something better, during a heavy drinking session at St Mary's.

"We sat up one night and we just got completely drunk and rolled around the floor," says Stipe. "We had all this chalk, and we took every name anyone could think of and we wrote it on the wall in the living room."

Although they had no specific type of name in mind, they did set themselves two parameters – it should be short and it shouldn't limit their options. "If you hear the name Circle Jerks," points out Mills, "you can kinda figure out what they're going to sound like. We wanted to have a name that wouldn't peg us immediately."

The pale light of a new dawn was creeping in through the windows before they'd whittled the list down to two contenders. "It was between R.E.M. and Negro Eyes," says Stipe, "and we thought that probably wouldn't go over too well outside our immediate circle of friends!"

The letters R.E.M., in medical parlance, stand for Rapid Eye Movement, a well-documented sleep state in which the eyelids are shut and the eyeballs move around rapidly beneath them. It is in this state that much dreaming takes place.

Despite its obvious symbolic potential for anyone involved in the creative arts, this was not why R.E.M. chose the name. They'd simply found it in a dictionary, chalked it on the wall, and liked the sound of it. "I wish we'd picked something we didn't have to explain all the time," grumbles Buck.

So the band that took the stage at the Koffee Klub on Clayton Street late on the night of April 19th was called R.E.M. But the show wasn't quite the runaway success that their first one had been. The band was only halfway into its set, at 2.30am, when the doors were thrust open by Sgt Pritchett of the Athens-Clark County Police. He and his fellow officers had been cruising by when they'd heard the noise and decided to investigate.

As it happened, the proprietors of the Koffee Klub didn't possess any of the relevant paperwork – notably a liquor licence or an entertainment licence – necessary to the running of a club. Protests that it was actually a private party, and that partygoers had brought the bottles of beer were dismissed by Sgt Pritchett, who ordered the place closed down.

The event was, however, not a complete washout, because in the crowd stood a young law student by the name of Bertis Downs, who had seen enough by the time the law arrived to know that this was no ordinary band. He even went to far as to tell them that they would be bigger than The Beatles. Their paths would soon cross again.

Having notched up all of one-and-a-half gigs, how did R.E.M. see themselves fitting into the local scene? "Pylon was a weird, angular dance band," says Buck. "The Method Actors were a two piece psycho-funk band. And then there was us. We were sort of considered the 'pop' band."

Linda Hopper has confirmed this assessment, observing that, "The art-school crowd in town looked down on them for being more straight ahead and fashionable."

Nevertheless, it must have been dawning on them that R.E.M. was their best hope for a prosperous and enjoyable future. Buck was in a dead-end job, Berry had been dumped from college and has said that Mills was, "barely hanging on". Michael was, miraculously, still progressing well but it must have proved difficult to concentrate on the academic life when, as well as playing in the band, they had to suffer the endless routine of all-night parties at St Mary's. Reminiscing about those hedonistic bacchanals, Linda Hopper has said, "By the end of the night there would be a girl naked in the punch bowl, and Peter Buck with a shoe, scooping up what was left of it."

Determined though they were to help Kathleen recoup her losses on the party, the thought of playing their first paying gig, had filled R.E.M. with dread. Their $100 fee to support Mercury

Records artists The Brains, at Tyrone's on May 6th, meant that this was the real deal, and none of them was entirely convinced that they were ready for it. So every waking moment not spent partying was spent rehearsing at St Mary's. "We'd sit up on the stage and get really drunk and play," explained Buck. To make it absolutely clear that the dividing line between party and rehearsal was exceedingly thin, he added, "Our friends would come over and we'd get drunk and just rehearse."

They needn't have worried about Tyrone's. Both Kate Pierson and Cindy Wilson of the B-52s showed up, and bestowed their blessings on R.E.M., much to the amazement of Peter Buck, who couldn't believe that the two goddesses of the Athens rock elite would both be so full of praise for his little band.

"The Athens foursome exploded with energy in only their third public appearance, " wrote William Haines of Athens paper *The Red & Black*. "Tyrone's may have been cramped and hot, but it hardly mattered when R.E.M. pulled out Johnny Kidd and the Pirates' rhythm and blues workhorse 'Shakin' All Over'. This was dance music impossible to resist."

If the band found those words mightily encouraging, they must have felt their spirits ascending to nirvana when Haines carried on with, "R.E.M.'s original material was even more amazing." The review ran under the headline, "Underdog R.E.M. Upstages The Brains". Even before seeing the review, Mike Hobbs had invited them to headline the next week's 'New Wave Nite'.

Nevertheless, and this is an R.E.M. hallmark, they didn't let this early acclaim inflate their own assessment of exactly who and what they were. "When we started out we were terrible," is how Mills remembers those days, "just like every band that starts out."

He wasn't the only one who thought so. Sean Bourne, who had been acting as roadie for The Brains on that occasion, had already picked up on an aspect of their performance that would be levelled against them for years to come. "I couldn't understand a word that Stipe was singing. There was a lot of energy and everyone was bouncing around, but I didn't ever think they would be anything."

When we started, we were terrible

Similarly, John Keane, a local producer whose studio, Keane Recording, would figure prominently in R.E.M.'s future, remembers them as "really raw … I didn't really like them that much because I was a musician." The remark may sound elitist, but Keane's attitude was shared by many local musos. R.E.M. was winning over Joe Public, but there was still little acceptance from other band members who regarded them as inferior musicians, or from the college intellectuals who saw them as too poppy to be taken seriously.

The second gig at Tyrone's, headlining on May 13th, took place under a different financial regime. "It was great," says Mills, "because the people that ran it would let anybody play there, and get the door. You charge two dollars and you get all the money. I made $30 and I thought I was rich. They made their money off the bar – and they made a ton."

As the band gained in confidence, Michael evolved rapidly as a frontman. "Michael was totally bizarre on stage," remembers Linda Hopper. "He threw his back out every night. He was compulsive to watch, a real focal point."

Just seven days later, The 40 Watt Club moved to its second location, above a sandwich shop on the corner of College and Broad. Although R.E.M. didn't grace the first night, Peter Buck and Michael Stipe quickly found themselves part-time employment as barmen, and The 40 Watt would go on to become the club most closely identified with the now-burgeoning Athens scene.

By the beginning of June, R.E.M. were ready for their first shows outside Athens, their first foray into the great beyond taking them to The Warehouse in Atlanta, headlining over The Space Heaters. Buck was reportedly drunk as a skunk, but the gig went well enough for local fanzine *Useless Knowledge* to declare them "Great for dancing and fun."

This was the start of a period during which, as Buck told David Fricke of *Rolling Stone*, "We played cheap, anywhere. We'd always get more people every time we went back. We were fairly decent and, if nothing else, our show was a nice way to spend an evening for a dollar."

Buck also soon began to notice that although they were considered virtually a pop band by the somewhat avant-garde standards of Athens, once they began to move further afield, "everybody thought we were really weird."

The end of June was also the end of an era, because St Mary's, having taken all the parties it could, was in such a dangerous state of disrepair that it had been condemned. Bill and Kathleen moved into a house together, while the other three sublet rooms in a house belonging to a couple of Michael's college girl friends.

The out of town gigs kept coming, taking them first to High Shoals, then to a couple more Atlanta venues, the Agora Ballroom and the 688 Club. On July 18, however, the R.E.M. magic was exported beyond the state line for the first time, when they played at The Station, Carrboro, North Carolina.

This proved to be a major turning-point for the Athens foursome, and the reason why can be summed up in two words: Jefferson Holt.

R.E.M.

Chapter Four

One Of The Best Support Bands Ever

"We had a whole year just to play around the South and get better – and to learn to deal with adversity, playing at pizza parlours and biker bars and gay discos."
MIKE MILLS ◼

Before the gig: at the I & I club in 1981

Before he became R.E.M's first manager, Jefferson Holt was the proprietor of Schoolkids' Records, generally agreed to have been the most happening teen hangout in Chapel Hill, North Carolina.

At the age of 28, he was tall, slender and by some accounts, eccentric. A former girlfriend, Ann-Louise Lipman, characterised him with the phrase, "He's odd but he's nice."

Lipman has also recalled one of his more unusual foibles. "He would have his Polaroid camera, and when girls came into the store, he would take pictures of them."

In his spare time, Holt dabbled with booking bands into local venues, operating under the name of Dasht Hopes Productions, although no such company actually existed. One venue he represented was a former railway station in the neighbouring town of Carrboro. It was as a result of Pylon unexpectedly pulling out of two gigs promoted by Dasht Hopes at The Station that he offered R.E.M. the opportunity to headline there on the evenings of July 18th and 19th. Before those dates, however, Stipe and Co had an opportunity to play as support to Gang of Four, an English punk-era band they had previously only been able to admire from afar. According to Stipe, Gang Of Four's debut album, *Entertainment*, "shredded everything that came before it." He's also not too proud to admit, "I stole a lot from them."

"We had the same agent, Ian Copeland," says Gang Of Four founder Andy Gill. "Ian felt we'd work well together on the same bill."

Naturally, then, when Gang Of Four came close enough to Athens to make it practicable, Copeland made sure they were supported by R.E.M. at Atlanta's 688 Club on July 15th and 16th. Gill recalls that the two bands found an immediate rapport, and well remembers his first sight of the band in action. "They had a slightly nerdish, geeky, anti-rock look on stage," he recalls, "but it wasn't contrived. It was just the way they were. You could tell right away that Michael was a great performer, but you couldn't understand a word he was singing. He really did mumble in those days."

Gill was also quick to identify a different chemistry at work in R.E.M. than in his own band. "Outsiders might look at Gang Of Four and see me and John running the show, but no-one seemed to be the leader in R.E.M. They seemed like a very democratic group."

Two days later, Gang Of Four had moved on, and R.E.M. drove up to Carrboro for the first of their gigs at The Station. As soon as the foursome took the stage, Holt was suitably impressed. "They blitzkrieged through some incredibly pop covers," is how he subsequently described it. "Then they had some of their own songs that were real pop but also some stuff that wasn't pop."

R.E.M.'s set was well under way before their faithful trio of followers, Kathleen O'Brien, Linda Hopper and Leslie Michel, drew up outside in Kathleen's Plymouth Satellite. "Jefferson and (his business associate) David Healy were doing the door," remembers Leslie, "and they weren't going to let us in because they didn't know us, but we just walked past them and started dancing." To be precise, they started dancing on the bar. "When the band saw us they all screamed and jumped, missed notes and everything, and all of us were dancing and got the whole place all whipped up."

It was, by all accounts, quite a night. Paul Butchart of The Side Effects has spoken of how, by the end of the evening, "the windows were dripping with perspiration." Even so, Carrboro's reaction to R.E.M. was mixed. "Everybody who was in a band hated them because Peter only knew three chords," explains Holt. "But a lot of people liked them because of their energy."

The booking required the band to play The Station for two consecutive nights so, rather than attempt a schlep back to Athens, they stayed awake all night, ending up in David Healy's swimming pool. Had R.E.M. known then how their lengthy association with Holt would end, alarm bells might have started ringing when they dropped into his lakeside home that Sunday for his birthday party.

"Jefferson was running around in his underwear," is one detail that stuck in Linda Hopper's memory. She also remembers that "Michael and I were looking at this book of pornography through the ages that Jefferson had, just watching him, saying, 'God, who is this guy in the black underwear?'"

Nevertheless, Holt's enthusiasm for the band was unmistakeable, and they hit it off well enough to arrange for him and Healy to visit them in Athens during August.

Having moved out of the church, Peter, Mike, Michael and various girlfriends were now at 169 Barber Street, with Bill and Katherine in a house nearby. Lacking the convenience of the big back room at St Mary's, they found themselves obliged to rent a practice space on Jackson Street, but the band's escalating income more than covered that expense.

Although offers were coming in thick and fast, Mike and Michael were

Michael was a great performer, but you couldn't understand a word he was singing

still attending UOG, which largely limited their gigging to weekends. "We were booking small tours, starting on Friday," explains Bill. "So we'd take Friday off and maybe the following Monday, and that started to turn into Thursday and Tuesday." With the weekend eating into the week, it wasn't long before Mike and Michael joined Bill as former students of UOG.

The relative remoteness of Athens made it difficult to find sizeable venues within a convenient driving distance, but Mike Mills also singles out that isolation as a positive element in the evolution of R.E.M. He has observed that any band that starts making waves in New York, Los Angeles or London is immediately championed by the local media and thrust into the international spotlight, often before they've properly developed. Rave reviews in *The Red & Black*, encouraging as they were, didn't have quite the same effect. "We had a whole year just to play around the South and get better – and to learn to deal with adversity, playing at pizza parlours and biker bars and gay discos."

When Holt and Healey drove down to Athens that August, they were warmly received at the band's Jackson Street facility, and found themselves, within hours, at a neighbourhood party that saw the debut of yet another new Athens combo, Love Tractor.

As R.E.M. grew in confidence, more and more of their own songs began to appear in the set list. Their August/September gigs around Athens and Atlanta would have included such recent compositions as 'Gardening At Night' and '(Don't Go Back To) Rockville'.

'Gardening At Night', said to have been written on a mattress in the front yard of the Oconee Street church, has been described as R.E.M.'s first real song. While that seems a tad dismissive its predecessors, Buck has described their musical modus operandi at this point as "three chords and a six pack of beer", pointing out that the first ten songs they wrote all start on an A chord – because, out of those three, A was the one he really liked.

He also singles out 'Gardening At Night' as a turning point. "Right around the time we wrote 'Gardening At Night' our songwriting started getting better. We wrote that and 'Just A Touch' in the same week."

Despite such typically impenetrable Stipe lyrics as, "We ankled up the garbage sound, but they were busy in the rows/ We fell up not to see the sun, gardening at night just didn't grow," it would seem likely that the song refers to the simple truth that gardening at night can be a good idea in Athens, Georgia, where the temperature is often too hot by day.

Before 'Gardening At Night', notes Buck, "The original songs all had lyrics that were simple and naïve, and then Michael moved away from that, and I really liked what he was doing. I was always listening to stuff that wasn't real straightforward, and reading poetry that didn't have literal sense. I'm not comparing what we do to T.S.Eliot, but I still don't know what *The Wasteland*'s about. I know what it's supposed to be about, but there's whole lines I don't understand."

Lyrically much more straightforward, '(Don't Go Back To) Rockville' was a Mike Mills song about his girlfriend Ingrid Schorr, who was considering leaving Athens for Rockville, Maryland. When R.E.M. first started performing it, the song was noticeably faster and rather more Buddy Holly-influenced than the version that ended up on *Reckoning* two years later.

By the time they played at Tyrone's on October 4th, Jefferson Holt was the club's new doorman. His belief in R.E.M. was such that he had thrown over his life in Chapel Hill, and moved lock, stock and barrel to Athens, where he had opened up a new establishment, Foreign Legion. "After he moved to Athens," says sometime R.E.M. soundman Woody Nuss, "he was known as the good guy who ran the door at Tyrone's, and those guys trusted him. My impression of why they hooked up with him is that he was the first doorman that didn't rip them off."

Local scenester Bryan Cook reckons that by this time, R.E.M. were unquestionably the biggest draw in town. "Whenever they played there'd be a traffic jam, and you couldn't park downtown. You'd see people walking, and they'd all be walking from wherever there was parking to down to Tyrone's."

Mike Mills has confirmed Cooke's assessment, pointing out that, "We were the first band among several that drew a cross-section of people. Pylon and the Method Actors would draw the creative left-wing people that cared. Then, when we started, we got everything from dormies and fraternity people to the arty types. We were accessible without trying to be.'"

Around the same time, R.E.M.'s Ian Copeland connection proved useful again. "I heard from Mike and Bill occasionally," Copeland told me, "and one time they asked me if I would get them in to see The Police at The Fox in Atlanta. After agreeing to put them on the list, we chatted some and they then told me they'd been gigging around Athens with a band called R.E.M., and I said, 'Why didn't you say so? To hell with putting you on the guest list, I'll put you on the show!'" (Presumably it slipped his mind that he'd already booked them for the Gang Of Four shows and thus must have known they were in a band.)

It should be noted at this point that Ian Copeland's brother, Miles Copeland, was the manager of The Police and owner of IRS Records – a fact that would shortly prove very significant to R.E.M. Like Ian, Miles had first met Bill Berry back in the days when he was the chauffeur at Paragon. The third Copeland brother is, of course, Stewart, drummer for The Police.

"As I recall," says Bertis Downs, "the support band had pulled out. Ian knew them already, so he was aware that the band was making waves. Sure, they were just doing small gigs, but every time they played, it was sold out, and they were starting to work further afield."

So it was that on December 6th, 1980, on Peter Buck's 24th birthday, R.E.M. supported The Police at the Fox Theatre, Atlanta. "The Fox show was really fun," recalls Downs. "R.E.M. had never played anything near that big – the place held about 4,500 people."

Woody Nuss, who at that time was a member of the backstage staff at the Fox, remembers, "They had no crew, but they brought this guy from Athens down to tune guitars and do stuff. Someone at the Fox described him as a shave-headed speed freak. He was loading out drums through dressing rooms full of people and doing stuff you shouldn't do. They got in trouble from everybody and things were flying around like, 'You'll never play in this town again.' It was great when you consider about three years later they were the biggest thing going and everybody in town was lining up to kiss their asses."

There may well have been backstage problems, but that day at The Fox, The Police were, apparently, impressed by their support band. "They really were rough, as I remember," says Ian Copeland, "but we were used to really bad imitation so-called punk bands. We insisted promoters find punk support even though they didn't exist most places, and 'close enough' had to do. Thus The Police thought R.E.M. were one of the best support bands they'd ever had at the time."

They could hardly have failed to have notice the fact that, as Downs remembers, "R.E.M. had brought down a bunch of fans from Athens, about a hundred I think, and they were all dancing on the orchestra pit …"

Such was the excitement whipped up by the band and its travelling caravan of devotees, that the crowd demanded an encore, during which Stipe rewarded their enthusiasm with an ill-advised suggestion. "Michael invited the audience up on stage at the Fox," says Nuss, "which you can't do because there's an orchestra pit. And the audience rushed the stage. The band got in huge amounts of trouble."

For Ian Copeland, however, that encore was a real eye-opener. "Police crowds almost never asked for encores from the support bands, no matter how good they were. The band had round-ed up all their gang from Athens, and Michael was so excited about being on a real stage in a real hall that he invited all his friends up on stage for their encore and that started a chain reac-tion. The Police's road crew were a little upset at the mess, but nothing that got out of hand. The promoter was more likely to be the one upset."

"For me it was a revelation," continues Copeland. "They changed from being my young bud-dies farting around to a serious proposition. I got that old feeling I rely on to tell me …'This band is going to be huge!' By then I had already signed Joan Jett, Iggy Pop, The Ramones, The B-52s, The Go Go's, Squeeze, UB40, The Cure, Siouxsie & The Banshees, XTC, Adam Ant, Midnight Oil, Robert Palmer, Thompson Twins, and I forget who else, but I knew the feeling well."

Once again, R.E.M. had turned an opportunity into a triumph, one that would lead them, in due course, to their first significant recording deal.

The early months of 1981 found R.E.M. venturing still further afield, gigging in towns like Smyrna, Georgia, Greensboro, North Carolina, and even Music City itself, Nashville, Tennessee.

Right away, points out Mike Mills, they found that their Athens origins stood them in good stead. "When we started touring, we'd say, 'We're from Athens.' People would go, 'Oh, Athens – the B-52s, Pylon – great. We'll book you.'"

It wouldn't be long, however, before their reputation would outshine even their illustrious forebears. Local Athens studio owner John Keane credits R.E.M. with being the most significant factor contributing to the blossoming of the Athens scene. "I think the B-52s on their own prob-ably couldn't have made that happen," reasons Keane. "I think it took the next wave of bands. We started getting media attention, and young people all over the world wanted to move to Athens and start bands."

For now, however, they were still trundling along the interstate highways in the lime-green 1975 Dodge Tradesman that served as the band van. "Shag carpet on the ceiling," recalls Buck.

On January 16 the trusty old Dodge pulled up outside The Milestone, Charlotte, North

Carolina, where they were booked for two nights. "We couldn't afford a hotel room," remembers Stipe, "so we slept on the stage and woke up with mice running around our heads."

Chaotic and undisciplined as it looked to outsiders, there was a certain method – or maybe just a low cunning – in R.E.M.'s touring madness. "We always tried to play on cheap drink nights," explained Buck, "because that would draw 'em in."

They also approached gigs with a gunfighter's determination to win. "We'd pull into some town and, if we were lucky, we'd open for the local hotshot band and blow the fuckers off the stage." The taking of prisoners was never an option.

In between gigs, of course, they still found time to put new songs together, one of the most promising bearing a title that Peter Buck had scribbled down in his notebook a long while earlier: 'Radio Free Europe'. The actual writing process, however, involved all four members of the band. "Mike brought in that ascending part of the song – where the chords go up and down," explains Buck. "I edited it a bit and said, 'Hey, try this as a chorus,' and Bill put in this other part, the verse. I threw in the bridge and suggested to Michael that we call it 'Radio Free Europe'."

Two hours later, Stipe had put a melody over the top of the instrumental backing but, as was fast becoming a trademark, the words were indecipherable. "I purposely did not want any of the lyrics understood," he has said, adding, "The main reason was that I hadn't written any of the words yet."

Thematically, the lyric was inspired by a conversation between Buck and Stipe about European disc jockeys playing American pop music on radio stations, such as the German-based US propaganda network Radio Free Europe, whose programmes were beamed deliberately across the Iron Curtain to the communist-controlled areas of Europe and Asia. It had dawned on Buck that America was effectively "spreading cultural imperialism through pop music" and that's what the lyric was intended to convey.

The lyric that appeared on the final single included such unforgettably mysterious lines as, "Raving station, beside yourself/ Keep me out of country in the word/ Deal the porch is leading us absurd," but how closely those words resemble what he sang while composing it is anybody's guess, as is precisely how they related to the concept of the song.

Not that any of this seems to have troubled Buck. "I was real supportive of what Michael did. His lyrics were full of allusions, lines that sound good together. Sometimes I've decided what I think the lyric is and then I look at the printed page and it's different from I thought. A lot of it means a lot to him, but it doesn't always have to be literal."

Also, when they played it live, Stipe felt no obligation to remember his lyrics word-for-word, and habitually free-associated or ad-libbed his way through the song, making each new performance a unique event in itself.

On a purely musical front, 'Radio Free Europe' perfectly embodied the sound and style that would make R.E.M. rich and famous. "The thing that's interesting," says Buck, "is the way the rhythm section works. The drums and bass are locked in, like Motown, but the bass is doing this melodic stuff against what I'm doing." Buck's point is that, although he was providing beautifully ringing guitar arpeggios, he was also playing on the beat more than Mills, leaving the bassplayer free to provide melody and harmony which is "completely the opposite of what you should do in rock'n'roll."

Although their show at Tyrone's on October 4th had been recorded (and has subsequently appeared as a bootleg) R.E.M. still lacked anything resembling a demo that accurately represented the sound they were now achieving.

To create that demo, on February 8th, 1981, R.E.M. drove 60 miles west to Joe Perry's Bombay Studios, an eight-track facility in Smyrna, just outside Atlanta. As Perry tells it, the special attraction of Bombay Studios lay in its unusually long hall, which produced a distinctive aural ambience that the band hoped would complement their style.

"They had never recorded in a studio before," recalls Perry, "and had an ambitious agenda." That agenda involved spending all day and all of the night recording eight songs, in the hope that two might stand out as potential singles. Perry particularly remembers Michael's anxiety about the level of his vocals in the mix – he wanted his voice buried. "He didn't even like hearing it in the control room for monitoring purposes," says Perry.

By sun up, they had versions of 'Radio Free Europe', 'Gardening By Night', 'Rockville', 'Sitting still', 'Shaking Through', 'Mystery To Me', 'Narrator' and 'White Tornado' in the can. Although Perry was struck by their obvious talent, the results were far from satisfactory, probably because they were trying to achieve too much in too short a time.

Of all the members of R.E.M., Bill Berry was probably the busiest during that spring. As well as playing with R.E.M., he was filling the drum stool for Love Tractor. Trying to combine both of these functions with his role as gigfinder general for R.E.M. was beginning to prove too much for one man. Things had to change.

His first step was to decide to focus full-time on R.E.M., so he bowed out of Love Tractor. Then, to further reduce his workload, he rang Jefferson Holt and asked if he'd like to become R.E.M.'s roadie.

With his new record store having lately gone belly-up, Holt didn't have to be asked twice. He dropped everything and was happily ensconced behind the wheel of the Dodge Tradesman in time for their gig at Cantrell's, Nashville, on March 27th. This was a role he relished, even if it didn't come with all the perks that accrued naturally to the band itself. "They'd sometimes get a girl in the van after the gig," he told *Q* magazine in 1988. "After a while, the girl would always ask, 'What does R.E.M. stand for?' That'd be my cue to shout over my shoulder, 'Really enjoy masturbatin!' Man, that was the true meaning for me. The driver never gets a girl."

Barely a week later, on April 4th, immediately after a show in The Station, Carrboro, Holt was offered a promotion from roadie to manager, which meant that, rather than a salary, he would now share band profits on an equal one-fifth basis. "Everybody was broke," he explained in Roger Lyle Brown's seminal book *Party Out Of Bounds*. "The band's money belonged to everybody, so whoever had control of the money eventually pissed off everybody else. But I could say 'No' to somebody and have it not disrupt the band itself. I could be the whipping boy and Mr. Moneybags at the same time."

It's widely agreed that, in those early days, Jefferson Holt was one of R.E.M.'s greatest assets. Betsy Dorminey, an Athens law student of the time, remembers: "He was the one who was really intent on making it happen for R.E.M. and he worked awfully hard … He really put his heart and soul into making it a success."

One of Holt's first official actions was very astute indeed. He advised them not to send the Bombay demos out to clubs because, rather than bringing them bookings, its poor quality would probably put gig promoters off. Holt then rang up an old Schoolkids' Records customer, Peter Holsapple, who was now playing guitar in an acclaimed New York band, The dB's, to pick his brains about recording studios. "He asked me where to take this new band he was recording," says Holsapple. "I suggested that he go to Mitch's place, the Drive-In."

Mitch was Mitch Easter, formerly of power pop band The Sneakers, but by then running a 16-track studio, Drive-In, in his parents' garage on Shady Boulevard, Winston-Salem, North Carolina. "It's the funkiest little place,"says Buck. "In his parents' house, with dogs all over the place and his mother who makes you coffee and donuts."

The one-day session was to be funded by Atlanta-based entrepreneur Johnny Hibbert, who was looking to find local talent with which to launch a new label under the name Hib-Tone.

On April 15th, R.E.M. arrived at Drive-In and, having learned from their Bombay Studios session that more haste makes less speed, they were planning to record just three tracks: 'Radio Free Europe', 'Sitting Still' and 'White Tornado'.

A mysterious ambient noise intro

On first hearing 'Radio Free Europe', Easter considered it "a really catchy song. It seemed like all the 1960s rock combos that were catchy. They didn't mess around, they got right to the point. And that's what I thought was great about that song."

The new version of 'Radio Free Europe' turned out to be a significant improvement on the Bombay version, and an obvious contender as a debut single. It started with a mysterious ambient noise intro which Easter describes as "static from the console amplified a whole lot and gated to the bass guitar pattern from the 'raving station' part of the song".

This was typical of the kind of inventiveness going on during the session, which, Easter points out, also included "plenty of backwards reverb, tape loops, household items as instruments" and more. When R.E.M. drove away from Drive-In, they were happy with what they'd achieved, but the feeling was not destined to last.

Hibbert felt that 'Radio Free Europe' was indeed a single, but he considered that Mitch Easter's mix could be significantly improved on and, as he had paid for the session, he was given the opportunity of overseeing a re-mix at Drive-In on May 25. Easter found the experience distinctly uncomfortable. "He came into my little studio and it was like, now the big city guy is going to do it right." Twelve gruelling hours later they emerged with a new mix.

They were evidently still not sure which of the two mixes was best, so in early June, for a third opinion, they took it Joe Perry at Bombay, who made it abundantly clear that he thought his original recording was superior to both. In th end, he plumped for "the one with the louder snare", which was Easter's mix. Hibbert ignored him and decided to go with his own mix.

Things went even further adrift when the track was mastered. Hibbert and Mike Mills, says Buck, "drove up to this place in Nashville with this 80-year-old man who had a cigarette and who actually dropped ash into the first master, so he had to throw it away and start over".

But even starting over didn't affect the outcome. Peter felt that the mastered version was "muddy and hi-end" but Hibbert was determined to release it. "The thing is," grumbles Buck, "none of us could afford to re-do it, and it was like, 'God, this isn't what it should be.'"

Before any final decision had been taken, another opportunity to support Gang Of Four came their way via Ian Copeland, with the added benefit that the tour would take R.E.M. to new territories, including Philadelphia, Washington DC and New York City. It was irresistible and it set off from The Ritz in New York on June 17th.

As this tour progressed, Andy Gill of Gang Of Four found himself beginning to grasp the R.E.M. chemistry a little better. "Michael was the quietest, shyest and most thoughtful. Peter was the last man in the bar, more voluble, outgoing, and up for fun and games.

"The other two seemed happy pretty much to keep themselves to themselves. To work with, they were 100 per cent reliable in terms of always turning up and playing. They seemed prepared to do any amount of work. Nothing was too much trouble."

Asked about the extent to which Gang Of Four might have influenced R.E.M., Gill says, "A lot of what Gang Of Four was about onstage was creating drama, through the use of contrasts of volume and tempo and so on. I think they picked up some of that from supporting us."

R.E.M. returned to Athens to discover that Hibbert had decided in their absence to release his mix of 'Radio Free Europe' in an edition of 1,000 copies on Hib-Tone. "I remember the first promo copy I got," Buck told *Bucketful Of Brains* fanzine, "I took it and ceremoniously broke it at a party at my house. I smashed it and taped it to the wall."

Becoming increasingly anxious about the publishing and recording contracts they'd signed with Hibbert, R.E.M. took them to their lawyer friend-cum-devoted fan Bertis Downs, looking for good advice. He told them quite plainly that they should never have signed them, because any band that gives away its publishing rights is selling its own future profits. Disappointing as this news was, the cloud did have a silver lining, because Downs so loved the band that he offered them his legal services for free. Another vital member – perhaps the most vital – of R.E.M.'s business team was now on board.

As much as the band hated the 'Radio Free Europe' single for its poor mix and bad mastering, there were members of the record-buying public who found other aspects of R.E.M.'s debut single unsatisfactory. "The first time I heard 'Radio Free Europe'," remembers Atlanta-based artist Sean Bourne, "I put it on for my ex-wife and she laughed and laughed. She put it on over and over again. There isn't a word you can understand on it."

Nevertheless, it's to R.E.M.'s credit that, despite their reservations, they now wholeheartedly threw their efforts behind the single. It was, they reasoned, too late to turn back, so they simply had to live with it. "We sent out a lot of copies ourselves," says Buck, "to every reviewer in America. And a lot of people liked it … which really dumbfounded us because we were really embarrassed by it." The influential *New York Rocker* praised its "ringing guitars and effortless rhythms", while Britain's *NME* hailed its "innocent charm and magic".

In retrospect, Radio Free Europe has been acknowledged as the moment in time when post-punk turned into alternative rock, but at the time, all that R.E.M. knew was that it was selling reasonably well in three locations. Athens was understandably the main bastion of support; Atlanta was coming in a close second; but third, and potentially the most important, was New York City. And that's where they returned on September 16th, to play at the New Pilgrim Theater, a Lower East Side joint on Third Street, described by photographer George Dubose as, "a really heavy heroin-purchasing area".

Jefferson Holt's girl of the time, Ann Louise Lipman, had given an R.E.M. tape to Dubose, knowing that in his role as a photographer he had contacts in the Big Apple music industry. When they came to play at the New Pilgrim, Dubose hospitably offered R.E.M. temporary lodgings at his 34th Street studio, in the shadow of the Empire State Building. They all accepted except Stipe, who stayed with friends in Greenwich Village.

Dubose even did a photo session with them, hampered somewhat by the fact that "it was the night after Bill Berry had passed out without removing his contact lenses, so he had suffered a laceration of the eye". Even a cursory look at those shots reveals that Berry does indeed seem somewhat more droopy-lidded than the others. Dubose chose to take the tape first to Ian Copeland at IRS, a happy coincidence, which must have further convinced Copeland – who had already mentioned them to his brother Miles – that the water around R.E.M. was heating up.

It certainly was. By the close of the year, no less an organ of the establishment than the *New York Times* had placed 'Radio Free Europe' in its top ten singles of 1981, and the hipper-than-hip *Village Voice* was calling it one of America's greatest singles ever. Suddenly it just didn't matter whether or not Sean Bourne's ex-wife thought it was funny.

Chapter Five

R.E.M.

Growing Pains

"Major labels would say, 'Well, gee, if you guys would get nice haircuts and start dressing up, maybe put a synthesiser in your band, maybe we'd sign you'."
BILL BERRY

After the fire: Tyrone's club, 1982

On the morning of January 8th, 1982, Athens, Georgia, woke up to find it had lost a dear friend. "It was a sad, sad day," said Mike Mills. "Everybody was upset."

Nobody had died, nobody had contracted an incurable disease but, dammit, Tyrone's had burnt down. "The suspended heater broke off its moorings, fell on to the stage and bang! There everything went," explained Mills. "It happened at about four in the morning. It would have been better if people had been there because they would have been able to stop it. It was a total loss."

Pylon had played their first gig at Tyrone's; there's a legendary R.E.M. bootleg that was recorded in Tyrone's; and it was generally regarded by the local music cognoscenti as the best gig in town, the hub of the rock'n'roll community. To make matters worse, the fire had destroyed not just the club but also the equipment and instruments belonging to two local bands, Little Tigers and Men In Trees. Capping it all was the fact that, in the words of co-owner Steve Ekard, the venue had been "between insurance companies" when the flames took hold, so there was no possibility of re-building the venue or recovering the cost of the two bands' gear.

Mills then, was absolutely right to say that everybody was upset, and no-one more so than he himself when he learned that just about the only thing that had survived the conflagration, by virtue of having been locked in an iron strongbox, was his hefty and long overdue bar tab.

Nevertheless, R.E.M., in common with other local bands including Pylon, Side Effects and Deboize, immediately offered to play benefit gigs that might help alleviate the financial burdens on Little Tigers, Men In Trees and the proprietors of Tyrone's.

R.E.M's benefit show took place at The 40 Watt Club on January 14th. Aside from serving its fund-raising purpose, it is memorable because R.E.M. used the event to plug an event the next day – the Athens debut of rockin' country-punks Jason And The Scorchers.

The previous July, when R.E.M. had voyaged north to Nashville to play at Cantrell's, a young man by the name of Jason Ringenberg was in the audience. "They were compelling right from the start," he told me. "Their set built from the beginning to the end – chock full of stick-in-your-head melodies and incredibly tight grooves. They were confident and poised. In those days they rocked pretty hard, some of the stuff sounding almost psychobilly. They closed the night with an Eddie Cochran song. Stipe was directly pointing at anyone not dancing and yelling at them to get up and move! They were the greatest rock'n'roll band on the planet at that moment. The night changed me as a musician and singer."

It changed him so much that he decided maybe he should, after all, start that band he'd been thinking about for so long. So he did, and on September 17th, Jason & The Scorchers played their first gig, as support to rockabilly legend Carl Perkins.

R.E.M. and Ringenberg crossed paths shortly after that, when The Scorchers supported R.E.M. at Cantrell's, and a lasting friendship was formed. "We hung out together and chased each other's girlfriends," recalls Ringenberg.

"In those days," remembers The Scorchers' original bassist Jack Emerson, "The Scorchers, R.E.M., Alex Chilton, The dB's, The Replacements and other indie bands were all sleeping on each others' floors, helping each other land gigs. All of that was based on fandom; we all wanted to communicate as much music to as many people as possible."

It must have gladdened the hearts of many in the audience at The 40 Watt Club on January 15th when Ringenberg announced from the stage that he wouldn't have been in a band if it wasn't for R.E.M. Right there in front of them was living proof that their very own Athens favourites were already having an impact on aspiring musicians hundreds of miles away.

"They had told their agent to book us," remembers Ringenberg. "They all came to the show and we had a major jam at the end of the night. On the last chord I tried to dive off the bar into a garbage can. I missed. I think it was Peter who helped me regain my senses."

'Radio Free Europe', meanwhile, was also continuing to make ripples in far distant places. Steve Wynn (later to support R.E.M. as a member of Dream Syndicate) was working as a product buyer in the Los Angeles branch of Rhino Records when the buzz about the single reached his ears. "I knew they were from Georgia, and I think I read something in *New York Rocker*," is his recollection. "My friend at another record store heard we had the single and was so excited he asked me to hold him a copy."

There was even evidence that the promo copies of the single had started to hit targets in higher places. Several major labels had written to the band and, on the whole, their letters had gone straight into the Barber Street waste paper bin. There was a definite feeling within R.E.M. that a major label deal at such an early stage in their development could work to their detriment. Berry has gone on record stating, "Major labels would say, 'Well, gee, if you guys would get nice haircuts and start dressing up, maybe put a synthesiser in your band, maybe we'd sign you.'" For a band whose appeal lay to a large extent in its idiosyncracies, this was really not an option.

Bill Berry has also offered a more succinct and perhaps more honest appraisal of why they were wary of a major deal: "We didn't think we were ready."

There was beginning to be a sense that the word about R.E.M. was going out, snaking across the nation, but the mundane reality, as Jefferson Holt told *Rolling Stone* magazine some years later, was that "The great reviews and Top Ten lists didn't change the fact that we were in a '75 Dodge Tradesman lugging all our gear ourselves."

On the plus side, they were parking that Dodge outside bigger venues, collecting fatter fees and calling more of the shots. On January 23rd, for example, they played Viceroy Park, located in a strip mall on Tyvola Road in Charlotte, North Carolina, supported by Mitch Easter's band, Let's Active. R.E.M. had played larger venues as a support act, but the audience at Viceroy

Park, estimated at 400 people, was high by their usual standards as headliners, and the fee of $680 well above their norm. Jefferson Holt even pulled a move on the venue's management, insisting that a local theatre troupe, Hit And Run, change their planned slot, moving from between the two bands to before either of them.

Four days later, R.E.M. returned to Mitch Easter's Drive-In Studios with the intention of recording enough material to release an EP for Holt and Healey's Dasht Hopes label. For once, though, they didn't travel in the lime-green Dodge. "They were going to drive up there but their van broke down," recalls their good friend Kurt Wood, whose stick-thin, Afro-topped frame was regularly to be seen throwing shapes in The 40 Watt, Tyrone's and anywhere else that good music happened in Athens. On the first day of recording, says Wood, "They came by at work and asked me if I could get off work and I drove them up in my dad's Volvo."

Perhaps in the light of the problems they'd encountered with 'Radio Free Europe', R.E.M. had considered trying another studio, Channel One in Atlanta, but a relationship of sorts had been forged with Easter, who had come to check out their live shows, and had even debuted his own band, Let's Active, as support at an R.E.M. gig in the 688 Club, Atlanta on November 13th of the previous year.

On hearing that they were considering Channel One, Easter had bent Holt's ear until he agreed to bring the band back to the 24′ by 24′ garage at Drive-In, even though its facilities were hardly 'state of the art'. Although some of his recording equipment was of a good standard, Easter himself has pointed out that, "There was nothing like a 'main' room! The drums were in an area of the garage, which was directly across from the control room window, basically in a 12′ by 24′ half of the garage. The control room was an actual room, which was one fourth of the area. Then the remaining one fourth of the space was another room, so amps could be in there and shut off from the drums."

Despite such primitive surroundings, the two days flew by effortlessly. "*Chronic Town* was really fun to make even though it sounds really basic," enthuses Easter. "They were really excited about being in the studio … They were just having a great time."

'Gardening At Night' is perhaps the best-known track from the resulting *Chronic Town* EP but the one that Easter really rated was 'Wolves, Lower'. "The first time I heard it was when they played it on stage. I thought, 'What an awesome song.' It was sort of more advanced than the songs they had before." Unfortunately, the version recorded at these particular sessions was taken at a breakneck speed quite unsuited to the song.

Less than a week later, R.E.M. had their first taste of a top-quality big city recording facility when they took up an offer from RCA of free studio time. They spent two days in RCA's Studio C in New York, with Kurt Munkacsi at the helm.

Munkacsi was a man of experience and taste, best known for his lengthy association with the contemporary composer Philip Glass. In his role as Glass's producer since 1973, he had redefined the parameters of recording orchestral music, moving away from the standard approach of attempting to achieve a realistic live performance feel, towards a rock-orientated approach of creating an artificial landscape that would work well on stereo speakers in a home environment. He had also worked with artists as diverse as Ravi Shankar, S'Express, The Waitresses and Lou Reed.

"One of my good friends in New York was Jim Fouratt, who ran several happening clubs, such as the Peppermint Lounge, Danceteria and Hurrahs," says Munkacsi. "He and I had long wanted to work on a project together. It was Jim who told me about R.E.M. and who I think had also put the idea of recording them to Nancy Jeffries, the A&R head at RCA."

Having been to see them play at Maxwell's in Hoboken, New Jersey, Munkacsi and Fouratt were sufficiently impressed to want to move to the next level.

The night before the sessions started, Munkacsi took the band out to try to get to know them a little better. "I took them to a Japanese restaurant on 45th Street in Manhattan, and I think it was the first time they'd ever been wined and dined by a major record company. What struck me right away was that although he was officially their manager, Jefferson Holt seemed much more like the fifth member of the band."

They asked me if I could get off work. I drove them up in my dad's Volvo

However much the expense account sake and sushi may have relaxed them that evening, R.E.M.'s anxiety meters were peaking in the red again by the time they entered Studio C the next day. "We were so nervous we could barely play," admitted Buck later. "We knew that (Munkacsi) had worked on a Lou Reed album and we thought, 'Christ! This guy worked with Lou Reed. He's seen it all.'"

Munkacsi, however, was genuinely impressed with what he saw and heard. "They played very well. The songs were obviously well rehearsed and they knew exactly what they were doing. The session was very spontaneous, with everything going down in one or two takes."

Like others before him, Munkacsi was struck by Stipe's vocal technique. "The funniest aspect of the whole session was trying to get Michael to sing the words clearly. But he made it quite plain that it was his intention that the words should be hard to understand, so I just accepted that this was his way of working."

Given his Philip Glass background, it was natural that Munkacsi would suggest embellishing R.E.M.'s basic tracks, and this was attempted at a second session on the 22nd. "We put down some keyboards and orchestration ideas but it was pretty obvious that the music didn't warrant it. Clearly nobody was going to orchestrate this band, so we gave up on that quite quickly."

The evidence of bootleg versions reveals these tracks as good, solid performances, well recorded, if a little more mainstream than the Drive-In versions of the same material. "RCA was very happy with the demos," recalls Munkacsi, "and even offered a recording contract for an EP, but they didn't go for it, which I think was the right decision for them at that time."

"If we'd been on RCA," Buck has since reasoned, "our album would've come out the same week as a Scotty Baio album. Now, I don't have a whole lot of dignity, it's just that I would prefer to have our record sold by people used to selling things like us."

It's fortunate, then, that RCA wasn't the only avenue open to them. Columbia and Arista had also made approaches but, showing remarkable strength of purpose and commitment to the idea of signing to the right label rather than just the biggest, R.E.M. held them at bay. "We wanted to go with someone who was our size," is how Stipe summed up their attitude.

On June 4, R.E.M. hooked up with Jason & The Scorchers again for a gig at Augusta College in Augusta, Georgia. "It truly had become a community of like minded southern – not southern rock – bands and R.E.M. was the central hub," says Ringenberg. "I will never forget that one night in Augusta.

"There was no money for a hotel and we were prepared to drive overnight the 400 miles back to Nashville. They gave us money from their fee to buy us a room, and this was when they had very little money themselves.

"They did things like that for bands and people everywhere, even before they could afford it. They were incredibly generous and led the charge. They did sleep on our floors when they played Nashville but frankly most of the help was from them to us. To this day they still are the most generous and communally minded musicians that I have personally known."

Meanwhile, Ian Copeland's faith in the band was such that he had signed them to an agency deal via his own company, FBI, even though they had no record contract. In an effort to rectify that situation, Ian had been badgering away on R.E.M.'s behalf, pushing their tape at his older brother Miles, head of the independent IRS Records. "Miles made the mistake I would have made," says Ian. "I said these were friends of mine from Macon, and I don't think he ever listened to it, just wrote it off as me trying to push some buddies."

Miles' attitude isn't difficult to understand because, after all, he didn't exactly need another band. Miles, who formed IRS in 1979, had already guided the careers of The Police, Go-Gos and Wishbone Ash, and was about to launch another internationally chart-topping act – of which more later.

Miles Axe Copeland III was the son of Miles Copeland Jr, a respected jazz trumpeter who later became a top US secret service operative, on friendly terms with George Bush, then head of the CIA. To be a successful rock manager requires an unusual combination of ruthlessness and diplomacy, plus, ideally, some understanding of music. Clearly, Miles's family background could not have been more perfect.

Miles has summed himself up in these words: "I'm very American and loud and believe you get what you deserve and work for, which is the basic American dream." What that doesn't reveal is the man's sense of humour. Given the family background, Miles had found it amusing to call his record label IRS, claiming that it stood for International Record Syndicate, when countless millions of his fellow Americans were paying tax to the original IRS (Internal Revenue Service). His brother Ian's agency, as already noted, was FBI, and Miles has also initiated a film and television company called CCCP, (Copeland, Copeland, Copeland and Power) and a Los Angeles-based management arm, LAPD (Los Angeles Personnel Direction).

In the early months of 1983, then, Miles Copeland was steadfastly ignoring his brother's pleas on behalf of his buddies from Macon. Fortunately, other forces were at work. Mark Williams, a DJ at one of R.E.M.'s regular gigs, the 688 Club in Atlanta, had sent a copy of 'Radio Free Europe' to Jay Boberg, the vice president of IRS. He recalls, "It was not the kind of thing you listened to once or twice, casually, and said, 'Oh my God, this is tremendous!' It had a depth to it." And that depth was what kept Boberg re-playing it over and over again.

Thoroughly intrigued, Boberg hopped on a plane to New Orleans on March 12th, 1982 to catch R.E.M.'s very poorly attended gig at the Beat Exchange, not the most salubrious of venues. "I walked into the bathroom," Buck told Jim Greer of *Spin* magazine, "and there was this syringe. Someone had darted it into the wall."

"There were about four or five people," remembers Boberg, "and half of those, including the club owner, were on smack. Jefferson was trying to work out the sound and it didn't sound great, but the band's star quality was so clear, and the music was amazing."

The band didn't think so. In fact, Buck has described it as "one of the worst dates we've ever done." By the time Boberg came backstage afterwards and said, "Hi, I'm Jay Boberg from IRS," Stipe was so disheartened by their poor performance that he responded, "Yeah, we were afraid of that."

But Boberg had already made up his mind to sign them. What he didn't know was that R.E.M.'s business affairs were, to say the least, complicated. 'Radio Free Europe' had been on Hib-Tone and the tracks that would become *Chronic Town* had been paid for by Dasht Hopes. The contracts for both deals were still in force, so signing them to IRS could prove much more problematic than signing a band with no legal ties.

This was where Bertis Downs's legal expertise first proved its true worth to the band. Using some front money from IRS, he bought the band out of their contract with Jonathan Hibbert of Hib-Tone who, luckily for the band, was experiencing extreme cash-flow problems. "Bert Downs drew up a contract so R.E.M. could purchase their publishing on the two songs, the metal masters, the artwork and the record," says Hibbert. "I sold it. I was talked into giving them what they wanted." The cost of the deal to R.E.M. was a mere $2,000. To Hibbert, the hidden cost was a comfortable future, but how could he know that retaining the rights to 'Radio Free Europe' would have kept him in beer and pretzels for the rest of his life?

David Healey, arguably, fared even worse. When the *Chronic Town* EP was eventually released, the back cover bore the legend 'A Dasht Hopes Production' and listed Healey as ex-producer. In fact he was already out of the picture. Details of whatever deal may have been struck with him are hard to find, but the man who funded *Chronic Town* ended up as little more than an almost-forgotten bit-player in the R.E.M. saga. "David Healey was a very gifted painter and, for a while, a very good friend," Mike Mills has said. "But his behaviour became extremely erratic and I think he was drinking way too much."

It took Healey many years to accept that R.E.M.'s treatment of him, harsh as it seemed at the time, was inevitable. To progress, they needed more than a backwoods record label, and it would have been madness for them not to go with IRS. Tragically, soon after Healey overcame his drinking problem and re-established friendly relations with R.E.M., he was killed by a hit and run driver.

With the band free of ill-advised legal entanglements, they were now free to sign to IRS, but not before Bertis Downs made sure they'd never make the same mistakes again. He set up two new companies, R.E.M./Athens Ltd and Night Gardening, the first of which would look after the day-to-day business affairs of the band, while the second was specifically a publishing company, to protect their valuable song copyrights. Downs also registered the band name as a trademark, cannily out-manoeuvering several other outfits around the world who were already called the same thing.

Although Jefferson Holt was still in complete managerial control of R.E.M., Bertis Downs' importance to the group was growing daily. West Virginia-born Downs had been largely brought up by his mother, because his father, a Presbyterian minister, had died in a plane crash when the boy was seven. Always a music fan, he got the business bug at college where he began booking bands for student gigs. "A friend and I got a job at the Fairmont Hotel as bellhops," he recalls. "We got to wait on the Rolling Stones, carrying their luggage, bringing them room service. This was about 1975 and they seemed old to me at the time … They were in their early thirties."

Like the members of R.E.M., Downs attended UGA in 1981, but unlike them, he left with an honours degree in law. "I knew Bill from the concert committee and Peter when he worked behind the counter at Wuxtry. I did their early contracts and helped them realize there was a business aspect as well as an artistic aspect to music. Now they are the board of directors and I run the company."

In New York, meanwhile, Jay Boberg had advised Miles Copeland of his intention to sign R.E.M. to the label. Miles now found himself being assaulted on two different fronts on behalf of the same band. But his major pre-occupation was his latest signing, an all-girl group by the name of The Bangs. It was his hope that Ian would organise gigs for them via his FBI booking agency. At this point, Ian realised that he might be able to do a bit of horse-trading with Miles.

"I didn't really want to handle them," says Ian, "so I did a deal with him. 'I'll do The Bangs if you sign R.E.M.' And The Bangs turned out to be The Bangles and R.E.M. were very beneficial for IRS, so it was a good deal all round."

While all these negotiations proceeded, R.E.M. continued to play live whenever the opportunity presented itself. On April 14th, for example, they could be found at Toad's Place in New Haven, Connecticut, supporting legendary guitar instrumental band The Ventures. The gig is etched in Stipe's memory. "I remember opening for The Ventures once and they played 'Classical Gas' and I was transfixed." He wasn't too over-awed, however, to put on a good show himself. "Michael gave it 200 per cent," remembers audience member Betsy Dorminey. "They worked really hard and they were just delightful and wonderful ... even if there was hardly anybody in the room."

Outside of Athens it wasn't unusual for them to play for mere handfuls of people, but Mike Mills insists, "We never lost money ever on a tour and we did that in the early days by staying in hotel rooms with two double beds. Peter and I stayed in one, and Michael and Bill slept in the other. Sometimes, if we had a manager with us, somebody else would rotate out to the van."

Michael Stipe's reputation as an eccentric was rapidly establishing itself by now. One acquaintance has claimed that he would happily pull out a toothbrush in

They are the board, and I run the company

a bar and brush his teeth in public. Another, Ken Fechtner, recalls waking up in bed one night to find Stipe staring at him. "I asked him what he was doing and he said, 'I'm watching you sleep.'"

The deal with IRS was signed in mid-May, followed immediately by a gig at Clutch Cargo's in Detroit, playing to an audience that yelled and screamed for more. R.E.M. repaid the crowd's enthusiasm by taking the entire audience – all four of them – out to a celebration dinner.

The signing was made public on May 31st, and there's little doubt in anyone's mind that, despite pocketing only a meagre $25,000 advance, R.E.M. had made the right choice. "IRS was about the boundaries of the biggest label we wanted," explained Buck. "Every band they have is really good. Maybe not all of them are to my taste, but they show real intelligence in signing them." Stipe put it even more plainly. "Any label who would sign The Cramps, you gotta have some respect for."

It was left to Jefferson Holt, however, to explain the financial thinking behind the deal. "We didn't want to owe anybody any money," he said. "And we don't want a large budget to record an album because we don't need it. The band knows the songs, they play the music live, and they don't really like the idea of futzing around in the studio for three months."

For Miles Copeland too, it was a win-win situation. Against stiff competition, he had secured a band with massive potential for a relatively small outlay. "R.E.M. were one of the very rare groups who practised what they preached," he recalled later. "They never walked into our office and said, 'Why aren't you doing this? Why aren't you doing that? Why don't we have more money?' Never once."

The first IRS release was slated to be *Chronic Town* but Boberg and Copeland felt that the proposed track listing – 'Ages Of You', 'Gardening At Night', 'Carnival Of Sorts', '1,000,000' and 'Stumble' – was let down by 'Ages Of You'. Like Mitch Easter, they felt that 'Wolves, Lower', was a stronger song, but that the speedy version they'd recorded wasn't doing it justice.

So on June 1st, they were back at Drive-In. "They returned and re-cut 'Wolves, Lower'," says Easter. "The first version is identical but unbelievably fast! Vocals were quick; it just took him a couple of takes, a couple of punch-ins, maybe another couple of tracks of funny noises and whispers. Backing vocals: same story. Really quick."

Back in Athens, the burning down of Tyrone's had left a gap in the club scene from R.E.M.'s point of view. They now drew too many people to play comfortably at The 40 Watt, and so had to find a new venue for hometown shows. They settled for The I&I, playing there for the first time on June 25th.

Located in a vast former warehouse at 244 Oconee Street, it had operated as a beer parlour since the early 1970s as The B&L Warehouse, gradually evolving into a live music venue around 1979 before re-naming itself The I&I Club in 1980. "The I&I was kind of a hang out for sorority and fraternity people, so it never really had a cool reputation," points out Mike Mills's former live-in partner Lauren Hall, "The good thing about it was that it was huge, so we'd get bigger bands coming to town." But it would never replace Tyrone's.

Early in August, the band re-located themselves briefly to Los Angeles, moving into the Oakwood Garden apartments on Barham Boulevard. With the release of *Chronic Town* imminent, the intention was to be near the IRS head office, to get to know the staff and be available for promotional activities. Like all men cut adrift from their womenfolk, they immediately reverted to slobbism.

"We found a liquor store that would deliver beer, sandwiches and cigarettes," recalls Buck. "So, about three o'clock in the afternoon, we'd order a case of beer, four sandwiches and a pack of cigs."

They also went out and played gigs, but soon found the local audiences bewilderingly different from anything they'd previously encountered. "In New York they kind of stand around and watch you," said Buck. "In the South everyone dances. In the Midwest they're kind of slow to warm up but then get very enthusiastic." In Los Angeles, however, Buck reckoned the response was "really more of a non-response."

By the time the *Chronic Town* EP hit the streets on August 24th, R.E.M. had laid the groundwork with a string of press and radio interviews arranged by IRS, which made sure that anyone who wanted to know about it probably would know. Compared to 'Radio Free Europe', it was definitely a step forward. Not only was *Chronic Town* better sounding," says Mitch Easter, "I thought the songwriting was expanding and progressing wonderfully! I really liked all the songs, especially 'Wolves, Lower'. *Chronic Town* almost sounds like a jazz recording to me, which I still like."

The critical fraternity, however, was divided between those who loved it, those who hated it and those who were clearly just too confused by its combination of tradition and sonic innovation to know what to make of it. IRS radio plugger Keith Altomare reported that many of his contacts at college radio fell into this latter category, although, understandably, "The Georgia stations and some of the more together college stations across the country jumped on it."

Chronic Town didn't set the world on fire, but it did notch up 20,000 sales inside a year and served its purpose of telling the world that R.E.M. existed. For those with ears to hear and the patience to listen more than once, this was clearly a band that was not about to go away.

Before leaving Los Angeles, on August 31st, they took the next logical step for a band in their position. They made a video. "Our idea was to have a non-slick video that portrays energy and change without fog and dwarves dancing," explained Buck. "We were trying to get across that we are a live band and we are energetic."

It was a one-camera shoot in the Club Lingerie, presenting the band in a performance of 'Wolves, Lower' that does achieve Buck's stated aim, but makes almost no attempt to be a faithful representation of the recorded version of the song. It's none too clear whether the director was aiming for art, documentary realism or commercial promo, and it was to be some while before R.E.M.'s representation in the form of moving images would start to make any kind of sense to their record company. MTV had been launched just a year earlier, but already it was noticeable that bands with videos did significantly better in the charts than bands without them. The success of the second British invasion of America, headed by Culture Club, Duran Duran and their ilk, is rightly attributed to heavy MTV rotation of their promo clips at a time when US acts hadn't fully grasped the implications of the video revolution.

This was not the case with R.E.M. They understood the phenomenon perfectly well but they were determined not to play the game by anybody else's rules. "Too much, too often these days is simply handed to an audience. MTV is a good example," said Stipe. "There's no room for imagination, no room for improvisation, for interpretation. Everything's rehearsed … people need to think for themselves again."

Allowing people to think for themselves isn't something that comes naturally to the music business. The tendency is to try to create and control what people think by the application of big budgets to promotional vehicles – videos being just one example. The reason for this is purely pragmatic, and largely to do with turnover.

The rock music industry in the 1950s could be likened to the world in medieval times, with literally hundreds of small local record labels all over America, whose owners were like the robber barons who populate Robin Hood movies. Yes, there were also major labels like Columbia and RCA, but those were largely bastions of the establishment, rooted in classical music, swing, crooners and jazz.

By the early 1980s the picture had changed. The music industry had become a massive worldwide rock-orientated business dominated by a small number of large labels – notably EMI, Columbia, WEA, RCA and MCA. And those companies, whose actions were formerly dictated by A&R men, were now dominated by accountants, because any huge business employing thousands of people needs to generate cash constantly.

Simple factors, such as the need to keep factories economic by having them churn out vinyl 24 hours a day, seven days a week, meant that music frequently took second place to product – the product being lumps of vinyl, flattened into a circular shape, and packed in cardboard sleeves.

To keep those factory wheels turning required the public to buy ever-increasing amounts of product, and video was one way to achieve that aim, by manufacturing instant disposable pop idols who could sell five million records in six months and then vanish almost without trace. Idols of this sort are not required to pay their dues by playing for five years in New Orleans drug dens and backwoods moonshine whiskey bars before earning star status. They could become stars overnight, so long as they accepted that they could just as easily disappear overnight. Zero to hero, and back to zero, just to keep the factories busy.

R.E.M. didn't accept that this was the only way. Stipe's dictum, that "people need to think for themselves again", is true, but it's certainly not the reason why R.E.M. became the biggest band on the planet.

Chapter Six

Faith In The Tastemakers

"That was the beginning of our odyssey with the record company, and, I suppose, the pressures between commercialism and art."
MIKE MILLS

Heritage trail: outside St Mary's Church in 1983

R.E.M. became the biggest band on the planet because some people have always thought for themselves. You see them everywhere you go. They're the ones not wearing the latest fashion, not trotting out the current catchphrases and buzzwords, not checking the pop charts every week to find out what they should be buying.

Record company marketing, aimed at psychologically bludgeoning the masses into buying product, virtually ignores those people because, statistically, they appear to be an insignificant minority. And yet, consciously or unconsciously, R.E.M. were directing themselves at them.

In fact, these people are anything but insignificant. Most of us can remember somebody a little bit different who we'd see in the corridor at school or college, or in the coffee shop, or at the record store. That person might well have been considered odd, an outsider or even an outcast. But whatever record that person was carrying was worth checking out, because somehow they knew more about this stuff than we did.

In the late 1960s, when their peers were buying The Monkees, those outsiders were buying The Sonics. By the mid-1970s, when everybody else was lapping up The Eagles, these people carried around a Kraftwerk album like a badge of identity. In August 1982, when millions were consuming Fleetwood Mac, these were the people clutching *Chronic Town*. They just knew that it spoke to them in a way no record had ever done before.

Let's call these people tastemakers. They couldn't achieve what Michael Stipe was hoping for: they couldn't actually make other people think for themselves. But given time they could – and would – influence what a lot of those other people bought. Using tastemakers as a marketing strategy is a slow process, a building process, and it requires that the artist doesn't betray their trust.

When a tastemaker perceives that a favourite artist has 'sold out', the relationship is usually over. The upside is that if the artist never betrays that trust, the tastemaker is probably hooked for life.

With a video-led pop act, let's say New Kids On The Block, the dynamic is very different. A huge fan base is built quickly, but there's never any relationship of trust or respect, because the artist never says anything to the consumer that hasn't previously been said by Bobby Vee or The Jackson Five or A Flock Of Seagulls. Boredom rather than betrayal becomes the deciding factor and, given an audience with a short attention span, that boredom can set in fast. Loyalty will last only until the next equally well-marketed phenomenon comes along, or until the artist no longer looks good in spandex. By placing their faith in the tastemakers, R.E.M. were accepting that their ride to the top might take years but, once there, they could expect to retain a faithful following for decades to come.

September 1982 found R.E.M. back out on tour again, supporting Gang Of Four for the entire month, before starting a string of headlining dates that would run through from early October into the middle of December. Old friend Peter Holsapple (on a solo acoustic sabbatical from the dB's) provided support on the majority of nights.

The touring regime, evidently, remained as squalid as ever. "We didn't really eat anything," remembers Buck. "We slept on people's floors. It was kind of romantic. It was cool. I guess a lot of people who weren't ambitious, weren't directed as we were, might've found it too much."

While R.E.M. were criss-crossing the country, of course, their women were stuck in Athens but, when they felt low, they always knew there was one person they could turn to – Bertis Downs. "Whenever the band would go out of town," remembers Sandi Phipps, Jefferson Holt's girlfriend of the time, "Bert would come and take us out. We would sit on his front porch on Prince Avenue all night. He would buy us flowers."

After a brief return home for a couple of celebratory nights at The I&I in mid-October, R.E.M. found themselves supporting The Beat (known as The English Beat in the US) and Squeeze, in front of 13,000 people at Nassau Coliseum, Long Island, on November 24th. "When you think about it," suggested an over-awed Peter Buck at the time, "that's almost as many people as have bought our record so far. What if they all went out and bought the record and doubled the sales?"

So far, the relationship with IRS was going smoothly but the possibility of a hiccup presented itself when Jay Boberg, keen to give the band a better production sound than had been achieved on *Chronic Town*, suggested working with up and coming producer Stephen Hague, former keyboard player of the critically acclaimed Joolz And The Polar Bears.

R.E.M. were perfectly happy with the way things had been going with Mitch Easter and saw no good reason to fix something that wasn't broke but, in an effort to maintain good relations, they agreed to try something with Hague.

"Jay Boberg was a friend of mine from LA, and he really wanted to get R.E.M. on the radio. The synthy stuff was starting to hap-

We didn't eat. We slept on people's floors

pen, so he thought of me, because he knew what I'd done in the Polar Bears," Hague told me, talking about the R.E.M. session for the first time.

"So, in December of 1982, I went down to Athens with an engineer, Walter Turbot, and had dinner with the band. The next day we went into a rehearsal studio in Athens and they played me the track 'Catapult'. We discussed maybe changing a couple of things, and we were getting along well."

Things began to go a little adrift when they moved to a better-equipped studio in Atlanta for the actual recording sessions. "The first problem I encountered was with Bill Berry," remembers Hague. "I was used to working with a brilliant drummer, David Beebe, in the Polar Bears, so I was pushing Bill very hard to get the best out of him. We spent a long time doing the drums and I think it demoralised him."

Nevertheless, at the end of the session, the general feeling was the effort had been worth-while. "Michael Stipe came up to me and said, 'I didn't enjoy the process, but I really like the way it sounds.'"

At this point, Hague was probably still in the frame to produce their next album, but then he took the tracks to The Cars' studio, Synchro Sound in Boston. "I was given carte blanche by Jay Boberg to do whatever I liked with them, so I added some keyboard parts. When I gave it to Jay, he was really interested in it but, when the band heard it, they didn't like it at all."

IRS now reluctantly arranged for a second test recording with Mitch Easter, this time mov-ing from the somewhat primitive 16-track facilities of the Drive-In to the 24-track board at Reflection Sound Studios in Charlotte, North Carolina. "It's mostly a gospel place," explained Buck. "We wanted to get the sonic quality of a bigger room."

From Easter's perspective, Reflection Sound was a little daunting. Virtually all of his record-ing expertise had been acquired in his beloved garage, so this was a move into unfamiliar terri-tory. To forestall any problems, he called up an old high school friend, Don Dixon, who had worked at Reflection. "Mitch asked me to help out," says Dixon. "I had consulted with him a bit on *Chronic Town*, and he felt like my added experience with big-time record companies might come in handy – at this point I had already made a few albums for major labels either as artist or producer."

Dixon might well have been tailor-made for R.E.M. Like Easter, he was a musician at heart, who believes his real function in the studio is "trying to save musicians from the kind of shit that producers had put me through". And like R.E.M. he was committed to the idea that, "Sometimes it's better for the long-term if people develop on their own terms. Not everything can be measured in the short term."

When Easter and Dixon, out of professional curiosity, asked if they could hear what the band had done with Stephen Hague, they opened up a can of worms. According to Dixon, they told him that Hague "did the typical thing of making them do 390 takes, and saying Berry sucked, and trying to get them to change all their parts and everything – and they hated it".

"They were so upset," remembers Easter, "we had to beg them to play it for us and it seemed to make them almost sick to even hear it … we had to sort of regain their confidence."

It's regrettable if this gives the impression that Stephen Hague was a poor producer – he was far from it. Hague's understanding of the emerging synthesiser technology was rarely less than brilliant when he went on to produce hits by virtually every British electro-pop band of the 1980s, including the Human League, the Pet Shop Boys, Orchestral Manoeuvres In The Dark, New Order and Erasure. In their own fields, Hague and R.E.M. represented pinnacles of achievement. Unfortunately, the distance between those pinnacles proved impossible to bridge.

Many years passed before Buck was able to admit,"It wasn't such a bad experience. I like Stephen and he's made some great records, but he wanted to work in a way that we weren't interest in."

The net result though, was that Easter and Dixon were now confronted by a band with a deep mistrust of studio trickery. "They were a little bit paranoid that the music business was gonna mess them up," said Easter, "and I think to some extent they don't exactly trust anybody as much as they used to. Back then [on *Chronic Town*] I think they thought 'Wow, this is great, we can play with this stuff' and now it's like, 'Don't put that high tech shit on our record.'"

Mike Mills remembers, "It was the beginning of trying to not be afraid of the studio, since we knew nothing about all the knobs and buttons and blinking lights. It was a very intimidating process, which is why we wanted Mitch – we felt it was someone we could trust. So that was just the beginning of a very long, ongoing learning process."

Utterly disenchanted with 'Catapult', R.E.M. decided to work on the haunting but hook-filled 'Pilgrimage' as the test song at Reflection and, thankfully, it proved to be a breeze. The track was captured on January 6th in one take and mixed the following day in a single session, leaving band and producers convinced they'd got it right. Mitch remembers, however, that IRS, probably miffed that their Stephen Hague idea had been rejected, "were just lukewarm about it".

Lukewarm was enough though, given the band's determination to work with Easter and Dixon, so sessions began on January 20th, aimed at completing an entire album, with a $15,000 budget. Don Dixon has said that, "Though IRS was skeptical about a bunch of hayseeds – a hayseed mafia, more or less – creating this record, they ultimately were very cool about letting us have at it. I believe that they just wanted to make a big splash at college radio – their investment was minimal. You should take note that the band was sharing one motel room while recording this thing … and not even a very *nice* motel."

On the whole, the sessions proceeded in a thoroughly professional manner, although Easter recalls prodigious quantities of beer being quaffed by the band, and frequent trips to the local thrift store to alleviate the cabin fever of being locked up in a studio. "There wasn't really any time for social life," confirms Mills. "We were in there from 12 to 12 and I think the only real time we took off is when we all went out to see the movie *Strange Invaders*, which was our very first song in a movie." This hilariously inept ultra-low-budget sci-fi schlock, directed by Michael Laughlin, has taken on a camp cult status, due at least in part to the inclusion of

R.E.M.'s *Chronic Town* track '1,000,000', which plays on a radio while a dog laps up a can of beer. "When the credits rolled and our names came up," adds Mills, "we all stood up and applauded like crazy! The other three people in the theater were baffled."

"They came with guitars in hand and a very specific vibe, a specific sound," recalls Dixon. "Mitch and I liked this band. We liked its quirkiness. We liked the songs they made up. We liked Michael's animal noises. We liked Bill's relentless drumming style. We liked Peter's arpeggiated guitar riffs, and we liked Mike's lead bass approach. We were very happy that we were able to preserve these unique qualities of the band."

As well as their "specific sound" – primarily guitar-orientated – they had the shape of the album already figured out. "I knew which songs were going to be on the record," Buck has said, "and had a good idea of what order they were going to be in." Above all, they were adamant that that they didn't want any synthesisers but, to Easter and Dixon's intense relief, they didn't rule out pianos, electric pianos or organs.

It's astonishing, given the ethereal beauty of Michael Stipe's voice in later years, that at the time of the *Murmur* session he genuinely did not know when he was singing in tune. "The guys would say I was out of pitch and I just kind of nodded," he has revealed. "I would say, 'What do I need to do?' They'd say, 'You're a little flat.' And then I would go out and sing it again and they would say, 'You're a little sharp now.'"

Murmur (so named by Stipe because, he claims, "it's one of

> # When the credits rolled and our names came up, we stood up and applauded like crazy

the six easiest words in the English language to say") was the first R.E.M. record bought in significant quantities, and it is still considered by many devotees to be the band's finest hour. So it's worth looking at the birth of each track individually.

'Radio Free Europe': previously released as their Hib-Tone single, it was re-recorded for *Murmur*, partly because the band felt they had improved since the first recording and partly because IRS asked them to. The tempo is slower and, says Buck, "I don't think we captured it the way we did on the single." Easter reckons this new version was "more pro, but it was a little too sedate".

As discussed earlier, the second track, 'Pilgrimage', was the sample song recorded by Easter and Dixon to win IRS approval for making a whole album. Anyone perplexed by such lyrics as, "They called the clip a two-headed cow/ Your hate clipped and distant, your luck, pilgrimage" can take comfort in knowing they're not alone. "'Pilgrimage' still baffles me," admits Stipe. "At one point, right after we recorded it, I heard it and it made perfect sense. I was so exhilarated. I thought I had accomplished what I set out to do. And then I forgot."

'Laughing': the richly textured guitar sound on this delicious track was achieved, says Easter, when "we did this sort of protest sit-in thing, with four people on acoustic guitars. It was me, Don Dixon, Pete Buck and Mike Mills. Then we tracked it again, so there are eight acoustic guitars on it." Stipe has claimed that lyric is, to some extent, about "Laocoon, a freak mythological figure who had two sons. All three were devoured by serpents. It was a popular theme in Renaissance painting."

'Talk About The Passion', which follows, is an exception to the rule that R.E.M. had all the songs for *Murmur* complete before they started recording. "They had been playing it some," explained Easter, "but they didn't have an arrangement. It was kind of rambling and went on forever." Easter and Dixon helped straighten that out. It's also notable for including Peter Buck's first actual guitar solo (taught to him by Mike Mills) and a lady cellist who was hired for $25. "We told her roughly what we wanted," says Buck, "and she was dumbfounded that we weren't going to give her a score."

'Moral Kiosk': Buck's distinctive guitar sound on this relatively rocking track was achieved by miking up Mitch Easter's little Ampeg amp from some distance, to let the ambience of the room have its effect. Mike Mills adds, "There is a clanking metal sound in the break of one of the songs, which is Mitch pounding on the metal leg of a chair with a metal pipe."

Buck has said that 'Perfect Circle' originated from a moment when he was standing in the city gardens in Trenton, New Jersey, and found himself moved to tears by the sight of children playing touch football as dusk fell. The feeling was so powerful that he asked Stipe to write a lyric that captured the same emotion. Stipe's response was to write about a former girlfriend, but both agree that the feeling achieved was exactly right. "I don't remember who thought of doing 'Perfect Circle' with the starting point being Bill and Mike playing two pianos at once," says Easter, "but the fact that Reflection had the 'nice' piano along with the 'saloon' one was essential to the direction that song took. Onstage, that song had been only vocal and a little Casio keyboard!"

'Catapult' is a re-recorded version of the song that had gone so wrong with Stephen Hague. Easter still feels it was "one of their really good catchy songs" and an obvious contender as a single, but it had become so tainted by the Hague experience that R.E.M. found it hard to love. Lyrically, it deals with one of Stipe's recurring themes, childhood.

'Sitting Still' was actually recorded in Easter's garage as the b-side of the 'Radio Free Europe' single. For *Murmur*, there was a little bit of tinkering with slightly out of tune backing vocals, and Buck recalls Mills re-recording his bass track. Otherwise, it's the same take. "We just mixed it again at Reflection," says Easter, "and we slowed the tape down a little bit." Lyrically, Stipe has admitted that the chorus was, "an embarrassing collection of vowels that I strung together ... basically nonsense".

'9-9' is the first of R.E.M.'s obvious Gang Of Four homages, and stands out as *Murmur*'s only serious rocker. The lyric is difficult to decipher even by Stipe's standards, but he claimed that in this case that was deliberate because the topic of the song is "conversation and fear of conversation". To make the aural texture even more blurry, the completed track was relayed back into the studio and re-recorded with a different miking arrangement.

'Shaking Through' is probably Murmur's least compelling and most formulaic track. An earlier version of 'Shaking Through' was completed during the Bombay sessions. Mitch Easter found it "a little too complacent sounding" and even Buck has subsequently grumbled that it feels twice as long as it actually is.

"The noise at the beginning of 'We Walk' is pool balls," says Dixon. "It's Bill playing pool, recorded really fast and then slowed down. That's what makes that thunderous noise ... We sped the tape up, recorded the pool balls hitting, slowed it down and added a lot of reverb, and then turned it into thunder." According to Stipe, the lyric was inspired by "a girl who lived on the second floor of this house and, every time she walked up the stairs, she would say, 'Up the stairs, into the hall.'"

'West Of The Fields' is said to have been about a trip Stipe took to New Orleans but, hey, you could have fooled me. It's another of those tracks that Buck has subsequently regretted, claiming that it features far too many chords. "There must be 15 chords in that song," he calculates. "We wanted no lead guitar and no heavy punk – just a fast, weird folk-rock record with tons of overdubs." Still, full marks to Mike Mills for his lovely counterpoint harmony.

The only real hint of tension in the *Murmur* sessions came when IRS began pressuring Easter and Dixon to give R.E.M. a more radio-friendly, 1980s-orientated sound, which they attempted to do while the band wasn't around.

"When we listened to the mixes of a couple of songs," remembers Mills, "I think 'Moral Kiosk' and 'Radio Free Europe', they were so discofied relative to what we wanted that Peter and I went up back up there and made Don remix them."

Up to this point, even given the Steven Hague debacle, R.E.M. had felt that IRS was giving them time to grow and evolve at their own pace, but now, says Buck, "It was a little depressing that all of a sudden they had to get involved. In a way, it kind of made us more guarded."

"That was the beginning of our odyssey with the record company," confirms Mills, "and, I suppose, the pressures between commercialism and art."

R.E.M. wrapped up the recording of *Murmur* on February 23rd, 1983, and retired back to Athens for a while to rest and prepare for a short tour with The Beat.

After a few warm-up one-nighters, the tour started on March 26th, 1983, and, despite their newfound reservations about IRS, Miles Copeland was now demonstrably happy with his new investment. "They were not spending fortunes in the studio and were making money on the road, because they didn't have expensive habits," he explains.

"So they were a good, tight, little business. They lived within their means and cut the cloth based on what they were going to generate, which is how you're supposed to run a business."

Having established a rapport with The Beat during the Long Island show back in November, Michael found that "Touring with the English Beat was exciting. We were playing places that were mostly all-age shows, and that is very hard to do. I think I can speak for all of us and say that we felt a certain camaraderie with them."

Jefferson Holt, meanwhile, was circulating tapes of the Reflection studio sessions to a few key people in and around Athens and Atlanta, in hopes of securing some early feedback. Not everyone was immediately smitten.

Anthony DeCurtis, later to become one of *Rolling Stone* magazine's most respected writers, was then just beginning his career and was already a huge fan of the band. "I had already heard many of the songs in performance," he says. "To my ears, the versions on the tape

They were a good, tight, little business

paled in comparison. They sounded precious and enclosed – the exact opposite of the exuberance and openness that excited me about R.E.M."

Buck almost seems to agree when he admits, "It was an old-fashioned record that didn't sound too much like what you heard on the radio. We were expecting the record company to say, 'Sorry, this isn't even a demo tape. Go back and do it again.'"

Steve Wynn of Dream Syndicate, however, was bowled over. "I remember being on tour in April of 1983, and our tour manager got an advance tape of *Murmur*," he recalled in *Talk About The Passion*, Denise Sullivan's excellent oral history of R.E.M. "We were on an overnight drive from Minneapolis to Denver and we listened to it. It was raining and it was three in the morning and it was perfect. That was the first time I became a fan of theirs." On April 2nd, Jason And The Scorchers supported R.E.M. again, this time at the University Of The South in Sewanee, Tennessee.

Murmur was released on April 12th, 1983. In another break with traditional marketing strategies, R.E.M. were nowhere to be seen on the front cover. Instead, the hope was that potential punters would be lured by an enigmatic monochrome shot of a rural backwoods scene, overgrown by a curious Japanese vine called kudzu.

"We wanted something definitely southern for the album cover, and kudzu is," Buck told Marianne Meyer of *Goldmine* at the time. "Eleanor Roosevelt brought it to America from China in her wisdom, to shore up erosion. She didn't realise that one acre of kudzu has one root, so it does nothing for erosion, and it just kills every plant it can touch. And nothing kills kudzu – you can burn it to the ground, and a week later it's back."

Kudzu, then, might be seen as a metaphor for the state of the American music industry when *Murmur* hit the shops. The land of the free was in the throes of the second British Invasion, with New Romantic combos like Duran Duran, Culture Club and the Human League wiping out the local competition.

Peter Buck grumbled at the time, "American bands don't get signed. American bands don't get promoted. American bands don't get played on the radio. The only thing the industry is interested in is leasing the latest British album to get a piece of the supposed invasion action. There's no money left for new American outfits."

At IRS, Miles Copeland's plan to work the album was based on breaking it out via college radio. His promotions man, Keith Altomare, felt he had in his hands an album that was worth busting a gut for.

"I knew it was better than everything else out there," he has said. "No-one was touching it at commercial radio, but they were touching it for me at college, so I could really run the show."

Altomare trucked R.E.M. to every college radio station that showed the slightest interest, and was delighted to find the band prepared to work the album as hard as he was. "We did so many radio interviews and so many appearances. I virtually had them scheduled to do at least one thing in every market."

Further fuelled by *Rolling Stone* calling it "intelligent, enigmatic, deeply involving", and the *New York Times* declaring that it would sound "as fresh ten years from now as it does today", college radio not only jumped on *Murmur*, but played it with such frequency that mainstream radio stations began picking it up too. Copeland's strategy had proved perfect.

In May, at the request of MTV, R.E.M. undertook their first serious attempt at a promo video, with director Arthur Pierson at the helm, for the newly released IRS version of 'Radio Free Europe'. Having told Pierson that they didn't want the video to include such rock clichés as naked girls in bed or guitars smashing through plate-glass windows, it was decided instead to make what was effectively a short art-house movie, with 'Radio Free Europe' as the soundtrack. The location for this earnest endeavour was Paradise Gardens, Summerville, Georgia, the home of Baptist minister and folk artist Howard Finster, whose extravagantly idiosyncratic life and work had already proved inspirational to the members of R.E.M.

Anyone particularly interested in Finster could do worse than to check out Thelma Finster Bradshaw's book, *Howard Finster: The Early Years: A Private Portrait of America's Premier Folk Artist*. But for the purposes of this book, it's probably enough to begin with Mike Mills's statement:

"Lots of students from here and the University of North Carolina, South Carolina and North Carolina State, all come down and help him with whatever projects he's doing. He's a tremendous guy. His idea is that he's a traveller in space and was put here to bring the word of God to people through folk art."

Stipe, arguably the most influenced by Finster, has described him as "completely outside the mainstream. There's something that really appeals to me about people who, in this day and age, work outside that whole miasma of everyday life."

Finster, born in 1916, believed that he was visited at the age of 60 by an angel who instructed him to make sacred art, and he devoted the last 30 years of his life exclusively to that purpose. As a visionary artist, Finster frequently made use of pop culture artefacts such as Coca-Cola or mass production cars in his art

He once claimed, enigmatically,"Elvis appeared to me in my garden several years ago after he died. He walked up behind me, and I looked around and seen him and said a very short word to him, and he said a very short word to me."

To Finster, R.E.M.'s decision to shoot a video in his garden was, if nothing else, another means by which to promote the word of the Lord. It was arguably more effective in that aim than in encouraging the youth of America to buy the record, because it consists largely of the band wandering aimlessly around Paradise Gardens, with Peter Buck clad in appalling white boots. "It was pretty boring," admitted Berry in retrospect.

Miles Copeland was little more than bemused. "I wondered about those obscure videos they were doing. But they were the only act I can think of, apart from Sting, who actually said, 'We'll pay the price. If it isn't a hit then it isn't a hit and, if it's a hit, great.'"

On May 28th, R.E.M. encountered another musician who would become a solid friend: Matthew Sweet. "I first got to know R.E.M. when I asked them to sign my 45 of 'Radio Free Europe' at the Drumstick Club in Lincoln, Nebraska," recalls Sweet. "It was a chicken restaurant by day. I was under age. They were like, 'Oh, wow, you have our record!' We ended up having dinner." Sweet then struck up a letter-writing relationship with the band and would, in due course, become involved the Stipe's Community Trolls project.

By June *Murmur* had shifted 85,000 copies and, in the fullness of time, *Rolling Stone* would vote it the eighth best album of the 1980s. "I think this was the album that created alternative music for this generation," muses Billy Corgan of Smashing Pumpkins and Zwan.

"They created 50,000 guitar bands after them. America was inundated with jangly R.E.M.-type bands. The record sounds so simple but so different. It has a murky southern soul, a real spookiness about it. You can't understand what he's singing and that's definitely something I can relate to."

They may well have been influencing a whole new generation of guitar bands, but they couldn't do much to influence the audience at Sheppard Air Force Base, Wichita Falls, Texas, in the first week of June.

A roomful of servicemen baying for heavy rock in the Def Leppard mould did not find them impressive. As Buck remembers it, "There were oranges flying out of the audience. They were passing notes – 'If you play one more song like this, you die, faggots.'"

Instead of buckling under the pressure, the band gave the crowd exactly what it didn't want. "Michael and I were rolling around on the floor, doing 'The Bump' onstage and kissing one another. It was like throwing meat to the lions."

Finding the jeers intolerable, Bill Berry abandoned his drumkit and stormed off to the dressing room, but Sara Romweber of support band Let's Active courageously stepped in, enabling the band to finish the show.

Looking back, Buck has said, "The major who took care of us was so nice and said, 'Look, we'll go over to the officers' club and get drunk; those people were idiots.'" In the heat of the moment, however, R.E.M. teetered on the edge of splitting up, because Buck felt that Berry's retreat under fire was unprofessional.

"Everybody got mad with everybody," is how Mitch Easter described it. "Everybody was gonna quit."

Fortunately, egos were soothed (perhaps by the major's beers in the officer's club) and nobody did quit, but Buck was evidently still seething. The following night, in Lubbock, he dived from the stage in pursuit of a heckler.

Given his attitude towards the new British invasion, it probably didn't amuse Buck to find himself in Los Angeles on June 11th, supporting The Human League at the Palace Theatre. But during the visit Stipe was struck with an idea for a song that would eventually become 'So. Central Rain'.

We thought we were so smart when we made it but we were actually really stupid

The sun was shining on southern California, but, as Buck told me, "We were all trying to ring home to speak to our families and friends, but the phones were all out, and the weather forecast was for heavy rain in the South Central region." Athens, it seemed, was in the grip of torrential rain that was rapidly turning to floods.

"The floods were just the starting point for Michael's lyric," says Buck, "and I started on the music, quite separately, later that summer in Athens. It has tons of chords in it, changes key three times, and yet it sounds like something you could strum round a camp fire."

On July 8th, when Jason And The Scorchers released their debut album, *Fervor*, eagle-eyed devotees were quick to spot that the song 'Both Sides Of The Line' bore a writing credit not just to Jason Ringenberg, but also to Michael Stipe. Ringenberg now says, however, that Stipe was an influence rather than an actual collaborator. "I wrote 'Both Sides of the Line' with Michael sleeping in my spare room. I felt somehow he was a part of the song so I credited him. Also I felt it was my own small way of saying 'thank you' for all I learned from him."

On July 30th, *Murmur* entered the US charts, where it would enjoy a 30-week stay, and peak at No 36, selling 200,000 copies within a year. The hail of critical acclaim continued unabated and, as 1983 drew to a close, it was the No 1 Critics' Pick in *Rolling Stone*, the No 1 album of the year in *Trouser Press* and No 2 in the *LA Times* Critics Poll. Even far across the Atlantic in England, the *Sunday Times* rated it the fourth best album of the year.

R.E.M. had every right to feel pleased with themselves, but it's typical of the band's attitude that, looking back on that first flush of success, Peter Buck has said, "We thought we were so smart when we made it, but we were actually really stupid. We didn't have a clue."

Chapter Seven

A Wretched Experience

"We didn't have the right equipment, didn't have a soundman really, didn't have a lightman. Then we were going to play to people who had never heard of us, never gave a shit."
PETER BUCK

Stadium rockers: supporting The Police in 1983

With Murmur on the charts, records were being sold and critical acclaim was pouring in from both sides of the Atlantic, but for R.E.M. the rock star lifestyle still seemed little more than a light at the end of a tunnel. "I was making $140 a month," remembers Peter Buck. "That was my salary for 11 months a year, and none of us had any money. We'd get good reviews, but then we'd go into town and play to 50 people."

It should have felt good, then, when their old friend Ian Copeland offered them another chance to play with The Police, this time on an extended tour rather than a one-off date, as they'd done at the Fox in Atlanta back in 1980. In those days, The Police were already a significantly bigger band than R.E.M., but now they were one of the world's biggest attractions. A support slot on a Police tour would put Athens' finest in front of countless thousands of potential record buyers.

Even so, the members of R.E.M. were not easily convinced. According to Bill Berry, "The record company tried every means of coercion to get us to do it and finally we said, 'OK, we'll do it, we're curious, maybe we will sell records and maybe people will respond.'"

Buck is even more blunt about how they saw this golden opportunity: "We knew it was gonna be horrible, but we got talked into it."

The tour kicked off at the Civic Center, Hartford, Connecticut, on August 12th, 1983, in front a typical Police audience that comprised everything from pop-smitten teens up through hip college kids and even a smattering of over-30s. "The main reason they were on the bill was because I made a decision to do so personally," says Ian Copeland. "No-one else chose the support bands in those days but me, and The Police almost never cared, unless they sucked, and then I caught hell. As at any stadium show, much of the audience were still coming in through R.E.M.'s set."

For Buck, one of the worst problems was that he felt the band simply wasn't ready to play venues of that size. "We didn't have the right equipment, didn't have a soundman really, didn't have a lightman. Then, we were going to play to people who had never heard of us, never gave a shit."

A review by Frank Rizzo of the *Hartford Courant*, who had seen and enjoyed R.E.M. on previous occasions, reveals that he could sense exactly how uncomfortable they were. "Michael Stipe was mysteriously and painfully remote for the half-hour set; clutching the microphone, as is his custom, but not being released by the music, which is also his custom," said Rizzo. "The band played well, especially in its last few songs, but there was a tenseness Friday night that was not in evidence when I caught this young hard-driving band at other shows."

Stipe wasn't the only one suffering. Berry has described it as, "The most wretched and abysmal experience of our lives – it was a joke. We shoulda stayed home and got drunk for all the fucking good it did us."

It should have cheered them up, the next day, to learn that the re-recorded version of 'Radio Free Europe' had just given them their first US singles chart placing: No 78. Unfortunately, they also had to play a second night at the Hartford Civic Center, and nothing could dispel their gloom on that front.

Buck has a painful memory of the gig two days later at the Scope Auditorium, Norfolk, Virginia. "There were all these really moronic Police fans sticking their middle fingers at us, booing us because they wanted to see Sting that much quicker ..." For both of the Copeland brothers, of course, this tour was the equivalent of throwing R.E.M. in at the deep end to see if they would sink or swim. If they could survive this tour, they could survive anything and, in a business as tough as the music industry, if they couldn't survive, then they probably didn't deserve to.

On the 18th, the tour arrived at New York's legendary Shea Stadium, famed as the location in which The Beatles had played to more than 55,000 fans back in 1965, when a 4,000-seat theater was considered the top of the tree. For The Police there would be 70,000.

"When we pulled up outside Shea Stadium," remembers Bertis Downs, "there were all these huge tractor-trailers for the other bands, and all we had was these two little vans, a green one and a tan one."

And then the heavens opened. "It rained like you wouldn't believe from start to finish of R.E.M.'s set," says Ian Copeland. "After that show R.E.M. wanted to strangle me, it's true, but I think it was a motivating experience for them."

Michael Stipe seems to echo that thought when he says, "Watching all those umbrellas going up and realising that the audience loved it – the rain that is – it was real strange."

Buck too found it a more enjoyable gig than they'd played so far on this tour. "Shea Stadium with The Police was kinda fun," he remembers, "because no one in New York really knew who we were at the time and we only played 20 minutes – that's all they wanted us to play – and it rained during our set and so everyone was screwing around with their clothes off when we played, which made it kinda neat ..."

Keith Altomare of IRS has spoken of how what Michael sang changed with every show. "If you would be at more than one show," he has said, "it would be different words. He might know the phone book in the town they were in or he would throw in whatever he was reading." He had also taken a liking to the sound of Altomare's surname, and would sometimes introduce it into the middle of a song. He did it at Shea Stadium and, says Altomare, "It was so touching. It really showed they were conscious of their people and their fans."

Although they enjoyed Shea Stadium more than the other gigs, R.E.M. still felt that it did them no particular good. But Ian Copeland disagrees vehemently. "They didn't hear what I heard, from out in the audience," he insists. "When they played 'Radio Free Europe', the whole crowd went fucking berserk. I looked up on the stage and there were these two kids I used to hang out with [Bill Berry and Mike Mills]. My heart was going crazy. That was the moment I finally realised, 'Shit! This isn't just my buddies out there. This band is going to make me rich! And I'm going to make them rich!'"

Evidence to support Copeland's contention comes from the fact that, as Bertis Downs remembers, "We did our first merchandising deal – two t-shirts – at Shea Stadium, with a company called Niceman. It's kind of indicative of the way R.E.M. thinks that one of the t-shirts didn't even have the band's name on it, just some kind of inscrutable signal. There's a line in the song '9-9' which goes 'Got a stripe down his back, all nine yards down her back', so this t-shirt just had a stripe down the back, and people could figure it out for themselves."

Copeland also feels that the band didn't appreciate or even understand how much good those massive shows were doing them within the industry. "Remember, every band in the world wanted to be in their slot. DJs and Police fans didn't know I made the choice, but rather assumed The Police made the choice, and it didn't hurt for R.E.M. to be getting such an endorsement."

Ironically, for The Police, Shea Stadium proved to be a watershed event. After the show, Sting, Andy Summers, Stewart Copeland and their families repaired to the house they were staying in on Long Island. "We sat round, put the fire on," Sting has said, "and we'd just had this huge triumph, and I turned to Andy and said, 'It doesn't get any better than this. We should really stop.' And, surprisingly to me, Andy said, 'Yeah, you're right. It can only go down from here.'"

Things didn't get any better for R.E.M. at JFK Stadium in Philadelphia on the 20th. "I remember we were sitting in Philadelphia and it was, like, 105 degrees and they were carrying kids over the barriers," says Buck. "It's one in the afternoon and you can't even walk around outside, it's so hot, and we had to go on in 10 minutes. And I'm going, 'Man, I just don't wanna go on, let's just break up the band.'"

In his review for the *Philadelphia Enquirer*, Ken Tucker observed that R.E.M. were less well-received than another of the support bands on that date: Madness. "Both R.E.M., the brooding Athens, Georgia band, and Madness, a giddy English group, played quick, light sets that allowed them just enough time to prove their talents," said Tucker. "R.E.M.'s quirky, dark music may have been too melancholy to go over with a cheerful crowd that had come to party, but Madness charmed the audience with its fast-paced tales of jolly English youth."

At the time of the seventh and final date, in the Capital Center, Largo, Maryland, on the 22nd, R.E.M. remained convinced that it had all been worthless. "It just taught us that we're pretty much right on these things," grumbled Buck in retrospect. "Everyone said that, 'Oh, this will make you have a hit record.' But we did the seven dates and we didn't sell one record out of that. It was a waste of fucking time."

Ian Copeland begs to differ. "I can only give my opinion as to why R.E.M. hated those gigs. Put yourself in their position. They were supposed to hate them! This was a time when you were supposed to be contrary, rebellious, even ungrateful. Many of the things bands say are meant to show how tough they are, how they're the real thing, and how they never got lucky. No band wants the public to perceive that they had a leg up in any way. Image is everything to R.E.M. Buck, by the way, has a particularly convenient memory, I've noticed over the years."

Jay Boberg of IRS lines up right along with Copeland, stating, "Those shows were probably a lot more successful in their career than they will ever acknowledge."

Bill Berry, however, remained stubbornly on Buck's side. "Just because we're hooked up with this vast business machine doesn't mean we have to go along with everything it says. Our intuition has been more valuable to us than any of the great words of wisdom passed on to us by the damned record company."

Matthew Sweet, whom they'd met as a fan back in May, had become so enthused by R.E.M. that he (and his band Buzz Of Delight) moved to Athens, partly to be around them, and partly in hopes of furthering his ambitions of

No band wants the public to perceive that they had a leg up. And image is everything to R.E.M.

making records. His friendship with Stipe bore fruit, in early September, with the creation of an R.E.M. side-project known as The Community Trolls, who played their first gig by busking outside The 40 Watt Club. "There was a real sense of a golden era in the early 1980s, and Michael and I ended up doing this Community Trolls thing," explains Sweet. "He was the real powerhouse behind it. I was pretty tentative in those days. We just sat around, Michael went through the little book he wrote lyrics in, with me just kind of strumming along behind."

During the same month, The Community Trolls provided a song, 'Six Stock Answers', which acted as the theme music for the Super-8 film *Just Like A Movie*, being shot in Athens by Laura Levine, whose day job involved being the chief photographer for *The New York Rocker* music paper. The film, put together on a $1,000 budget, was done strictly for laughs, with no intention of ever having it released. The film opens with Michael Stipe in a skirt and tights flipping through boards on which are written the lyrics to 'Six Stock Answers', in a blatant parody of the opening sequence of Bob Dylan's film *Don't Look Back*. The film continues in the same way, loosely following the 'plot' of *Don't Look Back*, and following two rival bands. "They were both playing on the same night," explained Levine to *Q* magazine in 1994, "and which band were people going to see?"

On the last day of the month, when R.E.M. started making demos of new songs at the Stitchcraft warehouse in Athens, they played an unannounced gig, during which The Community Trolls also played a four song set.

Rather more significantly, the six Stitchcraft demos were 'Camera', 'Letter Never Sent', 'Little America', 'Second Guessing', 'Cushy Tush' and 'So. Central Rain'. At that point, 'So. Central Rain' started out with what Buck now dismisses as "a kind of wishy-washy strum", and it would remain that way until co-producer Don Dixon suggested something better several months later.

Although Buck had written the chord sequence for the song months earlier, it didn't yet have a title and he hadn't even heard Stipe's lyric until now. It's fairly obvious that the "city on the river" is Athens, which stands on the Oconee, but what exactly is Michael so gut-wrenchingly sorry about? "I never asked him," says Buck, "but it felt strong, really emotional, and good to play. We hadn't decided it would be a single, but we knew it would go on the next album." Immediately, they began rehearsing the song with the intention of including it in their fall tour.

Just three days later, during a show at Legion Field, Athens, they played it live for the first time. Bertis Downs clearly recalls the impact it had on him. "It was an open air show, and I immediately loved the song. Those kind of mid-tempo, folky, melodic songs is something they're particularly good at, and it was hearing 'So. Central Rain' that confirmed for me that this wasn't any one hit wonder kind of band. I knew they weren't going to have any trouble coming up with great songs for their second album."

The band made their US national television debut on NBC's *Late Night With David Letterman* on October 6th, and their ascension to modern rock royalty began. Naturally, they played the single that was making them famous, 'Radio Free Europe', but they also decided to have a go at the wishy-washy strum song that didn't yet have a title. Legend has it that this bold decision threw IRS, into a state of shock by creating a surge of demand for a record that didn't yet exist. "Did it?" asks Buck. "I don't know. We didn't care."

Bertis Downs, however, puts a more diplomatic spin on the story. "People considered it brave to play a song that was so new and unfamiliar to them on a major TV show, but the idea that it caused problems for the record company is, I think, a myth that's grown up over time. We were just glad at that time to get any exposure at all."

Stipe also fingers that historic Letterman appearance as the moment after which the adjective 'enigmatic' began appearing as a prefix to his name. "I'm nowhere near enigmatic as people think I am," he insists. "I think I got tagged that in 1983 on Letterman, when I sat down instead of shaking his hand. From then on, I was an enigma."

The remainder of October was largely a month of relentless touring in support of the album and the single, at the end of which, presumably in dire need of light relief, R.E.M. took it into their heads to adopt a pseudonym, 'It Crawled From The South', and play unannounced as support for The Cramps at the Peppermint Lounge in New York City. They earned their $500 fee with a set consisting largely of covers such as T.Rex's '20th Century Boy', The Troggs' 'I Can't Control Myself' and The Velvet Underground's 'Pale Blue Eyes', although they did throw in one self-composed nugget, a heavy metal parody entitled 'Burning Hell'.

Work on the tracks that would become R.E.M.'s second album resumed on November 9th, in Rhythmic Studios, San Francisco. In what must have been a jam-packed day, no less than 24 demos were recorded with the highly respected producer Elliot Mazer, whose previous credits included Neil Young, Janis Joplin and Jerry Garcia.

As well as songs that would appear, in due course, on *Reckoning*, they laid down a number of items that are interesting for other reasons. In the less-than-earth-shattering cabinet can be filed 'Walter's Theme' (a jokey radio ad for a Broad Street, Athens, rib-shack favoured by the band) and 'Cushy Tush' (another whimsical commercial, this time for an imaginary brand of toilet paper).

They also laid down a tongue-in-cheek version of 'The Lion Sleeps Tonight'. This astonishingly durable song has proved a hit in several different decades. Based on the traditional African melody 'Wimoweh', it was popularised in the West by folksinger Paul Campbell in the early 1950s. Next, The Tokens topped the US singles chart with it in 1961, Karl Denver made it a British hit just a year later, Robert John took it to No 3 in the US in 1972, and Tight Fit reached No 1 in the UK with a 1982 disco version.

When I asked Peter Buck why R.E.M. had attempted it, he replied, "I remember hearing it when I was a kid. Everyone who's been to day care or a camp, they teach you 'Wimoweh'. It's a song we used to do when one of us would break a string or whatever. If I broke a string, the other three would just go into 'Wimoweh' while I was re-stringing and tuning up." It would, of course, resurface as a significant influence on the R.E.M. song 'The Sidewinder Sleeps Tonight'.

And while at Rhythmic Studios they also recorded 'All The Right Friends', one of their earliest compositions, which they'd first attempted at Reflection with Dixon and Easter.

"Michael and I wrote that back in 1979," Buck told me. "Back in the summer of 1980, maybe September, we had a whole set of songs like 'All The Right Friends'. Kind of first person, kind of naïve, maybe too many parts, because you don't really know what to do when you're first writing songs. Some of them are really kind of fun. 'All The Right Friends' was one of those."

Asked why such an obviously attractive song hadn't appeared on *Murmur*, he explained, "Our feeling was that we wanted to throw away the songs that we were learning on, write a lot more songs, start over. By the time we did *Murmur*, that was really our third or fourth album's worth of songs. 'All The Right Friends', being one of our older songs, we didn't pay much attention to it." It would eventually be re-recorded to appear on the soundtrack to the Tom Cruise movie *Vanilla Sky*.

On November 18th, during their first promotional visit to Europe, R.E.M. made their UK television debut, on The Tube, in Newcastle-Upon-Tyne. Clearly irked that presenter Jools Holland had introduced them as a band from Atlanta, Stipe seethed, "We're not from Atlanta, we're from Athens." His ire was understandable, but the remark probably achieved little more than making half of the show's viewers think they were Greek.

The songs had the energy of the band on the move

The British public, albeit a small and select gathering of it, had its first taste of R.E.M. live on stage the following night, when they appeared at the tiny Dingwall's Club in Camden Lock, London.

Barney Hoskyns of the *NME* was clearly quite overcome when he wrote, "Michael Stipe will set off a harmonic chain – picked up by bassist Mike Mills and rounded off by drummer Bill Berry – that moves with such flowing assurance it's like a single organic voice. These are figures whose shape and dynamic are things quite other than the small mercies rock has formerly yielded. I won't try and capture such a magnificent metamorphosis here; I'm still not certain it wasn't a dream."

On the 22nd, they played their only other UK date of the visit, at the legendary Marquee club in London's Soho, where Bill Black of *Sounds* was moved to report of R.E.M. that they "pack a live punch not hinted at on the under-played over-cautious *Murmur* album." The band were able to fly home content that England was definitely on their side.

The first eight days of recording sessions for *Reckoning* started on December 8th, back in Reflection Studios again with Easter and Dixon. It was here that 'So. Central Rain' evolved its final form. "Mitch Easter and Don Dixon had the idea that the intro was weak, which it was," recalls Buck.

"They came in early one day, and I think it was Don who took a little guitar hook out of the chorus and stuck it on the front of the song. In those days, you physically had to cut the tapes up and splice them back in to a new position, so it wasn't as simple as it is now. When we came in, they played it to us and we went, 'Wow! That's great!'"

The new intro was crucial to the song's initial impact, and it wasn't the only contribution made by the production team. Mitch Easter recalls that, in the early versions of the track, drummer Bill Berry "played every other snare beat. When we got finished, we thought, 'It needs something.' So we had him hit beats in other spots. Just by coincidence, there was some reverb on that channel, so you get this alternating reverb beat and non-reverb beat. I thought that worked very well." Even so, Buck was not 100 per cent happy with the track. "I think I felt that the little riff at the chorus should have come out a bit more."

After taking a two-week break over Christmas and the New Year, R.E.M. returned to Reflection, re-vitalised, for another seven days that would see the album completed. "We would work until three or four in the morning," recalls Buck, "then Don Dixon and Mitch Easter would get there at 10.00 ... So by midnight those guys would be exhausted."

While it was not unknown for heavy metal bands of the era to spend weeks just trying to find a perfect snare drum sound, R.E.M. had no such luxury. "We were making the records very quickly by the period's standards," says Dixon. "You can make records that are better thematically by making them quicker, where you don't have the luxury of second-guessing yourself."

Peter Buck, however, has pointed out that the possibility of interference from IRS, who wanted a more commercial sound, was an even better reason for making the record quickly. "We wanted to have it finished before they showed up to listen to it," Buck has said. "By the time Jay (Boberg) showed up, it was the last day and we just played him the record. He really didn't have anything to say about it."

The essential difference between *Reckoning* and *Murmur* is that the band was now playing more confidently, constructing its songs better and keen to go for a live feel in the studio, which was enhanced to some extent by Don Dixon's decision to make use of a technique called binaural recording. The essence of binaural recording is the use of a pair of microphones separated by about the width of an average human head and placed about as high off the ground as an average pair of human ears. The result is a stereo recording that is said to be more "realistic", because it accurately mimics the way in which people perceive sound.

Mitch Easter believes that the technique did result in a different ambience on the tracks. "The drums ended up fresher sounding," he says. "A lot of the songs had the energy of the band on the move."

Dixon too feels that the experiment was a success, enabling Mike Mills' backing vocals to be heard more clearly. He says that Mills was singing, "12 to 15 feet away from the microphones that were recording his parts but, because it was in a stereo binaural field, we would tend to hear him as behind Michael. He could be loud without covering Michael up."

The album opens in typically uplifting yet inscrutable R.E.M. fashion with 'Harbourcoat', which Stipe has declared to have been a re-writing of the Anne Frank diaries. It makes a good opener, but it's hardly a classic.

The equally impenetrable '7 Chinese Bros' is a song that gave Dixon and Easter no end of problems. Stipe, said to have been going through an emotionally withdrawn period, was singing it so quietly that it barely registered on the VU meters. In a desperate attempt at using a distraction technique to break Stipe out of the mood, Dixon threw him a gospel album, *The Joy Of Knowing Jesus* by The Revelaries. Intrigued, Stipe began to sing the album's liner notes over the music for '7 Chinese Bros'. Under the title 'Voice Of Harold', this improvised piece turned up on the *Dead Letter Office* compilation in 1987 but, more significantly, it had the desired effect of extracting a better performance from Stipe when he took another run at the original lyric.

Next up is 'So. Central Rain', which has already been discussed in some detail, followed by 'Pretty Persuasion'. R.E.M. had laid down a live recording of the track back in February 1983, during the *Murmur* sessions, and its popularity on stage convinced them to work up a multi-track version for *Reckoning*. "Michael had a dream three nights in a row," Peter Buck has explained, "that he was a photographer taking the last Rolling Stones picture sleeve. They were all sitting in a dock with their feet in the water and the (title of the song on the) cover was 'Pretty Persuasion'." This explanation is intriguing but, although the word 'sleeve' does feature in the lyric, it's hard to figure out exactly what the song has to do with the dream.

Raga rock meets the Velvet Underground in 'Time After Time (Annelise)', a particular favourite of Mitch Easter's. "We spent time getting nice guitar sounds so that the guitars could build up and have nice textures," he remembers.

'Second Guessing' is, quite possibly, an early example of Michael Stipe's disenchantment with being interpreted by journalists, although, as always around this time, the lyric is so elliptical that it's hard to be certain. Certainly not the most memorable track on the album, it presumably meant a lot to the band because the original title of the album, as confirmed by an IRS press release of the period, was 'Second Guess'.

'Letter Never Sent' is a classic example of the old rock'n'roll truism that many of the best songs are knocked together in a matter of minutes. Buck has stated that this one took, "about as long to write as it did to play". Lyrically, it seems to relate to one of Stipe's well-documented characteristics, the tendency to write letters and then never send them.

The identity of the Annelise in 'Time After Time …' remains a mystery, but Buck has confirmed that the subject of the emotionally overpowering 'Camera' is "one of our girlfriends that died in a car wreck". It doesn't need Sherlock Holmes to work out that Stipe is singing about his photographer friend, Carol Levy, who died on the day *Murmur* was released. He found the song so painful to sing that he couldn't bring himself to do the extra takes that might have made his vocal pitch perfect throughout. But this is one of those cases where being slightly out of tune is exactly what the song needed in order to communicate Stipe's sense of grief.

As recounted in chapter four, '(Don't Go Back To) Rockville' is a Mike Mills song. The decision to include this countrified version of the song on *Reckoning* was a gesture of affection to Bertis Downs, who had a soft spot for country music. Stipe has pointed out that, for anyone who'll take the trouble to listen, there's always been a lot of country influence in his singing, from female vocalists such as Patsy Cline, Skeeter Davis and Wanda Jackson, but this track is a particularly good place to start looking for it.

The album closes with the rockier 'Little America', the most overtly political statement on

Reckoning. Lyrically, it can be interpreted as a series of snapshots of things seen by R.E.M. on their travels across the land of the free. "Take what you see on TV, mix in a guy who's turned thirty and still doesn't have a job, throw in some Uncle Remus stories and add a few flies in amber and you have America," is how Stipe explained it.

The song also includes a reference to Jefferson Holt in the line "Jefferson, I think we're lost", which refers directly to Holt's tendency to get them all lost while driving the band's van, but indirectly to the erosion of the lofty ideals that inspired America in the Reagan years. "Basically," said Buck, "the whole unseen premise of his presidency is that if you're not a white American, you're not an American at all."

On January 16th, 1984, the last day of working in *Reflections*, the band used the location to

Michael insisted on singing a new vocal

film a video for *Reckoning*'s first single, 'So. Central Rain'. Once again, their approach to the video illustrated just how unorthodox R.E.M. really were. "Michael would never lip-synch a vocal," Buck told me. "We played a recording of the track, and the rest of us faked it, but Michael insisted on singing a new vocal to make it more real for him."

While no doubt inwardly panicking at the thought of how MTV might react to yet another unconventional R.E.M. promo-clip, IRS wisely presented it to the world in a positive light. "We did a big publicity thing because Michael refused to lip-synch to the record," recalls promo-man Keith Altomare. "We did major publicity to promote the fact that we had this really cool band that was breaking tradition by not lip-synching."

With the album completed, R.E.M. had the best part of a month with nothing much to do, but Michael Stipe quickly found an interesting diversion. He took himself to New York City where he recorded vocals in the Radio City Music Hall studio for a couple of tracks on the album *Visions Of Excess* by The Golden Palominos, an ever-changing musical collective formed in 1981 by the ex-Feelies' percussionist Anton Fier. At that point, the group included such luminaries as Jack Bruce, Richard Thompson and Syd Straw, but Fier was definitely in charge. "Everybody on the record is a favourite musician of mine," he said, "and they also happen to be my friends."

Stipe's first attempt at a vocal for the song 'Boy (Go)' didn't meet with Fier's approval. "If people don't sound like themselves and do what they do, I'd get very angry," explained Fier.

Stipe was presumably pleased with what he was doing, because he has said that the track "brought out a voice that I didn't know I had – the swing of the song, the rhythm of it".

Fier, however, stuck to his guns. "Now, Michael also could have gotten angry and walked out," he says. "But he didn't. He stayed."

The middle of February saw the formation of yet another R.E.M. side project – Hindu Love

Gods. According to Buck, "We were just bored because we had a month off. Me, Mike and Bill had talked about forming a side band that did all covers and played Holiday Inns." The Holiday Inns part of the dream didn't materialize but, after three days of rehearsing with vocalist Bryan Cook from local Athens band Time Toy, they had a set that boasted a bunch of hits by The Troggs, Sweet, Mud, T.Rex and Slade, with a few older R.E.M. originals thrown in.

This formulation of the Hindu Love Gods made their world debut at The 40 Watt Club on February 14th, but a week or so later events took a significant new twist. Athens studio owner John Keane remembers, "They called me up and said they wanted to bring Warren Zevon into the studio to record some demos."

Acerbic 1970s singer-songwriter Zevon was, by his own admission, going through a career trough, during which he was "permanently loaded". The R.E.M. trio had offered to back him on some demos, which would then be used to get him a new recording contract. Having completed the Zevon demos, they remained in Keane's studio where he joined them on backing tracks for the songs 'Gonna Have A Good Time Tonight' and 'Narrator'. Bryan Cook popped in to contribute vocals and it was done. "The whole session took about 15 minutes," says Keane. "I think it's a kind of studio world record – Shortest Time Ever Spent On A Recording."

Before returning to Los Angeles, Zevon also joined the Hindu Love Gods for a

These guys seem to know exactly where they're going, and following them should be fun

show at The 40 Watt Club on the 29th, by which time Stipe was back in town, so he too stepped on stage to add to the glitz of the occasion.

Aside from another bunch of East Coast gigs, March 1984 is memorable largely because it included another attempt by R.E.M. to get to grips with the idea of presenting themselves on film. At Ruben Miller's Whirligig Farm, Rabbitstown, Georgia, they were filmed by Stipe's former art tutor, James Herbert. "We did a 20 minute film," says Buck, "a weird image thing that doesn't have us playing instruments or anything." Instead, with much use of arty close-ups, silhouettes and slo-mo, it shows them wandering around the farm. The result was titled *Left Of Reckoning* and, as usual, it mystified MTV. "It didn't do our careers a lot of good," Buck concedes, "because it didn't have naked women in it."

Reckoning was released in the UK first, on April 9th, 1984, to coincide with a second European jaunt, with the US release following on the 17th.

As with *Murmur*, the album cover art did not feature an image of the group. "Michael drew the outline for this two-headed snake," explained Mike Mills in 1985, " and gave it to Howard (Finster) to fill in."

While Finster worked, the four members of R.E.M. stood and watched him. "They wanted serpents on it, so I made them cloud serpents," explained the artist, in Denise Sullivan's book *Talk About The Passion*. "It was only a ten or fifteen minute job and they liked it, so they used it. I made another one for them with all four of their pictures on it and they didn't use it."

Another intriguing aspect of the sleeve is the note "File under water", printed along the spine. This is clearly a parody of the instructions that formerly appeared on albums, advising record store owners to "File under pop" or "File under rock", but, perhaps to prove that he can be as enigmatic as Stipe, Peter Buck has gone so far as to say that File Under Water is "the real title of the record."

Finally, instead of having sides 1 and 2, *Reckoning* has sides L and R, which explains the title of that 20-minute film they made with James Herbert. The soundtrack of the film is a whole side of the album. Guess which.

Reviews of *Reckoning*, of course, appeared first in the UK press, with Mat Snow of *NME* taking it as evidence that R.E.M. were "one of the most beautifully exciting groups on the planet." and Fred Dellar of *Hi Fi News* noting that, "R.E.M., bless their cotton-pickin' socks, offer nothing new or fashionable ... on the other hand, it's virtually impossible to dislike them."

On release in America, *Rolling Stone* said, "These guys seem to know exactly where they're going, and following them should be fun." Meanwhile, for Californian teenager Stephen Malkmus (who would one day form Pavement) *Reckoning* was "my badge of hipness. R.E.M. were pretty esoteric for an 18-year old. I was starting to discover music beyond Californian punk and SST Records." So, in the first week of release, were about 100,000 others. R.E.M. were now officially big business.

Chapter Eight

Dark, Dank & Paranoid

"We had a batch of songs that we'd written really fast, with not even the beginning of an idea on how to make them. We couldn't agree on tempos. We'd argue about things like keys."
PETER BUCK

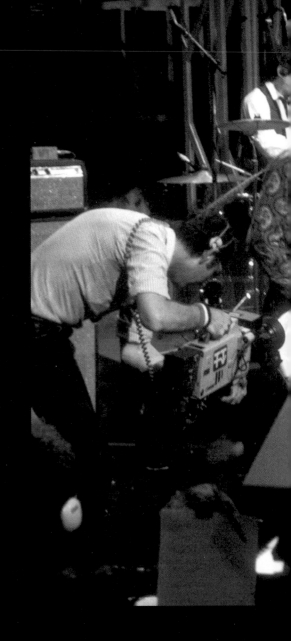

Television personalities: The Tube, UK, 1983

The day before Reckoning hit the streets in England, R.E.M. had started their first European tour with a gig at The Paradiso in Amsterdam, in Holland, supported by My Bloody Valentine.

Oliver Gray, a British rock manager and musician, was in Hamburg on April 13th and, having read about them in the UK rock press, decided to check them out at the Knust Club. In his excellent rock memoir, *Volume*, he writes: "The Knust Club was a minuscule room, holding at most 100 people. R.E.M. were doing two nights and two sets each night, there being no support band. To get to the stage they had to walk through the audience. This being a very long time before stadium rock status for R.E.M., they were all dressed in black jeans and leather jackets, rather in the manner of The Ramones. They creaked as they pushed past me, Peter Buck apologising, 'Excuse me, man, it's a bit hard to get through here.' Their understated but supremely atmospheric music was precisely what I needed to hear."

While they were still in mainland Europe, 'So. Central Rain' was extracted as *Reckoning*'s first single in America, with its title slightly amended to 'S. Central Rain (I'm Sorry)', because, in Buck's words, "The record company people told us that we had to have the main chorus line in the title because radio programmers were so stupid that unless you did that, they wouldn't know which song it was."

The British leg of the European trip started on the 24th. With a total of seven dates, it took them further into the country than before, travelling as far north as Glasgow in Scotland. But in London they were still playing in one of the city's smallest clubs, The Marquee, where the *NME*'s Cynthia Rose – a fan of *Murmur* – was decidedly unimpressed. "For much of the evening Stipe and secondary vocalist Mills were singing out of tune," she wrote. "Rack this one under Rick Johnson's seminal definition of Wimp Rock: dentist's office music minus the drill."

Jack Barron of *Sounds*, on the other hand, saw them at the same venue one night later and concluded, "Even at their most strident, there is a winning casualness about the group. It's everywhere in evidence, from singer Michael Stipe's incomprehensible diction to their motley clothes sense."

At this point it must have seemed to R.E.M. that Britain might already be slipping away. Jay Boberg confirms that, "Although we did have some underground and 'tastemaker' success, it was hard going. So the band's overall impression of Europe and the UK was not easy." *Reckoning* was racking up major sales in their homeland, where it would eventually rise as high as No 27, but it peaked at a disappointing No 91 in the UK, a position that might have been achieved even if no-one but friends and distant relatives had gone out to buy the album in the week of release.

Buck, however, seemed to have a good grasp of the phenomenon, telling one UK fanzine that,

"Some of our early reviews were so amazingly over the top and positive. No-one's that good, and people tend to have a backlash against anything that's claimed to be great. If you sit in obscurity for years a lot of people appreciate you. If you start getting on the front page of magazines, people start whispering about a hype job."

Returning to America in the early part of May, R.E.M. spent much of the rest of the month mired in a seemingly endless round of promotional activities for *Reckoning*. No fewer than 67 interviews were conducted at the New York HQ of IRS alone. Keith Altomare has testified to the band's willingness to do anything necessary to help promote the music, but Stipe in particular was beginning to feel the pressure of being pursued by earnest journalists all of whom, he felt, wanted to "delve into my psyche".

"Provincial American papers ask you the most boring things, like 'What is your music about?'" Buck moaned. "So you tend to make up things like, I don't know, 'Our music is a conscious creating of the myth of modern man against that of the penile mother.' OK, so we're making fun of these guys, but we're also making fun of ourselves. This is a pretty silly way to make a living."

From the earliest days of their relationship with IRS, after the initial euphoria of signing a record deal had worn off, R.E.M. had felt themselves beleaguered by record company pressures. Now that they were selling records in large quantities, instead of being set free by their commercial success, they found those pressures becoming demands and consuming ever-larger chunks of the band's time. "It was getting to be professional time," Buck told *Pulse* magazine. "We were starting to hire people and sign paychecks. None of us was familiar with that and it was confusing. We started wondering if we'd rather go back to playing clubs."

One thing which went a long way towards making all of this bearable was that Jefferson Holt and Bertis Downs were now fully in charge of every aspect of R.E.M.'s business affairs. They acted as a sturdy buffer between the band and the record company. They also made one particular decision, which was crucial to the way the band would develop over the coming two decades. They decided to stay in Athens.

That decision would probably have been disastrous in any previous era, but it made sense in the mid-1980s. Traditionally, successful rock

Dentist's office music
minus the drill

acts could come from anywhere, but to maintain and increase that success they would have to base themselves in or near one of the main centres of music business activity: New York or Los Angeles.

In the mid-1980s, however, the arrival of fax and, a few years later, the development of email, meant that a great many business functions could now be conducted at a distance. Property and salary costs in Athens were minuscule compared to the major cities so, even with a considerably higher phone bill taken into account, staying put made sound financial sense. On top of all of that, Athens was where they felt at home. It was comfortable and familiar. It proved to be exactly the right decision.

In the middle of May, an event occurred that would have a remarkable impact on R.E.M.'s future, although no-one could have predicted it at the time. The anarchic American stand-up comedian Andy Kaufman, best known as Latka Gravas in the television series *Taxi*, died of cancer, aged 35.

"Andy was a really big TV hero of mine when I was a teenager," Stipe told me when I interviewed him for this book. "He was so audacious and so ballsy when he was on TV. I saw him the first time he was on *Saturday Night Live*, miming along to the *Mighty Mouse* theme. I was 15 years old or something, I didn't know comedy or anything, didn't know what were the rules, but I knew watching this that it was absolutely ground-breaking, that it was just the ballsiest thing I had ever seen. I followed his career from then until his death."

Stipe was not alone. All of the members of R.E.M. shared a love for Kaufman's work. "People think of him as a comedian," says Mills. "I don't. I think of him as a performance artist. He changed a lot about comedy and yet he wasn't actually that well known in America, apart from *Taxi* and *Saturday Night Live*. And what he was well known for, he wasn't liked for. He got kicked off of *Saturday Night Live*. They had a nationwide vote for kicking him off and never coming back!" Kaufman's death would lead, eventually, to the writing of one of R.E.M.'s best-loved songs, 'Man On The Moon', which would in turn inspire a movie of the same name, for which R.E.M. would write another potently moving song about Kaufman, 'The Great Beyond'.

Meanwhile, another sign of R.E.M's changing status was that the office in Athens was increasingly deluged with fan mail, to such an extent that, in early June, a fan club (known as the Fun Club) was started. And now began the most intense period of touring the band had ever known, headlining larger venues, in the 1,500 to 2,000 seat range, all across America. By the end of the year they would have returned to Britain, and added Norway, Hawaii and Japan to their overseas conquests.

But before the grind was fully under way, they had a TV show to do. MTV was putting together an edition of the show *Rock Influences* with a folk-rock theme, which would be based round a concert at the Capitol Theater, Passaic, New Jersey on June 9th. The show was to open with a 1960s supergroup, featuring Roger McGuinn of The Byrds, John Sebastian of The Lovin' Spoonful, three members of The Band, Richie Havens and Jesse Colin Young. This ensemble would then give way to R.E.M., as exemplars of contemporary folk-rock. The finale, predictably enough, would bring old and new together, as McGuinn and Sebastian guested live onstage with R.E.M.

The one element of the show that didn't quite make sense was R.E.M. Could this be the same

R.E.M. who, for the last year, had been steadfastly denying that their music had any connection whatsoever to folk-rock and, even more specifically, to The Byrds? Just two months earlier Buck had fumed to the *New Musical Express*, "Comparisons to The Byrds are, as far as I'm concerned, a blot on our career. I liked The Soft Boys a whole lot more than The Byrds."

Strange then, that the guest slots with McGuinn and Sebastian revealed R.E.M., and Buck in particular, to be revelling in the joy of the moment. In 1999, Dave DiMartino of the Yahoo! website asked Buck to choose a moment in his career where he thought, "Man, this is it – I have arrived." He had no hesitation: "A lot of people would say getting a Grammy or playing some big place. For me, I've played with Roger McGuinn, and I can't help but get a real thrill playing *Rock 'N' Roll Star* and see Roger McGuinn singing it."

I knew watching this it was absolutely ground-breaking — the ballsiest thing I'd ever seen

Then they were off into the deep blue yonder, heading for a severe case of white line fever, with Los Angeles becoming Fresno becoming Santa Cruz; Portland blurring into Seattle cross-fading to Tuscaloosa; falling asleep in Boise, Idaho, and waking up in Salt Lake City (where, I'm reliably informed, it is illegal to carry an unwrapped ukulele in the street on a Sunday). "Hi there, we're R.E.M. and you're listening to KQAK in San Francisco ... WBCN in Boston ... WXRT in Chicago..." "Hello Buffalo ... Pomona ... Boca Raton ... Are you having a good time?"

"When you tour," Stipe has said, "there are a lot of times when you have absolutely nothing to do. It's useless time. You can't sit down and read, you can't go out and eat, you can't write and you can't sleep. It's really not that much fun."

It certainly can't have been fun for Stipe to sing with blood pouring from an injury to his foot in San Diego, or for any of them to play to what Buck described as "kids on Quaaludes, already passed out" at the Mountain Aire Festival in Calveras County. But they soldiered on, becoming increasing tired but always determined to turn in a good show.

"They were playing great," is how Steve Wynn of Dream Syndicate remembers the June/July dates on which his band supported them. "They were playing a few songs that hadn't been recorded yet, and they were really good."

Closing the set during this early part of the tour was '(Don't Go Back To) Rockville', which had been released in the UK as the second *Reckoning* single in mid-June, but new material was indeed emerging along the way. During the MTV concert at Passaic in New Jersey, for example, they played (and recorded) a live version of 'Driver 8', a train song that Buck has described as "probably the quintessential R.E.M. song of that particular period. The chord changes, melodies and harmonies are very representative of what we were doing then." The live recording would turn up as a b-side of a UK 12-inch of 'Wendell Gee', and the studio version would appear on *Fables Of The Reconstruction*. The same show also saw the first airings of 'Hyena' and 'Old Man Kensey'.

On June 14th, during an appearance on *The Cutting Edge* TV show in Los Angeles, they premiered the haunting 'Wendell Gee', which, remarkably, is also said to have been written that same day. Mills has said that he came up with the music for the song after listening to Fleetwood Mac. 'Bandwagon' surfaced on July 16th at the Playpen in Wildwood in New Jersey, but was relegated to b-side status.

R.E.M. took a break during August and, early in the month, Buck managed to participate in perhaps the shortest-lived of the many R.E.M. side-projects, Adolph And The Casuals featuring Raoul. "The Adolph thing was just a gig by Dream Syndicate and me at a bar," he explained. "I was showing them around Athens and, since there's nothing to show, we ended up in a local bar at 6am." The scheduled band was unable to play, so Buck and his chums filled in with a set that included 'Gloria' plus several Stones and Lynyrd Skynyrd covers. "We were so drunk we played 'Ghostbusters' twice."

'(Don't Go Back To) Rockville' got its US release on August 7th and, on the 19th in New York, Buck joined The Fleshtones onstage for a version of 'Windout', but much of the month was used to put together more songs for the next album, probably including the Bill Berry composition 'Cant Get There From Here'.

The first week of September found them back on the road, with old friend Peter Holsapple's band The dB's taking over as support for a month and a half after the September 7th gig at the Fox Theater in San Diego. And still the new material was being road-tested. 'Kohoutek', another *Fables* track, was first heard at the Greek Theater, Los Angeles on September 6th, and 'Auctioneer (Another Engine)', also destined for *Fables*, was premiered for the good folks of Tokyo on November 10th.

Five days later, and half a world away, they began their most extensive UK tour yet, at Tiffany's, Newcastle. With 15 dates, all in reasonably-sized venues, this should have been the moment for R.E.M. to crack the UK wide open, but their November 16th show at the Caley Palais in Edinburgh was reviewed unfavourably by *Melody Maker*. Audience member Stewart Cruikshank confirms the reviewer's view. "I'd loved R.E.M. from the start," he says, "but they were definitely a bit iffy that night. I think it was because there tended to be guitar overdubs on the albums which, of course, Peter Buck couldn't replicate on his own, so it felt as if something was lacking in the live show."

By the time they reached Nottingham's Rock City on the 21st, however, they were back on form. "I'd seen almost all the dates on that tour," remembers their UK publicist Kelly Pike, "but nothing like this. Everyone expected a good gig, but the air felt charged. It was as if something had changed them overnight. People were gaping open-mouthed because we all knew we were watching a band that was actually making history."

While in the UK, they also made an appearance on the BBC TV show *Whistle Test*, after which they revealed to Sandy Robertson of *Sounds* that they had a dozen new songs ready to record, but felt that it was time for a change of producers. "There've been no definite decisions," said Buck, "but it's time for a change. The producers we've worked with have been very nice, but we're not confident enough to produce ourselves yet."

They had, in fact, already been approached by Elvis Costello and were keen to work with him, but the plan fell through. "I loved the first two albums when you didn't know what the hell he [Stipe] was on about," Costello told *Q* magazine many years later. "It was much less interesting when I found out what he was singing."

After they'd returned home, R.E.M.'s star could be seen to be in the ascendant again in the UK when the NME's annual critics' poll chose *Reckoning* as seventh Best Album Of The Year on December 22nd, with the same paper's readers voting them eighth Best Band Of The Year soon after.

As 1985 dawned, with Costello out of the frame as a possible producer for the third album, R.E.M. were casting around again, considering Beach Boys collaborator Van Dyke Parks, Police producer Hugh Padgham, and Elliott Mazer, with whom they'd made demos in San Francisco, as mentioned earlier. Peter Buck, however, had a particular hankering to work with 1960s veteran Joe Boyd, whose track record with British folk-rockers Fairport Convention, the highly eccentric Incredible String Band, and others, seemed to make him an ideal choice.

Boyd's folksy eclectic sensibilities certainly seemed in sympathy with the kind of music that Stipe says was influencing him at that point. "The people that I'm more connected with are acquaintances I go out and visit, older people. One man, the Reverend Ruth from Philomath, has a little K-Mart organ he puts on his kitchen table. He sits there and plays it, and his wife stands with her hand on the stove and sings gospel songs. It's about the most amazing thing you've ever heard. It's much more influential on me than any rock music I've heard in the last five years."

It must have been disappointing for them when a prior commitment to record Mary Margaret O'Hara in Toronto obliged Boyd to turn them down, leaving them scratching their heads again. But, as was fast becoming an R.E.M. tradition, when faced with adversity they decided to have a laugh by inventing yet another imaginary band. "We sent out a press release that said it was a combination of Jerry Lee Lewis and Joy Division," said Buck. "God knows how we got the date."

They saddled this extraordinary concoction with the name Hornets Attack Victor Mature, largely because Buck figured that "anyone who'd pay a dollar to see a band with a name that silly is our kind of person".

It was, of course, nothing more than another excuse to spend a night playing cover versions, which is exactly what they did on February 12th, at the recently-opened Uptown Lodge in Athens. "The Uptown Lounge is right across from the police station," explains Mills. "It used to be a porno theatre and they've been working on it steadily since then, trying to re-arrange it. I guess they've got all the stains off the floor."

Sometime around then, Joe Boyd rang. The Mary Margaret O'Hara project had fallen through. He was now in Toronto at a loose end and maybe he could fly down to Athens and meet them? So, come February 17th, R.E.M. could be found in Broad Street Garage Studios, spending the day knocking together some rough demos of songs for the album.

The following night Boyd caught their live show at the Moonshadow saloon in Atlanta and then, he recalls, "I flew back to England, booked the studio, and they arrived a week later to make the record."

It turned into a nightmare of epic proportions for all concerned. "Have you ever been to London?" Berry subsequently asked one journalist who inquired why the sessions had wrong. "It's nothing but rain and fog. We had to drive 30 miles to the studio every morning, having had pork and beans for breakfast because that's all we could get."

Michael seemed to be on automatic pilot

This was something of an exaggeration. Livingstone Studios was a converted church in the North London suburb of Wood Green. The band were staying in a more than acceptable hotel in Mayfair (central London), and the seven-mile trip to the studio took between 45 minutes and an hour, depending on traffic.

Recording started on February 26th and, as Joe Boyd gradually came to know them, he perceived Mike Mills as the effective leader of the group, because he was cheerful and practical and worked hardest to keep everyone's spirits up. Stipe he saw as a strong character, enormously respected by the others, but understated. Buck, in Boyd's estimation, was the group intellectual but he was gloomy, while Berry was equally gloomy but generally took a back seat. As a result, most of his communication was with Mills and Stipe.

What Boyd wasn't seeing was that the band was falling apart. "We weren't sure if we really liked each other or not," said Stipe later, "and that was really reflected in the record."

Soon after they arrived in London, they rang to invite Kelly Pike, their former A&M press officer to visit them at the studio. "The distribution deal that A&M had with IRS had now moved to MCA, so I was no longer their press person," she recalls. "I'd been around them a great deal at the time of the first and second albums, and they'd been such happy guys, but the atmosphere now was dramatically different. The first thing I noticed was that Michael had shaved the crown of his head, like a monk, and he was behaving oddly. They were working on 'Wendell Gee' and he would only listen to it while lying down under the mixing desk. The others made light of it, but it wasn't right."

Pike also noticed that, for the first time, she could hear and understand what Stipe was singing on the tracks they played back for her. "Michael didn't like that at all," she remembers.

Later in the evening, while playing pool, the band made it clear to Pike that they had grown increasingly unhappy with their IRS deal. "They felt they were being manipulated, and they hated the fact that 'Rockville' was coming out as a single in England, because they felt it didn't represent them accurately at all."

Leaving Livingstone Studios at about 1am, they offered Pike a lift home and she climbed in, only to find herself utterly speechless when she saw a truck bearing down on a collision course with the car. "They'd turned onto the wrong lane of the road, as if they were still driving in America," she recalls. Only a last minute swerve across the road saved them from almost certain death.

Summing up how she felt about the band at this point, Pike says, "They remained friendly and charming and polite but, having got to know them well before, I could feel an underlying tension. They obviously liked Joe Boyd and admired his work, but something was definitely wrong. Michael in particular seemed to be on automatic pilot."

Boyd, perhaps distracted by the fact that his own record label, Hannibal Records, was undergoing serious financial problems, didn't seem to notice R.E.M's internal discontent at all. "They were absolutely comfortable, it seemed to me, with where they were going," he has said. "It was a surprise to learn later of tensions that surfaced during the recording, both within the band and about the production."

Peter Buck has acknowledged that the band had arrived at Livingstone Studios with "a batch of songs that we'd written really fast, with not even the beginning of an idea on how to make them. We couldn't agree on tempos; we'd argue about things like keys."

Most contentious of all, though, were the arguments about mixing. Stipe felt that Boyd was "a very meticulous producer, especially when it comes to mixes. He has this idea that there is The Perfect Mix for each song, and he'll work and work and work to get that mix and … it drove me up the fucking wall."

From his perspective, Boyd saw it quite differently. "I had problems with the vocals," he says. "Michael Stipe wanted them quieter than I did. It was a strange experience – everyone in the group wanted themselves turned down."

Most band members, cursed with inflated egos, demand exactly the opposite – that their part should be louder. R.E.M., however, believed that the strength of their music came from its overall coherence, its blend, rather than from the contribution of any single member.

There was another problem. The studio had recently been upgraded and Boyd didn't like the new set-up.

And another. Apart from a half dozen songs that had been road tested on the last tour, most of the material was still new to them, and in some cases not even complete. "We were writing and arranging the songs right in the studio," says Buck, "so it came out sounding tentative."

When Jay Boberg of IRS dropped by to see how things were going, he immediately sensed, as Kelly Pike had done, that something was wrong. Unlike Boyd, he had seen them recording on previous occasions and knew how they generally behaved. "It was the first time I was in a studio where I didn't feel everyone was having a good time," he said.

Beyond the bounds of the studio, R.E.M. were finding London an utterly alien environment. Apart from the constant rain and sleet, Berry found it particularly taxing that their only form of entertainment, the hotel TV, had only two channels and "one always had snooker on, while the other was showing a sheep-herding contest".

Stipe did manage to fit in some visits to galleries and museums, but the regime was tough. "I was just real tired," he explained. "We were travelling constantly, we were exhausted all the time, living on $5 a day each and sleeping in one hotel room. I had a breakdown."

Mills sums the whole experience up very concisely when he says, "It was a mistake going to England. It was a very bleak period of our lives."

There may well have been even more factors contributing to their depression at this time than just bad weather, business hang-ups and creative differences. Rumours had been circulating around Athens that, since the money had started rolling in, R.E.M. had started using cocaine. One of the best-documented side-effects of cocaine is its tendency to induce paranoia in users, which might explain why Stipe once classified the album as "dark, dank and paranoid".

Bill has confirmed that he was using cocaine in the 1980s, and has stated that drinking had become a major problem for him. He's also honest enough to admit that, despite the band's remarkably democratic set-up, being in R.E.M. meant, "I never had a chance to grow up and have any perspective of being other than the least important member of R.E.M."

With all of these problems brewing before the band even arrived in the UK, it would be simplistic to blame Joe Boyd (as had happened to Steven Hague some while earlier) for the way things went. Looking back, Buck has been able to admit that Joe "had the unfortunate task of being saddled with a band that was pulling in about eight different directions … We were all kind of unsure where to go and Joe was stuck in the middle and I felt kind of sorry for him."

Towards the end of March, Bill had had enough and went home. The others were not far behind but, despite their intense misgivings, they had created a remarkable piece of work that owed a great deal to the circumstances in which it was made.

The discordant opening track seems to capture their unease, harnessing it to good use given the title, 'Feeling Gravitys Pull' (note the lack of punctuation), which seems to imply a heightened state of awareness. The next up, 'Maps And Legends', sets the tone for much of what is to follow, introducing an 'American Gothic' flavour, derived from Stipe's fascination for older people, especially creative older people: artists, singers, sculptors and suchlike. Stipe has suggested that many people can be read just as you can read a map, so this song can also be seen as an indication that the album is going to be about people.

This in itself is a remarkable development, especially for Stipe, who had hitherto written lyrics whose meanings were far from clear. Now he seems to be spinning little stories, fashioning oblique cameos, about people he had met. The precise meaning of his lyrics on this album remains hard to understand, but it's easier to hear that they are about something. 'Driver 8', 'Old Man Kensey', 'Wendell Gee', 'Auctioneer': clearly, these are all songs that are about people.

Although it doesn't mention eccentric Georgian author Brivs Mekis by name, 'Life And How To Live It' is certainly about him. Even 'Kohoutek', while notionally about the comet of that name, is the surname of the Czech astronomer, Dr Lubos Kohoutek, who discovered that celestial body.

Fables Of The Reconstruction is also the first R.E.M. album to feature strings and horns, and this is one area in which Joe Boyd's participation can hardly be faulted. The soul/funk horns on 'Can't Get There From Here', for example, are a perfect complement to a song that namechecks Ray

We were travelling constantly. We were exhausted all the time, living on $5 a day each

Charles and was intended as a tribute to Al Green, James Brown, and other soul legends.

The one song that sticks out like a sore thumb is 'Green Grow The Rushes', not because of any musical incongruity, but because its subject matter is so overtly political. While the rest of the album seems to exist in a mythological America, this one attacks America's attitude to the third world and, specifically, the exploitation of migrant workers.

Over the years, *Fables Of the Reconstruction* has grown in stature to occupy a place in the band's catalogue as an unusual album, but certainly not an inferior one. It is perhaps some indication of how uncertain R.E.M. were about the album that *Fables Of The Reconstruction* would not be released for another three months.

Chapter Nine

Rough-cut Glory

"The most crippling
thing for a band like
us would be to feel
that we have to do a
really professional
set. Once we decide
that because people
paid money we have
to give them the
most perfect set we
can, we're finished."
MIKE MILLS ■

Paying those dues: UK tour, 1984

With hardly a break after the completion of Fables Of The Reconstruction, R.E.M. entered Waveform Media Rehearsal Studios in Atlanta to begin rehearsing for the opening half of the tour that would accompany the album.

On April 22nd, they cranked into gear with the first show on their home turf, at Legion Field in Athens, supported by yet another of their heroes, Alex Chilton, formerly of Big Star. If the previous year's touring schedule had seemed gruelling, it paled by comparison with what the rest of 1985 had in store for them.

They were now commanding fees of around $12,000 per show, and playing major venues. But what had seemed like the ideal lifestyle five years earlier was fast becoming little more than drudgery. For Ken Fechtner, a friend of Peter Buck's since college days, it was obvious that things were changing. "It got really big," he says. "They were in theatres, you needed passes and, in a way, I felt I was intruding." The thrilling intimacy of the club shows where they'd made their name was gone. Audiences were larger and physically further away. To get across to those audiences, R.E.M. would have to change.

Their first inclination was to make the drama bigger. The set now began in darkness with train sound effects blasting through the PA system. In the middle of that, the band would take the stage using flashlights to find their way to their instruments. It was cheap and effective.

Thomas T. Huang of *The Tech* magazine provided some interesting insights in his review of their show on May 3rd at the New Athletic Center, MIT, Cambridge, Massachusetts. He describes Stipe as "hiding in a large overcoat, his hair covered by a drooping baseball cap put on backwards. White charcoal stains the skin under his eyes like mourning tears. His hands are taped."

The set did not include 'Radio Free Europe' and more than half of what they did play was completely new to the crowd, but Huang saw this as proof that R.E.M. were "willing to take a risk. It explored new musical ground at the possible expense of the audience's rejection. Their experiments are getting better known as they tour the colleges. They may well be setting a new trend in contemporary music."

Just as R.E.M's success was changing within the band, so it was also changing things in Athens. By the middle of 1985, the sleepy little southern town was attracting young bands on the make, who would then discover that the scene wasn't as huge as they had imagined. Peter Buck observed at the time that "Kids go there to form bands and they think, 'Hey man, you can get famous and be on MTV like R.E.M. When we first started out, it was a weird funky little town. It was us against the rest of the world. There were 200 people we knew who were in bands and did weird stuff and dressed funny. We had to travel in packs so we didn't get beaten up. Now it's like I'm famous. Five years ago I'd walk down Fraternity Row and they'd yell, spit and throw cans at me. Now they try and get me to come inside and drink beer with them."

Mills, meanwhile, had noticed another side-effect of their increasing popularity. "A lot of the local bands resent us," he said. "It's a backlash because it's, like, our fault that we made Athens a 'scene'. And a lot of people here go, 'Oh, there go those hot-shot rock stars.' Sorry! I just live here because I like it. I didn't ask to be in this band. It just happened."

As well as coping with hometown resentment, Mills was feeling a new kind of tension within the band. The personality differences between him and Michael Stipe, which had been relatively easy to brush under the carpet in the euphoric camaraderie of the early days, were now pushing them apart. "We were very different people," is how he explained it. "Michael was trying to deal with being a really shy person thrust to the front of the band. And I was trying to deal with how somebody had an attitude when it was unnecessary."

Fables Of The Reconstruction was released in the UK on June 10th, and a day later in the US. Stipe has insisted on a number of occasions that the title of the album is actually *Reconstruction Of The Fables*, and a cursory examination of the cover supports this contention to some extent. The back cover is emblazoned with the words 'Reconstruction Of The' while the front bears the words 'Fables Of The'. Flip it over repeatedly and the title reads endlessly, like the literary equivalent of a moebius strip: "Reconstruction Of The Fables Of The Reconstruction Of The …" ad infinitum. Or ad nauseam, if you don't find it amusing.

Stipe backs up his version of the title by pointing out that the idea came from a phone conversation in which his father used the word 'reconstruction'. For reasons he can't explain, it appealed to Stipe so much that he decided there and then to use the word as the title of the album. The 'Fables' part came later, when he was ruminating about how many of the songs had a fable-like quality, probably caused by the fact that he had been reading a great deal of fantastical childrens' literature, including *Brer Rabbit*, *The Wind In The Willows* and *Aesop's Fables*, in the run-up to making the album.

As ever, the album was clad in a sleeve whose front cover conspicuously lacked a tasty, shirts-off photo of the band. Instead, Stipe had been instrumental in designing an image that looked like a cluttered attic, with hacked-off human ears and a burning book among the debris. True, the band members' faces were on the cover, but they were obscured by slide projections. It was (arguably) marginally more mainstream than the snakes on *Reckoning*, but it was hardly what IRS must have been hoping for. Nevertheless, Jay Boberg remained diplomatic. "R.E.M. have a very firm vision of what they want to do and how they want to do it," he stated. "If their album covers are not good marketing tools, hey, too bad for us. They're not willing to compromise that."

Whatever the band felt about the stuff in the grooves of *Fables*, the majority of the world's music critics embraced it wholeheartedly. The *New York Times* gave it a rave, and *Rolling Stone* considered it to be "unretouched R.E.M. in all their rough-cut glory".

In the UK, although the *NME* grumbled that "in this plainly-produced set the group struggle to make their mystery interesting", *Sounds* enthused, "never has Michael Stipe's lyrical imagination had more freedom".

Joe Boyd read the reviews and felt able to relax a little. "I was very relieved when most reviewers really liked the album, but I don't think the group was that happy with it," he said later.

At the time, he was right. But, by 1987, Buck was able to see *Fables* with the 20/20 vision of hindsight, telling *Bucketful Of Brains* magazine that "It's a misery album in a lot of ways — but I like it. The songwriting's great. It's one of our stronger albums as far as songwriting." Joe Boyd has also reported that, in later years, Michael Stipe has told him that he had grown to love the album.

Before *Fables* had even entered the charts, R.E.M. were back on the road again, returning to the UK to kick off another tour as one of many acts supporting U2 in a concert known as The Longest Day, at the National Bowl in Milton Keynes, on June 22. Mat Snow of the *NME* was pleased to note that, "Milton Keynes' big stage and excellent sound system show off R.E.M. to advantage, especially on songs which sit gleaming and slow

It's a misery album in a lot of ways — but I like it

to yield on their new LP." Garry Bushell of Sounds was even more impressed, raving, "There's no disputing R.E.M.'s prowess, their mastery of mesmerizing melody."

Two days later, and rather further north, R.E.M. took the stage at the International Ballroom in Manchester, where Jack Barron of *Sounds* was struck by the physical changes in Stipe. "The singer looks drastically different from the time R.E.M. last visited this country. Gone is the flowing mane of hair, to be replaced by a severe crop, the final solution to a bad cut. He says people think he's a marine in America. The 'slaphead' skull, together with the scars on his face, the result of a car crash at 18, make him seem like a suitable case for treatment."

And two days after that, at Tiffany's ballroom in Newcastle-Upon-Tyne, Andy Gill of the *NME* provided a fascinating printed Polaroid of the debris atop R.E.M.'s dressing room table. "Among the litter of tins and towels are a little Walkman and two of the tiniest speakers you've ever seen. Stacked in front is a pile of cassettes … there's *Swordfishtrombones*, a David Thomas tape, *Astral Weeks*, Peter Buck's current faves Mojo Nixon, Georgia gospel outfit the Fantastic Violinaires … and what's this? Bob Dylan and The Hawks, live at the Albert Hall."

On the 29th, *Fables* entered the UK album chart, where it would peak at a respectable No

35, although it would do rather better in America, entering the Billboard album chart on July 6th, peaking at No 28 and selling more than 300,000 copies in its first three months on the shelves. Once again, R.E.M. had substantially improved on their previous sales figures.

The first single pulled from *Fables* was 'Cant Get There From Here' which, promoted via an entertainingly wacky, slightly surreal, Monkees-style video directed by Stipe, racked up enough MTV plays to push it into the lower reaches of the Billboard singles chart. Stipe, with his love of and training in the visual arts, could see the potential of videos as TV commercials for songs, especially if done with some intelligence and taste.

As far as Buck was concerned, videos were something they were obliged to do; but they didn't have to like doing them. So, naturally, while it was being aired on MTV, Buck was berating the channel in press interviews. "I honestly don't think that MTV does anything at all," he told one reporter. "It's no marketing tool at all, except in the case of someone who would be marketed that way ... They sell images and we're not a band that takes to the selling of images. Also, frankly, I don't give a shit about videos. I like playing."

The second half of the US tour commenced on July 11th at the Arlene Schnitzer Concert Hall in Portland, Oregon, and would carry on relentlessly, 43 dates in all, through to the prestigious Radio City Music Hall in New York City on August 31st before they could take another break.

By now they were traveling in a Silver Eagle tour bus with a destination board on the front that read "Nobody You Know". It was spacious and comfortable, but there were obviously times when they wished they were back in the old Dodge Tradesman. "Compared to what used to be a really ripe situation for weird things to happen," lamented Buck, "this is kind of predictable."

It was inevitable, but it took a month before things went seriously adrift. At Barrymore's Club, Ottawa, Canada, on August 17th, they snapped. Somewhat the worse for drink, R.E.M. abandoned their planned set and ripped into an unscheduled evening of impromptu and extremely ragged cover versions. The problem was not just that they were drunk, but that they were bored rigid by having to play the same songs the same way night after night.

The audience didn't know what had hit them. If R.E.M. had done exactly this at The 40 Watt Club five years earlier, the crowd would have loved it, but Barrymore's was full of strangers, half of whom were probably only there because a friend had told them they should go. They'd paid good money to get in, and they wanted to hear what they expected to hear. Then, instead of 'So. Central Rain' they got Zager And Evans' bubblegum novelty, 'In The Year 2525'. Instead of 'Rockville' they got 'Smokin' In The Boys' Room' by Brownsville Station.

Cries of "Fuck you" rent the smoky air as the band essayed an a capella version of 'Moon River', and Michael Stipe's recitation of the lyrics of the Sex Pistols' 'God Save The Queen' fell on humourless ears. Before long Buck was inviting audience members backstage for a good thumping.

In an interview soon afterwards, the ever-diplomatic Mike Mills tried to pass the incident off with the explanation that "The most crippling thing for a band like us would be to feel that we have to do a really professional set. Once we decide that because people paid money we have to give them the most perfect set we can, we're finished."

The stark reality was that R.E.M. were close to throwing in the towel. On August 25th, the day of a show at JB Scott's Theater in Albany, New York, the band had a crisis meeting, literally to decide whether they would continue or split. "If you don't talk you are doomed," reckons Mills. "Secondly, once you start talking, you have a few decisions to make, such as, 'How much am I going to put into this? Is it worth it? Do I want to keep doing it?' Once you answer those type of questions, it's easy to decide what to do."

The meeting may well have had a therapeutic effect on the band, making them realize that they had already shared so much together and invested so much time, effort and emotion into making this band work that it wasn't possible just to walk away. Much more likely though, is that they were reminded by Jefferson Holt and Bertis Downs that contracts had already been signed which would keep them touring for many months to come, and that they had a legal obligation to deliver two more albums to IRS. Stopping was simply not an option, unless they were prepared to shoulder the cost of the financially crippling legal suits that would inevitably follow.

They chose, wisely, to keep on keeping on, at least for the moment. After all, they were fast approaching September, a holiday month during which they could do nothing except maybe recharge their batteries, think about the future and prepare themselves for the onslaught.

First though, they had to get through five more dates that would bring them to the end of the second US leg of the *Reconstruction* tour, at Radio City Music Hall in New York on August 31st. During the encore, for no obvious reason, Peter Buck unstrapped his Rickenbacker, tossed it violently across the stage and brought the show to an end by storming off the stage.

Two more singles were released around this time, 'Driver 8' in the US and 'Wendell Gee' in the UK. Both were strong songs in the context of the album, but neither was an obvious hit, so neither of them troubled the compilers of the charts to any great extent, much to the annoyance of Miles Copeland at IRS. "Miles was frustrated by their unwillingness to take the steps that would have brought them greater commercial success sooner," explained Jay Boberg in David Buckley's insightful 2003 R.E.M. biography *Fiction*.

A deeply committed capitalist, Copeland presumably took his success with acts like The Police as confirming what he had always believed, that musical artists perform in the public arena in order to make money out of their art. If they didn't want to make money, they'd be perfectly happy playing for their own enjoyment in each other's kitchens. Given the desire to make money, most rock bands will conform to the system by consciously tailoring their songs to make them more commercial and by making videos that present them as sexually attractive rebels against the system.

There are many ways to view this kind of activity. It can be seen as hoisting the music business with its own petard, by slyly subverting the system to your own ends and getting your anti-establishment message across to vast numbers of people via the very mechanism you despise. It can be seen as a pragmatic compromise in the face of the realities of media-driven international music markets.

It can also be seen as selling your greedy little soul to the devil and, as long as they remained at IRS, that's how R.E.M. saw it. It may be that, as they have always maintained, they simply couldn't stomach the idea of compromising their own artistic principles. It's also hard to imagine that their egalitarian values wouldn't pitch them directly into a head-to-head clash with Copeland himself, something they hadn't foreseen when they signed the five-album deal.

Two of Copeland's strongest traits, however, have always been persistence and logic. His relentless banging away at the group about videos and commercially oriented singles, much as they hated him for it, would be seen to be having its effect on them within just a few more months, although they'd probably hate to admit it.

R.E.M. returned to the fray on October 1st, setting off across Europe on a tour during which the steadfastly didn't play the current single, 'Wendell Gee'. If it had been hoped that the relative tranquillity of their September rest would restore their inner equilibrium, that hope was cruelly shattered during the UK leg of the trek.

On October 23rd they arrived at Barrowlands in Glasgow, in Scotland, where the punters were treated to the bizarre sight of Michael Stipe hurling himself across the stage with his body festooned in watches and the word "dog" scrawled in felt-tip pen across his forehead, the ink dripping down into his eyes under the heat of the spotlights.

"I was so sick that night," is how he rationalised it. "I couldn't stand up. I hadn't eaten anything but potatoes for a whole week, 'cos the food is so bad in England. All I could eat was a sprig of parsley before I went onstage and I was vomiting and shitting. It was just awful. I felt like a dog so I took a felt tip and wrote it on my face. But I started sweating it off while I was onstage, which looked weird."

I felt like a dog, so I took a felt tip and wrote that on my face

True, ever since the pork and beans days during the making of *Fables*, it was on record that the band was not fond of British cuisine. But there are other edible substances on the island than potatoes. There are health food shops, fruit and veg markets and some of the world's finest restaurants, but then you might not notice those if you were already feeling a bit under the weather and, as Michael told *Q* magazine many years later, "I spent much of the 1980s feeling hugely depressed and disillusioned. I would drink myself into stupors, and then I started in on drugs. I was very keen to experiment, and I went through every narcotic except maybe mescaline. But it was just a phase and I got out of it very quickly."

The kind of behaviour he exhibited in Glasgow suggests that perhaps he wasn't quite out of it yet. Three days later, at the Royal Court, in Liverpool, John McCready of the *NME* seemed to be detecting some element of derangement in the singer when he noted, "Stipe shakes and stutters on the end of some theatrical tether. He disappears to recollect his marbles and the remainder of R.E.M. feed their detractors with a smiling and functional cover of 'Ghost Riders'."

In between Glasgow and Liverpool, they fitted in another appearance on UK TV show *The Tube*. Nicky Wire, later to play bass for British mega-band the Manic Street Preachers, was watching, and has since said, "When R.E.M. were on The Tube doing 'Driver 8' and Michael Stipe had purple eyeliner on, that was the first time I'd seen them on telly and I thought, 'Fucking hell, that's fantastic.'"

November found them back in America with another solid month and a half of dates stretching ahead of them. First though, they had an appearance to make at the CMJ (College Music Journal) New Music Awards in New York's Beacon Theater, to collect an Album Of The Year award for *Fables*. It was hardly a Grammy, but meant a great deal to R.E.M. because it reflected the fact that *Fables* was now the most-played album on college radio stations across America.

Although the show was televised by MTV, the band (no doubt to the chagrin of Miles Copeland) declined an offer to play during the broadcast, electing instead to do a set purely for the theater audience after the ceremony was over. To the astonishment of the collected music industry movers and shakers watching the event, Buck repeated his Rickenbacker trick in the middle of 'Cant Get There From Here' and stormed off again, bringing the crowd's 'special treat' to an uncomfortable end.

He subsequently explained the event as a result of his frustration with the onstage sound, claiming that he couldn't hear the monitors and that the soundman refused to do anything about it. Naturally, what one does in such circumstances is to throw a Rickenbacker at the naughty soundman, so he did.

It's plausible, but, for a man who so dearly loves his guitars, two Rickenbacker smashings in fairly rapid succession does seem to confirm the general feeling that Buck was a far from happy bunny around this time.

"We weren't being very nice to each other around '85," he has admitted. "We were just mean to each other. We didn't really talk. I seem to remember seeing most of that year from the bottom of a glass."

Audience member Scott Martin reports an equally telling moment from the gig on November 12th at the Memorial Gymnasium, Vanderbilt University in Nashville. Old friend Jason Ringenberg of Jason and the Scorchers joined them onstage during the encore and, reports

Martin, "Michael Stipe went back to Bill Berry's drum set, picked up a beer bottle and poured the contents on Berry's head. Berry stood up, reached over the drum kit and grabbed Stipe by the collar or throat while Stipe grabbed Berry. Jason had to pull them apart."

Martin goes on to record that, when the concert was over and the bulk of the crowd had gone, Bill Berry ran back out on stage, grabbed a microphone and yelled "Fuck Michael!" whereupon Stipe re-appeared and tussled with Berry while roadies endeavoured to pull them apart.

When I interviewed him for this book, Jason Ringenberg told me, "I sang 'Broken Whiskey Glass' and 'Rockville' with them. I do remember picking Michael up and carrying him off stage like a sack of potatoes. Maybe that is how that story started. I don't think there was any Michael/Bill fight that night, although Michael certainly would at times pour beer on our heads! Or maybe I did that …"

Ringenberg also confirmed that, "The shows we did with them were absolute rock'n'roll extravaganzas. There must have been an army of guardian angels watching over that outfit to keep them out of trouble because the post-show R.E.M./Scorcher parties were as wild as any LA metal scene. No one could out party Peter Buck or (Scorcher) Jeff Johnson alone. Imagine them together … For a kid off an Illinois hog farm it was quite an education."

Their last gig of the year was in Augusta, Georgia, on December 14th, from where it was a short hop back home to the oasis of relative calm that was Athens. In the wake of *Fables* though, R.E.M. were finally reaping some of the benefits of a higher level of affluence. Buck is reported to have earned $24,000 in 1985, not including his songwriting royalties, and was now the proud owner of not just a house but a house with a pool.

Mills had bought himself a turquoise 1966 Thunderbird and Berry had splashed out on a lavender 1960 Ford Galaxie (both of which can be seen during the drive-in movie sequence of the video for 'Cant Get There From Here'). Stipe, charmingly, could still be seen cycling around town, although he admitted that in the winter he would often borrow his mother's car.

Having no immediate R.E.M. commitments, the band started 1986 with a flurry of outside activites. Following on from the studio recordings he'd made with them in February 1984, Michael Stipe went out on tour with The Golden Palominos for half a dozen shows in January of the new year and, while he was away, Peter Buck produced an album, *The Good Earth*, for The Feelies up in New Jersey.

Feelies' founder Glenn Mercer says that Buck had been a fan of their debut album, *Crazy Rhythms*. "He approached me with the idea of working together. He has a good perspective. We knew that the association (with R.E.M.) could have its drawbacks, but it didn't bother us." Although some have claimed that Mercer and his writing partner Bill Million did the lion's share of the production on *The Good Earth*, anyone who knows their previous album would easily hear the R.E.M. inflections that Buck's involvement brought to the music.

Buck also spent some of his free time working back at WUXTRY records, taking his payment in the form of freebie records. Evidently he regarded working in a record store to be a recreational pursuit rather than a job, and it also afforded him the opportunity of hearing lots of new music which he'd been missing while out on the road.

Mills, when not playing golf, found time to co-produce *Hermitage*, the debut album from Norfolk, Virginia, band Waxing Poetics, with Mitch Easter at his Drive-In Studio. Mills had apparently taken an interest in Waxing Poetics when he joined them onstage after playing at Chrysler Auditorium in Norfolk back on December 4th.

And Bill? Well, let the record show that Bill went fishing, but he did manage to settle on his drum stool long enough to play as part of the Hindu Love Gods (without Warren Zevon) at The 40 Watt Club on January 20th. The occasion was a benefit show in memory of Dennes Boon, guitarist with The Minutemen, who had died in a road accident in the Arizona desert on December 22nd. The Minutemen had supported R.E.M. on some gigs during the *Reconstruction* tour, so this gig was put together to raise money for medical treatment for the crash survivors.

February was an even quieter month, memorable mainly for a one-off recording session at John Keane's studio in Athens by a Jefferson Holt project calling itself The Vibrating Egg, in honour of the battery powered female-orgasm-producing sex toy of the same name. For those who might find this odd, it's worth remembering that Steely Dan were named after a dildo in a William Burroughs' novel, the Lovin' Spoonful is a reference to the fluid produced by a male ejaculation, sometimes also called Pearl Jam, and 10cc is said to be the average amount of such fluid produced per orgasm. I rest my case. There's absolutely no way that Jefferson Holt could be accused of being obsessed with sex, just because he called his band The Vibrating Egg.

One further incident that bears re-telling is that on February 14th, Peter Buck and his friend Ken Fechtner went to see Husker Dü play at the 688 Club in Atlanta. Fechtner recalls that Peter, who was notoriously hyperactive, had been prescribed Halcion, a sleeping pill, by his doctor. After the gig, they went back to Fechtner's place and Buck couldn't sleep, so he took one pill. It didn't work, so he took another. When Fechtner got up the next morning, he found Buck still crashed out on the couch, and the previous day's newspaper "neatly shredded into one inch strips and tossed all over my living room".

When Fechtner asked Buck, the guitarist had no memory at all of shredding the newspaper, and Fechtner later learned that Halcion could cause bouts of amnesia in some people. This incident, trivial in itself, takes on new significance when seen in the light of Buck's arrest following an alleged air rage incident in 2001.

Things started hotting up in March. Not only did Mills and Berry debut their legendary Led Zeppelin-tribute band The Corn Cob Webs at The 40 Watt Club on the 8th, but Bill Berry married his girlfriend Mari on the 22nd with the whole band in attendance. Finally, a productive session at John Keane's Studio resulted in no fewer than 16 demos being recorded for the next album.

The session was conducted under the watchful eye of Don Gehman, who had formerly worked with Neil Young, Stephen Stills, Eric Carmen and John Cougar Mellencamp. Mike Mill claims not to remember who suggested Gehman to them, but thinks it may have been Jay Boberg. He does, however, remember what they were looking for: "We wanted a clearer, more powerful sound."

R.E.M. were certainly not big fans of John Cougar Mellencamp, but they were smart enough to know that, compared to their own down-home, funky recordings, Gehman's productions boasted a demonstrably superior sound. Gehman was able to make records that were simultaneously rootsy-sounding and AOR-friendly. If R.E.M. were to make the jump into the mainstream, Gehman was a better than average bet.

So Gehman had been invited to check out the band at a gig in December. "I was intrigued," he has said, adding, "I wouldn't say impressed."

Gehman was certainly not a choice that the average R.E.M. fan would have considered to be in the frame but, having come so close to breaking up during the last tour, it was time for the band to take the biggest decision of their career so far.

Assuming that they wanted to continue, R.E.M. could choose not to seek another deal when the IRS contract ended. If they did that, they could then return to the club level of two years earlier, which was something they all knew they enjoyed.

Alternatively, R.E.M. could continue with IRS or another label along the path of total integrity and total artistic control which was slowly building their name but destroying their friendship because of the ruthlessly commercial orientation of the music industry.

Their third choice was to go for broke. Bring in a producer who knows how to make hits records. Go for the big drum sound. Go for the upfront vocals. One man who could do that for them was Don Gehman.

There were only two albums left to run in the IRS contract. If Gehman delivered a major hit, they would be in a very strong position when the time came for renewal, able to dictate their own terms to one of several major labels who were almost certain to be bidding for them. And if Gehman didn't deliver a hit, they were no worse off. The IRS contract would end, they wouldn't renew, and they'd be free agents again.

Whichever way it worked out, one vital aspect of R.E.M.'s identity would be changed irrevocably. Until this moment, R.E.M. had managed to remain fiercely independent, even by the standards of a relatively small label like IRS. So far, and to their enormous credit, they had achieved everything without playing the game and without compromising their principles. They were outsiders, strangers at the party, innocents abroad.

When they invited Don Gehman into the studio with them, all of that was put behind them. They were now players.

Chapter Ten

Loud And Clear

"I'd never want to be one of those guys who plays six-minute solos. Or even one-minute solos."
PETER BUCK ■

Ricky and me: Peter Buck, 1986

Still shattered by the previous year's heavy schedule, Michael Stipe was finding it hard to come up with lyrics in the spring of 1986. This was, in effect, his first encounter with writer's block. "Every record is challenging and hard to write," he has since claimed. "I always get writer's block, and that's that. I expect it." Back then, though, it was a new experience.

Nevertheless, John Keane remembers that when R.E.M. and Don Gehman entered his studio in the middle of March, "the guys were tight and well-rehearsed. They really seemed to be hitting their stride with the new material."

To describe some of the tracks that ended up on *Life's Rich Pageant* as "new material" is something of a misnomer. R.E.M. – and Peter Buck in particular – were so prolific that they now had a backlog of songs that, for one reason or another, had never been recorded. They had also amassed a significant number of good but half-formed ideas that had never been properly worked up into fully-fledged songs.

Considered chronologically, 'Just A Touch' was the oldest: a song about the day Elvis Presley died, dating back to the early months of 1980. It appeared on R.E.M's very first demo tape, and they took another crack at recording it for *Reckoning*, but that version didn't make the grade. Then, during the *Fables* tour, says Buck, "We got tired of the songs we were doing, so we decided to pull one out of the past." Playing it live injected a new spirit into 'Just A Touch', making it one of the fiercest, punkiest R.E.M. tracks yet recorded.

Similarly, 'What If We Give It Away?' started out as 'Get On Their Way' towards the end of 1980. Never a favourite of the band's, it was resurrected for *Pageant* because Don Gehman took a shine to it. Peter Buck damned it with faint praise by describing it as "innocuous" and, unlike 'Just A Touch', it doesn't seem to have benefited significantly from being re-visited.

The lyric for 'These Days', perhaps the most anthemic song R.E.M. had written so far, was apparently put into Michael's book in July 1984, but it would seem that no suitable music was offered to him until the latter part of 1985. For those who don't see the humour in R.E.M., it's worth noting the line sung by Mike Mills at the very end, "Take away the scattered bones of my meal", a whimsical reference to the messianic status Stipe was being accorded by fans and critics alike.

'Underneath The Bunker' had its origins in London during the *Fables* sessions. "We went to this Greek restaurant and got drunk," recalled Buck. "And this is the type of stuff they were playing. We just came back and did our own version of that kind of music." Including such a lightweight track on the album was a deliberate attempt to balance out the more serious political aspects of some of the other songs.

Of the genuinely new songs, Peter Buck's basic music track for 'Fall On Me' dated back to July of 1985, when Stipe had written a lyric about acid rain. But the song had been virtually re-written, melody and lyrics, by the time it came to be recorded. Stipe, who declared in 1991 that "this may well be my favourite song in the R.E.M. catalogue", has described the final version as "pretty much a song about oppression". Trainspotters might like to know that the counter-melody used in the second verse is actually the song's original tune.

'I Believe' started life in early 1985 with the title 'When I Was Young', a reference to the fact that the first verse describes a bout of scarlet fever suffered by Stipe when he was two. A good deal of rewriting took place before the final lyric emerged in February of 1986, and that snatch of Peter Buck playing banjo at the start was recorded without Buck's knowledge, then stuck on to the song for fun.

Buck has described 'Swan Swan H' as "fake Irish music", knocked together by himself and Michael in 20 minutes on November 4th, 1985, in Elk's Bow, Wyoming, while their tour bus was broken down during the *Fables* tour. Lyrically, according to Stipe, it's about "a war our country inflicted on itself a number of decades ago. It's about a period of our American history that was very, very ugly." Mills hates it.

We got tired of the songs we were doing, so we decided to pull one out of the past

'Begin The Begin', planned as an eight-minute epic, was written by the whole band in Michael Stipe's living room during a cold spell in February 1986. To begin with, explained Buck to *Creem* magazine, "I had that one little riff and that was it." As the writing process continued, however, the composition became ever more complex: "Nothing was the same all the way through except the riff. There were five different choruses, no bridge, no melody." Thankfully, by the time it was recorded, the song had been pared down to three minutes, with a powerful lyric that evoked America's nightmarish origins via a reference to Miles Standish, a soldier who had arrived on The Mayflower in 1620. After profiting significantly from the freely given local knowledge of two Native Americans, Wittuwamet and Peksuot, Standish arranged to have them killed.

Thrust along by Mike Mill's bass, 'Cuyahoga' is another of R.E.M.'s many eco-conscious political songs, which Stipe has described as "a metaphor for America and lost promises". The

Cuyahoga River flows through sacred Native American land in Ohio. Once pure and clean, it had become so polluted by industrial effluents as far back as 1915 that one method of cleaning it up was to throw a torch in and set the river on fire.

Although it's not glaringly obvious from the lyric, 'Flowers Of Guatemala' is, like 'Green Grow The Rushes' on *Fables*, about America's oppression of third world countries. "There's big fish and medium fish and little fish," explained Stipe. "Big fish is the United States. Medium fish is Mexico. Little fish is Guatemala. One eats the other up. One gets bigger."

Only two songs on *Pageant* were not demoed at John Keane's studio. 'Hyena' had been recorded during the *Fables* sessions, but doubts about the tempo at which the song should be played led to it being abandoned. As with 'Just A Touch', playing 'Hyena' live brought the band to a better understanding of its dynamics and enabled them to make a worthwhile version with Don Gehman.

'Superman', the first cover version to appear on an R.E.M. album, was also not from the Keane demos. A shameless slab of catchy pop, originally released by Texan band The Clique, it was recorded, says Buck, as a possible b-side but turned out so well that they elevated it to album status.

One song recorded at Keane's that didn't make it to the album is nevertheless worthy of mention. 'PSA', an anti-media rant inspired by a day when Stipe answered his front door and found a camcorder lens poking into his face, is said to have been prototype of 'It's The End Of The World As We Know It'. 'PSA' would also be re-vamped as 'Bad Day' in 2003.

"It kind of got top-shelved and we never looked at it again," Stipe told me. "Although we knew it was there, we knew it was in our catalogue collecting dust and had a great idea and a great chorus but we just never finished it, there was other material that seemed more appropriate to the record we were trying to make."

Working on the demos with Don Gehman proved to be a dramatically new kind of studio experience for R.E.M., and John Keane reckons that, "Gehman was a little taken aback by their insistence on doing things their own way. They definitely weren't accustomed to taking directions from anyone."

Nevertheless, the demo recordings were deemed more than satisfactory. As Mike Mills saw it, "We wanted someone who would make us sound like a band, really clearly and crisply, and he did that." It was decided to proceed to the making of finished recordings in April at Belmont Mall Studios in Bloomington, Indiana. This was a facility Gehman had built for John Mellencamp. They had a $100,000 budget. It would prove to be a learning curve unlike anything they'd encountered before.

With years of experience and success behind him, Gehman was not intimidated in any way by R.E.M.'s cliquishness. He didn't fully understand how they worked or how they thought, but he knew the formula for hit records, and saw it as his job to apply that formula to R.E.M. One of the first rules in Gehman's book is that listeners like to know what words a singer is singing – even if they can't understand those words. As a result, says Stipe, he was "the first person to challenge me on my lyrics, just saying, 'What the fuck is this about?' I crossed my arms and walked out of the room."

For his part, Gehman insists that he wasn't trying to squeeze the poetry, the allusion or the richness out of Stipe's writing. He felt all of that could be retained but, with a bit more discipline and bit less self-indulgence, the words could also make sense. As Gehman puts it, "He didn't want to write banal lyrics, in other words, something literal. Whereas all I was looking for was, if it was metaphorical, that it made sense."

Bill Berry has pointed out that, although it isn't a feature of his speaking voice, Michael Stipe has a slight lisp when singing. "He would taper it out of his vocal style by mumbling. That's literally what was going on." With his keen ear, Don Gehman picked that up and resolved the problem by bringing in a special microphone to eradicate the lisp.

Thus, aggrieved though he was by Gehman's bluntness, Stipe came to realize that the producer knew what he was talking about. The other members of R.E.M. traditionally deferred to Michael in matters lyrical, partly because they respected him as a friend, partly because they were in awe of him as a poetic visionary, and partly because what he wrote had seemed to work perfectly well so far. None of this applied to Gehman. He had been brought in with the band's agreement to make them more commercial and he knew how to do that. If they chose to ignore his advice, he'd move on and produce hit records for somebody else. He had nothing to lose by challenging Michael Stipe.

Jay Boberg of IRS has stated that, in his opinion, there was another factor at work that dictated Stipe's willingness to play ball with Gehman. "The band wanted more and more to be successful, despite their assertions to the contrary. Michael Stipe in particular was starting to sense that they could be a big band, and I think he was really striving for this."

Nor did it do any harm that the circumstances in which *Life's Rich Pageant* was recorded much more closely resembled R.E.M.'s usual modus vivendi than the London locale they had suffered for *Fables Of The Reconstruction*. "We were in sunny southern Indiana," remembers Berry, "and we all had our own condominiums. I even bought a boat out there. We'd go in at one every afternoon, knock off at eight, then hit town and have some drinks. It was done with a more positive attitude."

The end result was a generally satisfactory working environment, in which Mills and Gehman seem to have hit it off best, with the producer happy to indulge Mills' enthusiasm for tinkering with unusual keyboard instruments in order to find interesting new tonal colours and textures.

Those keyboards, Buck feels, contributed more than a little towards giving the album an overall coherence that *Fables* had perhaps lacked. "We always think of an album as a whole," he explains, "and how the songs can be linked together." Thus, having decided to use an oldfangled pump organ for one song, they went further and used it on every track but one. "We found a lady whose husband was a preacher. The church burned down, so the organ got covered in slime from the fire. She put it in her barn and kept it there for about 50 years, but it played great."

Berry has declared himself particularly pleased with the improvement in the drum sound. "In the past we always tried to stay away from big, booming, stupid-sounding drums," he said, "but, as a result, they ended up sounding wimpy and lackluster. Don gave us a big drum sound, but it's natural – he didn't make us sound like a disco-pop mechanism."

I wouldn't call myself a lead guitarist

Peter Buck has also acknowledged that "Don helped me question why I play at certain places" and it's evident throughout the album that, rather than the traditional layers of guitar, Buck is tending towards finding a single distinctive line, with only occasional embellishments.

"I still wouldn't call myself a lead guitarist," he admits modestly. "All my solos are basically melodic/rhythmic devices to fill up space, and that's the way I like it. I'd never want to be one of those guys who play six-minute solos. Or even one-minute solos."

It seems, however, that although Gehman had been brought in to teach them a few new tricks, some of R.E.M.'s unique ways also rubbed off on him. "R.E.M. taught me how things don't have to be that focused," he says. "I taught them a lot about how to make records; the chorus has to come in and lift, doubling, making shifts in songs – all that Producer 101 stuff. But they taught me about chaos. You can let a lot of it go on and still come out with a viable, commercial project. It will have a level of magic you would never have had any other way."

Although Stipe has always accepted that *Pageant* is a beautiful-sounding record, he still feels that he compromised his principles too much when singing the vocals. "The direction that Don Gehman pushed me in for *Life's Rich Pageant* really paralysed me for several records, because he had such an idea for what a vocal should be, that it threw me into this place of wild insecurity. And I think it really affected the ways that those subsequent records were produced."

Having completed the album in May, R.E.M. had a relatively light diary for the next three months. A video for 'Fall On Me' was made in a stone quarry in Bloomington, Indiana, with Michael Stipe acting as cameraman, director and editor. This is the one that IRS boss Miles Copeland later singled out for a tongue-lashing, saying, "They had videos that they literally weren't in, that weren't very good, in my view. I just didn't think we were going to see a lot of action out of those videos, and I was right."

For Michael, though, it was "a fuck you to MTV". And that was evidently more than enough reason to do it. The only other significant activity in June came on the 16th when the Hindu Love Gods single 'Gonna Have A Good Time Tonight' was finally released in the US.

'Fall On Me', which Don Gehman had rated as the "closest thing we had to a hit, but even that was a long shot" was released in the UK as the first single from *Life's Rich Pageant* on July 14th. "I did argue that the first single should at least have something that makes sense for the chorus line," Gehman grumbled later. "I mean, give me a hook, come on!" Instead, what they gave him for a chorus in 'Fall On Me' was the deeply impenetrable "Don't fall on me (What is it up in the air for?) (It's gonna fall.)"

Stipe set off on another brief string of dates, mostly in Europe, with the Golden Palominos on July 14th. On the 28th *Life's Rich Pageant* was released in the UK. The title of the album refers to a line spoken by Peter Sellers as the bungling French policeman, Inspector Clouseau, in the Pink Panther films. After driving his car into a lake, a completely sodden Sellers tries to make the best of a bad situation by wryly observing, "It's all part of life's rich pageant." Having cracked the band up when they saw the film, the phrase had rapidly become their stock response to any of life's little problems.

Among those problems, of course, was the fact that R.E.M. could see little point in releasing the album in Europe at all. As mentioned previously, IRS had switched, as far as Europe was concerned, from distribution by A&M to distribution by MCA. Peter Buck clearly recalls "being told by MCA's head of promotion at the time of *Life's Rich Pageant*, 'We're not going to promote this record, because there aren't any hit singles.' I mean, he's sitting there telling me this." Artist motivation, it would seem, was a low priority at MCA in those days.

At the time, comparing *Pageant* to *Murmur*, Buck said, "This one came out more like we wanted it to, song-wise and production-wise." Mills went further, declaring it to be "the strongest, best album we've ever made".

One of the first things that reviewers picked up on was that although Michael Stipe's words, thanks to Don Gehman, were now beautifully audible, their meaning was usually so hidden in metaphor and allegory that it was still impossible to have any idea of what he was

This one came out more like we wanted it to

singing about. In Stipe's defence, Mills has said, "He's got to write words for the songs we churn out, and a lot of them are going to be personal. If I was him, I wouldn't want to lay my soul bare for 100,000 record-buying people. So, if I could express some feelings without telling everyone what I did last night, I'd want to do it that way. If you're at all a private person, the last thing you'd want to do is to tell strangers your innermost feelings."

The British press spoke as if with one voice. "One of 1986's benchmark offerings," said

NME, while *Melody Maker* rated it "R.E.M.'s greatest LP to date". Similary, after US release on the 29th, *Rolling Stone* had no hesitation in proclaiming it "brilliant and groundbreaking". It would rise as high as No 21 in the *Billboard* album chart, significantly out-performing *Fables* sales-wise, and would go on to earn R.E.M. their first gold record.

Frustratingly, however, when 'Fall On Me' was released as a single in the US, on August 19th, it rapidly became their most-airplayed track ever, but still didn't rise above No 97 in *Billboard*.

The Pageantry tour, another three-month coast-to-coast marathon, set off from the Oak Mountain Amphitheater in Birmingham, Alabama, on September 5th, 1986. The gig has passed into history as the first time R.E.M. played 'The One I Love' which, with its repeated yells of "Fire!" would go on to become their first Top Ten hit single. "Originally, I wasn't saying any word at all, I was just screaming," Stipe has revealed. "The whole chorus was me screaming, and then that developed into the word 'fire' when it became time to put it down on tape."

R.E.M. were evidently in better shape on this outing because, whereas the previous year's tour had all but wiped them out, they seem to have taken this one in their stride. Although some observers, like IRS art designer Geoff Gans, found it "strange that the band wasn't spending any time together", the conscious decision not to live constantly in each other's pockets was probably an important factor in maintaining good relations when they did come together.

Woody Nuss, R.E.M.'s first soundman, was now working with Guadalcanal Diary, who played support during the early part of this tour. "One of the best R.E.M. shows I've ever seen was in the rain at Mesa, Arizona," he says, speaking of the September 23rd gig at the Mesa Amphitheater. "They didn't care that it was raining. They were doing a lot of songs that would be on *Document*. It was a really good tour, they were playing really well, and all of the shows were sold out in nice amphitheaters."

At the Civic Auditorium, Portland, Oregon, on October 3rd, R.E.M. debuted another new song, 'Oddfellows Local 151', although at this point they were still calling it 'Firehouse'. The song had grown out of Stipe's concern for the poorer elements in society, the tramps, the winos and the bums. "When a neighbourhood starts having people pass out on the ground," he explained, "it means that the society in that neighbourhood is already on the downswing. Not because these people are bad, but because it represents the fact that people aren't taking care of their duties to take care of them."

Peter Buck has explained that the song's title derives from the Masonic Lodges of America, saying, "There used to be Oddfellow's Lodges all over the town, just like the Mooses or the Shriners. The song is actually about these winos who used to live down the street from us. They used to live in cars."

In Stipe's lyric, the winos congregate behind the Oddfellows Lodge, a poignant reminder that those who have live side by side with those who have not. Even an organization like the Masons, originally intended as a brotherhood of tradesmen helping each other to prosper in the face of an oppressive system run by rich and powerful autocrats, turns away from those who have fallen completely through the holes in society's safety nets.

Michael Stipe was, by now, finding life on the bus a bit too intrusive. So that same night he elected to travel for most of the rest of the tour with his Canadian schoolteacher friend Georgina Falzarano, in her car. This turned out to be a smart decision because, as well as affording him a quieter existence, their travels together inspired a new song.

Five days later, after the show at the State Fairgrounds Coliseum in Salt Lake City, Michael and Georgina drove through the night to Boulder, Colorado, the next stop on the tour. Stipe subsequently described the journey in his notebook in words that eventually became the song 'You Are The Everything'.

Camper Van Beethoven, an off-the-wall Californian combo with a large college following, took over as support from October 9th at the Colorado University Events Center, in Boulder, Colorado. Victor Krummenacher, Camper Van B's bass player, was impressed by Michael Stipe's willingness to address political issues onstage.

"I was just beginning to read about and understand the Iran-Contra affair," he remembers, "so I was pleasantly surprised that they would be political about that onstage. It was really intense. He would do this rap and recite the Pledge of Allegiance. At the end of it, he would mimic blowing his head off."

One of the few notably odd incidents on the Pageantry tour took place at the Welsh Auditorium Grand Center, Grand Rapids, Michigan on October 18th. In the middle of R.E.M's set, a man made his way onto the stage and grabbed Stipe's microphone. Stipe's response was to leave the stage but, once the security staff had removed the man, Stipe returned and wiped off the microphone with a towel. This seems fair enough, except that one observer says that he continued with this cleansing activity for several minutes before starting the next song.

The following night, during the gig at Chicago's Viceroy Pavilion, Michael improvised a rap at the start of 'Auctioneer (Another Engine)'. Tapes of the concert, closely scrutinized by R.E.M. obsessives far more diligent than I, reveal that Michael's rap included four lines that would later serve as the opening of 'Finest Worksong', on the *Document* album.

Around this time, Peter Buck told *Pulse* magazine, "Our album isn't any kind of political manifesto, but it reflects our experiences of the past year." Then he added, in an obvious reference to 'Flowers Of Guatemala', "which include picking up the newspaper and reading how we're bombing foreign countries, and giving aid to the Nicaraguan contras. It's a shameful thing, how we're sitting here drinking beer while we're paying for other people's misery in foreign countries."

Political manifesto or not, there's no doubt that R.E.M. were being perceived as political activists by a large portion of their audience. On November 2nd, the second of two nights at the Wang Center in Boston, when they sang 'Flowers Of Guatemala', it had a startling effect. "I looked into the audience and people were weeping openly," recalls Stipe. "It was like, 'Oh my god!' You could hear a pin drop. It was the most incredible feeling."

The tour wound down without further incident, and ended with a celebratory three-night stand back in Georgia at Atlanta's Fox Theater, after which the band were required to record a song as part of the soundtrack to the low-budget Timothy Hutton-Kelly McGillis movie *Made In Heaven*. Having chosen 'Romance', an oldie dating back to 1981, they planned to re-unite with Don Gehman to record it in Athens, but Gehman was busy with other projects. Instead, on Gehman's recommendation, they chose Scott Litt. With a resume that featured work with Let's Active, The dB's and Katrina And The Waves, Litt was a natural fit for R.E.M. and the recording went so well that Litt was immediately on the short list of potential producers for their next album. The band took a well-earned month off to enjoy Christmas and the New Year. It would be another nine months before they'd hit the road again.

For Peter Buck, although the band was functioning efficiently again, there had been a couple of personal upheavals in 1986. He split with his long-time girlfriend, Ann, and he lost his father. The other three members of R.E.M. came from very supportive families, but Buck's parents had been deeply disappointed when their son decided to pursue a career with a rock band. "They'd worked and gone to college, got masters degrees," he explained. "To see the next generation go back to what they saw as blue collar work was upsetting. They were right in a way, because you work weird hours and get no pension. They kind of raised me to be a college professor; they couldn't believe I was throwing it all away."

During the early years of R.E.M. he barely saw his parents and, even by the time of his father's death, "We weren't really close in a lot of ways, but the last thing he said to me before he died was, 'Make sure you make a million because there's nothing else on earth that you are able to do.' He was trying to kind of say 'stick with it' but he was saying it in the nastiest possible way."

As 1987 dawned, R.E.M. moved back into high gear, first of all working up new material at their West Clayton Street Rehearsal Studio in Athens, then quickly moving into John Keane's studio to record the demos that would become their fifth album, *Document*.

This time, however, they had a new agenda, a determination to make a record that critics couldn't dismiss as jangly or comfortable – which had been just about the only consistent complaint against the otherwise well-received *Pageant*. "We wanted to make a loose, weird, semi-live in the studio album," is how Peter Buck explained it. To achieve this end, they adopted what has come to be known as their chaos method of songwriting. Explaining the method to me, Buck said, "Sometimes you sit down and you have a piece of paper and you sit at the piano and you write things out, and those are very songwriterly songs, but sometimes you just make a whole lot of noise and something occurs."

They had first tried it out in the summer of the previous year in rehearsal room sessions which produced ten potential songs, all of which were quickly abandoned except for 'The One I Love' and 'Lightnin' Hopkins'. Nevertheless, the idea of music emerging from chaos still appealed to them, and they had a higher success rate with it in January, working almost every day of the month, and turning out the musical backings for 'Finest Worksong', 'Welcome To the Occupation', 'Exhuming McCarthy', 'Fireplace', 'Disturbance At The Heron House', and, most notable of all, 'It's The End Of The World As We Know It (And I Feel Fine)'. It was now up to Michael Stipe to find words and, in some cases, melodies. "If Michael is in the room when we are doing songs," says Mills, "he writes lyrics as we work but it's usually something he takes away to a certain place."

Life's Rich Pageant was certified as R.E.M.'s first gold disc on January 23rd, but the popping of the celebratory corks had barely

I looked in the audience, and people were weeping openly. You could hear a pin drop

died down before they were back into John Keane's. The heavily ironic 'The One I Love', which Stipe describes as having been born out of frustration and anger, was demoed on February 4th. "It's about using people over and over again," he says. "That's probably a sentiment everyone has felt at one point or another, so you can apply it to yourself, but it's not an attractive quality."

Irony, of course, is a technique much beloved of modern songwriters, who usually forget that large swathes of their audience will take the lyric's sentiments at face value. So, much to his dismay, whenever Stipe sang the opening line, "This one goes out to the one I love," an audience of young men and women brought up on radio love song dedications reacted like Pavlov's dogs and began staring moistly into each other's eyes. By the time he got to the punchline, "A simple prop to occupy my time", they were in each other's arms, lip-locked and oblivious to the outside world.

Stipe had been misunderstood by fans and critics in the past, but 'The One I Love' took those misunderstandings to a whole new level. And it gave R.E.M. their first huge hit single.

Chapter Eleven

Mr Evil Breakfast

"The whole album
is about chaos ...
and the hypothesis
that there is order
in chaos."
MICHAEL STIPE ■

Guitar to the fore: Buck at the time of Document, 1987

Before R.E.M. could crack on with the recording of Document, their next album, Buck, Berry and Mills had an appointment in California with their old chum Warren Zevon.

The plan was to go into Record One Studios in Los Angeles and record tracks for Zevon's forthcoming album, the star-studded *Sentimental Hygiene*. R.E.M.'s involvement in the proceedings came about, says Peter, because "he wanted to have a working band, rather than guys he pays by the hour."

Even so, it seems Zevon often treated them like guys he would have paid by the hour. After they'd completed what they considered a perfect take, Zevon would want to do it again because, for example, he was unhappy with the drums. "Literally, you'd be off a hair, you couldn't even hear it," grumbled Buck, "but he'd be timing it with a stopwatch."

These and other minor quibbles aside, R.E.M. appreciated the opportunity to hang out with Zevon's other guest-artists, a roster that included Bob Dylan, Neil Young, George Clinton, Don Henley of The Eagles, Stray Cat Brian Setzer and some of Tom Petty's Heartbreakers.

Sentimental Hygiene was seen as a triumphant comeback for Zevon, and the sessions also brought him an unexpected bonus. "We spent a couple of weeks rehearsing and a couple of weeks recording," explained Zevon to *Vox* magazine. "We were finished ahead of schedule and we still had studio time. We were in the habit of meeting in the studio every day, so we just kind of came down to see what was for lunch, they started rolling the tape, and we started playing."

The results would, in due course, be released as an album by the Hindu Love Gods banner. The material consists largely of Zevon and the R.E.M. trio jamming on a bunch of cover versions, which, according to Bill Berry, "took us about as long to do as it takes to listen to."

According to Zevon, "We joked about doing 'Raspberry Beret' or 'Bungle In the Jungle', which turned out to be too difficult to learn." Ever pragmatic, they soon found a solution to that problem. "We sent somebody out for the Prince songbook which had 'Raspberry Beret' in it. The performance is literally a reading of the song from the lead sheet."

Meanwhile, back in Athens, things were going badly for the beloved 40 Watt Club. From its humble beginnings, The 40 Watt had gradually expanded and gone a little more up-market over the years. To do this, the club had moved around town, and was now in its fourth location, 382 East Broad Street, under the ownership of local entrepreneur and health food proprietor Doug Hoescht. Towards the end of March, however, Hoescht shut up shop, claiming that business was on the decline and that the recently raised drinking age had seriously affected profitability. Shortly afterwards, he left for the Caribbean.

Fortunately, when an establishment is as important to the good cultural health of a community as The 40 Watt, it isn't that easy to kill. Two of Hoescht's former employees managed to raise the finance to re-open the club at 256 W. Clayton Street later in the year.

Recording of *Document* began on March 31st, at Sound Emporium, Nashville, Tennessee, where they would spend all of the following month, with Peter and Mike sharing a house while Bill and Mike moved into a condo. The decision to record in Nashville was not specifically connected with the city's country and western heritage but more generally intended to provide a new and stimulating environment in which to work. "If you work out that you're going to spend a month recording," said Buck, "you may as well go somewhere different each time and soak up a different atmosphere."

In an interview with *Melody Maker*, Buck also noted, "Every record is a process of reacting against the prior one. I was really happy with *Pageant*, but none of us wanted to make that record again."

Having worked so well with Scott Litt on *Romance*, he was invited in as producer. "We wanted to work with someone who's primarily an engineer," said Buck. "Scott's a very good producer, but he would allow us to mess around. Don Gehman was good, but he was real directed and straightforward in that he would say, 'This song, to get on the radio, has to sound like this.'"

As Litt saw it, when they started work, the album was "a document of how R.E.M. play live off the floor in an ensemble situation".

A document of how R.E.M. play live

Like Gehman, Scott Litt liked to work in an orderly way, which suited R.E.M. just fine. "Every night we'd finish at around one," said Buck, "go to a bar and meet the same five people."

The overtly left-wing political stance, first been articulated on *Fables* and very evident on *Pageant*, was now prominent: it was arguably the most significant aspect of Stipe's lyric writing. In justification of this new direction, he pointed out that, in a world where the news, even when it could be trusted, was frighteningly sanitized and ineffectual, "pop culture is still the one way in which someone who is without power can attain it and bring change".

The album opens with the stirring call to arms of 'Finest Worksong', in which Buck's guitar, somewhat subdued on *Pageant*, takes centre stage again. "The minute we wrote that," said Buck, "we pretty much knew that it had to be side one, track one." Drawing some of its energy and inspiration from Peter Gabriel's 'Sledgehammer', the song is an attack on the American work ethic, which Stipe perceived as "the idea that you can work and work and get what you want and then try for even more. It's the American dream, but it's a pipe dream that's been exploited for years."

The folksy, traditional-sounding 'Welcome To The Occupation' obviously derives from the same concerns about American foreign policy in Central American as 'Green Grow The Rushes' and 'Flowers Of Guatemala'. Although the band generally shared Stipe's sentiments, an early version of the lyric offended Bill Berry with a line that read, "Hang your freedom fighters". Although Stipe countered that he had intended the line as a double-entendre (hang as in "execute" and hang as in "place on the wall in a picture frame") Berry's concern that it was too blatant convinced him to change the line to "Hang your freedom higher".

That ominous clacking sound at the start of 'Exhuming McCarthy' is Stipe's typewriter, which he used in the studio to finish off lyrics. The subject of this chorus-free song was what the band saw as a return to the "reds under the beds" paranoia that had swept America in the 1950s, when Senator Joe McCarthy's political witch-hunts attempted to purge America of communist influences. "It's the 1980s and McCarthy's coming back," said Stipe, "so why not dig him up?" Like that of 'Welcome To The Occupation', the music of 'Exhuming McCarthy' (defined by Buck as "vampire-surf-guitar-funk") is deceptively sweet in tone, sugaring the pill of the dark and bitter political invective of the lyric.

'Disturbance At The Heron House', criticized by some for sounding like a slower version of 'Gardening At Night', has been described by Stipe as "the most political song I've ever written." His lyrics, by this time, were becoming less obtuse, but it's hard to blame anyone for not deciphering the "meaning" of this one. Set in a dreamlike Orwellian zoo, it tells of monkeys being numbered, perhaps to see how many might have to be locked in a room full of typewriters to guarantee the eventual production of all the works of Shakespeare. Or even one Michael Stipe song? Good heavens, no. "Something very ominous is hinted at in 'Disturbance at the Heron House' that can be taken and applied all types of ways," he says. "It's not connected to who was in the White House at the time or what they were involved in, catastrophic or otherwise. It can be applied a little more universally."

'Strange', a speedier cover of a song by the UK art-punk band Wire, features a vocal Stipe knocked off in two takes. "It's a great song," said Buck at the time. "If we were going to write another song for this record, I couldn't have written one better."

Clearly descended from Chuck Berry's 'Too Much Monkey Business' and Bob Dylan's 'Subterranean Homesick Blues', 'It's The End Of The World As We Know It (And I Feel Fine)' features a rapid-fire lyric that is not only one of Stipe's most powerful, but also one of the quickest to write. "When they showed me the song in the studio, I just said, 'It's the end of the world as we know it and I feel fine.' I wanted it to be the most bombastic vocal that I could possibly muster, something that would completely overwhelm you."

'The One I Love', R.E.M.'s first top ten hit, has already been examined in Chapter 10, but it's worth noting that the band seemed to have very little faith in its commercial potential. "It will go higher than we ever had a single," allowed Buck, "but we never got above 90 anyway."

'Fireplace', blessed with another of Buck's bizarre genre definitions when he called it "Chinese heavy metal jazz", is based on guidance about good domestic practice given by Mother

Ann Lee, the 18th century leader of the American Shakers. The track features an old friend of the band, Steve Berlin of Los Lobos, playing saxophone with wild abandon. "It was 2am," explains Buck, "and I told Steve Berlin to think of [jazz sax genius John] Coltrane and go to it, get right out there. And he went, 'Great! I never get to do this.' Because he plays rock'n'roll sax."

Peter Buck has forcefully insisted that the only connection blues guitar legend Lightnin' Hopkins has to the track named after him is that, "I just happened to have a Lightnin' Hopkins album in my hand when we went into the rehearsal studio that day, and Michael wanted to call the song that, so I said, 'O.K., fine.'" A look at the lyric, however, reveals the word "lightnin'" being used several times, in a song whose first line is "When I lay myself to sleep" – an inversion of the standard blues opening, "I woke up this mornin'" – along with such evocative terms as "crow" and "badlands". It's all very suggestive of the blues, as indeed is Buck's passable attempt at a slide guitar solo.

'King Of Birds' dated back to the *Pageant* sessions, where it had been put to tape as an eight-minute backing track, then abandoned. Stipe didn't forget it, however, and encouraged the band to cut it again in a more concise and folksier version that would suit some lyrics he had worked out. The new treatment, an eclectic concoction of tribal drums, psychedelic guitars and dulcimer, perfectly suited Stipe's fantastical lyric about "Standing on the shoulders of giants", a line nicked from Sir Isaac Newton. Look it up.

The album closes with the doom-laden 'Oddfellows Local 151', already discussed in the previous chapter and, with recording wrapped up on May 2nd, there came a pleasant surprise for Peter Buck. Back in 1986, the guitarist had been approached by illustrator Jack Logan, who had asked if he could do a comic based on Buck. For some reason, Buck thought he meant a single cartoonish drawing, and gave his consent. What the delivery service brought to Buck, however, was a full-blown comic magazine with Buck as its star.

Mixing of the album was set to begin in May, but, in the meanwhile, IRS was set to release *Dead Letter Office*, a compilation that included all of the *Chronic Town* EP plus any R.E.M. b-sides that had never appeared on an album. "I had some doubts about that," admitted Buck, thinking maybe people would think we were trying to cash in, to sell records."

On the contrary, R.E.M.'s fan base had now swollen to such an extent that hundreds of thousands welcomed the opportunity to get hold of tracks that were fast becoming impossible to find. "Listening to this album should be like browsing through a junk shop," suggested Buck in his sleeve notes, making the point that much of it was throwaway discarded stuff, but the diligent seeker will always find some little object of desire. Here there be covers of classics by artists as diverse as the Velvet Underground, Aerosmith and Roger Miller, plus a clutch of R.E.M. originals that either didn't make sense on any particular album, or weren't quite up to scratch.

Work resumed on *Document* in early May, when the band flew out to Master Control studios in Los Angeles for the mixing sessions. Buck feels that for the first time, the band became fully involved in the mixing process. "We were there from the word go," he said. "We were there when they were bringing up the kick drum and when they were starting a drum mix that takes two hours."

Litt, who seems to have appreciated their involvement, says that, at this stage, "I began to experiment a little until we found a consistent character in the band's studio sound."

The process of bringing Stipe's vocals to the forefront of the mix, which had been started by Don Gehman, progressed further with Scott Litt. Halfway through the mixing process, says Mills, "we looked at each other and said, 'Wow, it seems like the vocals are pretty loud here' but we said it was OK, because we hadn't noticed it up to that point and it just seemed to fit."

For Scott Litt, "It was probably the most fun I've had making a record. I didn't want it to end." The band felt much the same way, so Litt remained as their producer until 1997.

Despite the fun they had making it, Stipe summed up *Document* as "a very vitriolic statement". He told writer Bill Flanagan that, thematically, "The whole album is about fire, about everything you think about fire as being cleansing, something that destroys everything in its path."

To another interviewer, however, Stipe insisted that,

The whole album is about chaos ... and the hypothesis that there is order in chaos

"the whole album is about chaos ... and the hypothesis that there is order in chaos." While it's true to say that the one need not exclude the other, it's worth remembering that the members of R.E.M. like nothing better than winding up journalists.

Buck once told a hapless hack that his father had been "a Shakespearian actor, but he made his fortune playing the Tidy-Bowl man [a cartoon character who rows a boat around the toilet bowl in a US commercial for toilet cleaner], and he couldn't come to grips with that kind of success, so he committed suicide and it tragically marred my teenage years".

To his amazement and delight, the story was printed. If, God forbid, a government of rock stars is ever elected, Stipe and Buck would be joint No 1 on the shortlist for the job of Minister For Disinformation. During the mixing of *Document* in Los Angeles, Stipe took time out to record 'A Campfire Song' with 10,000 Maniacs in Los Angeles, for the album *In My Tribe*. The friendship of Stipe and Maniacs' singer Natalie Merchant had got off to a bad start back in 1983. So many people had described her as a female version of him that he went to extraordinary lengths to avoid meeting her, even hiding in the bathroom at a party they both attended.

Once they finally did meet, however, they clicked to such an extent that they became lovers, on and off, for a couple of years. The happy coincidence of Stipe being in Los Angeles, while 10,000 Maniacs were recording there, meant that it was almost inevitable that he would end up visiting them in the studio. But Merchant's most vivid recollection of that encounter was something that took place on the street.

"We went out to get something to eat," she told Toby Manning of *Q* magazine in 2001. "It's so light in LA, Michael forgot to put his headlights on, and the police pulled us over and Michael was trying to negotiate what he was drinking and a cigarette. By the time the police came over, he didn't have his hands on the steering wheel and the cops put a gun to his head and he cried out, 'I'm from Georgia!' And the cop was yelling, 'Keep your fucking hands on the steering wheel!' So I almost saw Michael Stipe blown away by LAPD."

Happily, Stipe survived to join Natalie again in a noteworthy, and oft-bootlegged, benefit show for the financially threatened Texas Records, owned by their friend Michael Meister, in Santa Monica's legendary McCabe's Guitar Shop on May 24th. The event also included ex-Plimsouls' singer-songwriter Peter Case, Jenny Homer of ethereal popsters Downy Mildew, Steve Wynn of Dream Syndicate, and Californian psychedelic combo Opal, fronted by Kendra Smith, who had also been a founder-member of Dream Syndicate.

The all-acoustic show took the form of a review, with all of the participants mixing and matching their talents in various combinations, performing weird cover-versions and original material. Most entertaining of all was perhaps a rendition of John Denver's 'Leaving On A Jet Plane' by Natalie Merchant and Jenny Homer, while Stipe, Buck and Wynn simultaneously sang The Velvet Underground's 'Sunday Morning' to the same backing.

The entire affair was delightfully low-key and ad hoc, with Peter Buck recalling how, at one point, "I was upstairs getting nervous and stretching, and Michael wanted to surprise me. He had taught a friend of his (Geoff Gans of IRS) how to play the song ('The One I Love')." It did indeed surprise him to hear the song playing through the wall, when he couldn't imagine that anyone other than himself would have known how to accompany Michael on it.

The McCabe's show, as well as being a barrel of fun, can also be seen as presaging the move towards the more acoustically orientated R.E.M. of the early 1990s.

The one sour note of the day is that although the show had been advertised on flyers as featuring R.E.M., Bill Berry was nowhere to be seen. At the last moment, he'd decided to go home. He'd pulled the same stunt on the second last show of the Pageantry tour, walking out of the Fox Theater in Atlanta just as the band went back on for the final encore. Berry's commitment to the band in general was not seriously in doubt at this time. His strong sense of loyalty and duty meant that he could be relied on for the big things, but there were more and more little incidents which suggested that, when push came to shove, there were many times when he treasured his home life much more than he valued R.E.M.

Despite Peter Buck's ongoing conviction that "the whole of idea of videos is despicable", the video compilation *Succumbs*, including all of the band's little films and promos (except *Wolves, Lower*) was released in the US on June 2nd.

Stipe, who had been personally involved in the making of many of them, was coming round to the idea that videos were not necessarily a bad thing, and was much happier than Buck with the release of *Succumbs* because, "a lot of people have never seen them. They never played them on the national video channels."

What did get played on the national channels, however, was the video for 'The One I Love', which was made on July 18th and 19th in Athens, by director Robert Longo of New York's Pressure Pictures. The band's decision to allow an outside company to take control of this video was a sign of their increasing acceptance, reluctantly or otherwise, that to maximize the success they'd achieved so far, they had to be on MTV.

To achieve that, they had to make videos that MTV would be prepared to show. Buck complained that IRS would prefer them to make, "a glitzy video where we all sing and look sincere and there's a pretty girl", but they weren't ready to go quite that far yet.

Although Longo's promo did include performance shots of the band, there was no attempt to lip-synch, and the feel of the thing remained vaguely art-house. Nevertheless it was close enough to a traditional pop video for MTV to put it into heavy rotation.

On the second day of shooting for the 'One I Love', Stipe played with Cowface, his sister Lynda's band, at The 40 Watt Club. Mat Smith of *Melody Maker* was there, and was distinctly unimpressed. "Unfortunately they are awful," he wrote. "Stipe whacking out a guitar drone while two beefcakes bash sheet metal with 10lb hammers."

The following day, Stipe was back in the director's chair for filming of the 'Finest Worksong' video, which also took place in Athens, and employed a goodly number of his male friends from the town stripped to the waist, working hard and glistening with sweat. Mike Mills has categorized it as "page 14 in the R.E.M. book of homoerotica", although the director himself declares it to be "just erotic".

'The One I Love' was released as a single in the UK on August 24th, and appeared a day later in the US and, despite the fact that it would become their breakthrough hit, Stipe has since stated that, "I didn't want that song to come out. I thought it was too mean. I thought it was too creepy."

Release of the album followed a week later. Among many possible names for the album, R.E.M. had considered and rejected *Mr Evil Breakfast*, *Pig Wrangler*, *Skin Up With R.E.M.*, *No 5* and *Herd Politics*. Tragic though it is that there will now probably never be an R.E.M. album called *Mr Evil Breakfast*, *Document* is probably a title better suited to the words and music in the grooves.

Anticipating yet another significant increase in sales, IRS shipped out 500,000 copies. To R.E.M. this seemed astonishing, but *Document* came out on the same day as *Bad*, Michael

Jackson's follow-up to *Thriller*, which had shipped in the millions. Buck claimed not to be dismayed that, when he went to a record store on the day of release, "every single person in line had the Michael Jackson album". He rationalised, with some justification, that Jackson fans were not the audience R.E.M. was pursuing. "He will sell eight million to people who are only going to buy three records this year and, if they're only going to buy three records, they're not going to buy ours."

Intriguingly, the sleeve notes showed Scott Litt as co-producer with the band, although when questioned about it later, Buck stated, "I don't think we did anything more on this record than we did on the last couple."

Don Gehman seems to confirm Buck's assessment, when he says, "I cracked the ice and got things rolling, then Scott Litt came in and took it the rest of the way."

With a European tour looming, R.E.M. played themselves in with an unannounced, but packed to the rafters, warm-up show at The 40 Watt on September 3rd. Around this time Stipe was starting to notice another way in which R.E.M.'s success was changing the way he was perceived in their home town. "It's kinda gross, what money does to you," he complained. "Businessmen say hello to me in the street now. They acknowledge me when I go into a nice restaurant. They let me put my bike in the kitchen at the best restaurant in town. I can wear a smelly t-shirt and they'll take me to the best table. It's really gross."

R.E.M.'s return to the UK after two years was welcomed with a rave review in *NME*. They delighted a rapturous crowd in London's Hammersmith Odeon on September 12th, and were no doubt buoyed up by an *NME* album review describing it as "a harder, louder R.E.M. record, free of the wispiness and the more obvious 60s references ... and I think it's brilliant."

The European tour was short and sweet, just five dates covering England, Holland, France and Germany, interspersed with high profile TV and radio appearances before heading back to America where, no doubt much to IRS' surprise, the video compilation *Succumbs*, had reached No 1 in the Billboard video chart.

The US leg of the Work tour was rather more arduous but, with a mere two months duration, it was something that such grizzled road warriors could do without breaking a sweat. It set off from Tipitina's in New Orleans, with 10,000 Maniacs in the support slot, on September 28th, just five days before the US release of *Document*.

The size of R.E.M's road crew was expanding with every tour. Instead of just one tour bus, there were now two and, inevitably rumours began to spread when Stipe moved out of the bus in which his three bandmates were traveling to be with Natalie Merchant in the other bus. Stipe vehemently denied any kind of romantic entanglement between himself and Merchant, but she has since categorically stated that they were lovers.

The media buzz around R.E.M. at this time was intense. They were clearly poised on the brink of a massive success whose implications ran far beyond the band itself. Dance-orientated music had been dominating the American music scene for many years, and the only rock acts able to generate significant sales were artists like Springsteen who really belonged to a different era. Now, at last, here was a bona fide rock band that looked like contenders. In classic rock tradition, they were a group of friends who had met while young, wrote their own songs, and appeared to be beating the system at its own game by focusing on the heart of the matter, music-making, rather than pandering to the "style without substance" ethic that permeated the pop charts.

Photographer Stephanie Chernikowski got a taste of what it was like to be at the centre of so much attention when she ran into Stipe in a room at Radio City Music Hall on October 6th. "Michael had been hovering with a couple of his friends and no-one was approaching him," she recalls. She spotted him, walked over and briefly engaged him in conversation. When she turned around, the others in the room had noticed him and "it felt like the entire room was converging on us. I understood in that moment, the absolute terror you must feel as a star."

On the 17th, R.E.M. had their first taste of serious singles chart success when 'The One I Love' entered the Billboard Top 40. "The fact that we had any sort of single success at all was a huge surprise," admitted Mills later. "Only college radio was playing us at the time. But it was cool, because we thought that maybe some of the walls were coming down."

Buck agrees: "We were selling a fair amount of records and we were playing to 10 or 15,000 people a night without really literally being on commercial radio. There was a great resistance there because those stations were run by people who hated punk, hated new wave, whatever new wave was. Husker Dü was never going to be on the radio. We were never going to be on the radio either, except that we tended to remind those programmers who are older than we are of stuff that they might have heard when they were younger. We have a little folk music influence."

As it spread across the airwaves of the nation, 'The One I Love' found its way to someone R.E.M. had admired from a distance for as long as they had been listening to music. "I hadn't been listening to much rock'n'roll throughout the 1980s," says Patti Smith, "but then I heard 'The One I Love' on the radio and it really drew me in, without even knowing who the song was by. My husband (guitarist Fred 'Sonic' Smith) and I were working with Scott Litt. When Scott heard me humming this song in the studio, he said, "You're singing R.E.M. – I produced that!"

At Chrysler Arena in Ann Arbor, Michigan, on October 29th, The dB's took over from 10,000 Maniacs. When they'd supported R.E.M. two years earlier, there had been very little difference in popularity between the two bands but by 1987 all that had changed. The dB's drummer Will Rigby remembers, "'The One I Love' went Top Ten while we were on tour and this was their first top ten single. By that point, it was a whole different ball game. They were playing much bigger places and we were like this little opening act that nobody really knew."

Over the years, the other members of R.E.M. have frequently had to defend Michael Stipe against accusations that he is humourless. Their general response tended to be that Stipe's humour is so deadpan that most people didn't even notice it. On November 4th, 1987, at the Circle Pavilion in the University of Illinois, Chicago, Stipe imparted a few words of advice to the audience that sounded like his own version of Desiderata. "Remember, civil disobedience belongs in the town square and the home, not the concert hall, so please file out accordingly," he told them. "Think about your neighbours, don't get your elbows stuck in their eyes and like-wise. Don't drink and drive, wear a seatbelt at all times, don't eat meat. Above all, don't wor-ship false idols and don't forget to vote. Call your parents every weekend. Don't worry about school. It'll be OK. And, if you want some friendly advice, it's gonna be a hell of a winter, so I suggest you move south."

It's kinda gross, what money does to you

In the vexatious matter of the unbelievers vs Michael Stipe's sense of humour, the defence rests its case.

On December 5th, 'The One I Love' peaked at No 9 in the US. And in that same week, R.E.M. appeared on the cover of *Rolling Stone* magazine alongside this headline: "America's Best Rock'n'Roll Band."

If their ever-increasing celebrity status was giving them problems before, now it was assum-ing unbearable proportions. In the wake of the *Rolling Stone* headline, the *Athens Observer* fol-lowed up with: "It's official – R.E.M. Hit Big Time."

Earlier in the year, Michael Stipe had reluctantly erected a sign outside his property asking fans to respect his privacy. Of all of them, Stipe was the one who liked to lead a simple, some might say austere, life. When Geoff Gans had visited, he found the house to be "kind of stark". The room Gans stayed in was completely devoid of furniture. Stipe's own bedroom featured a mattress on the floor, surrounded by paintings and sculptures. Another room was bare save for piles of cassette tapes. This was a man who valued and enjoyed his solitude, but now his home had become virtually a tourist hot spot.

At the start of 1988, Michael Stipe would move out of Athens, and he would keep the loca-tion of his new home a secret.

Chapter Twelve

R.E.M

The Turning Point

> "We were suddenly in this great position, where we were telling labels that we wouldn't sign unless they'd give us complete artistic freedom. And a lot of them were willing to give us that."
> BILL BERRY

New deal, new look: R.E.M. in 1988

Considered as a point on their career curve, the most significant thing about Document was not that it was the first R.E.M. album to go platinum, which it did on January 25th, 1988, but that it was the last album they were contractually obliged to do for IRS.

"They weren't into being stars," says the label's founder and co-owner, Miles Copeland. "I used to beg them to appear in their videos, but they wouldn't. On the other side, when they started happening, they wouldn't add any more albums to the deal, even for more money."

IRS's other co-owner, Jay Boberg, frequently flew down to Athens that spring in an effort to convince the band that they should re-sign to his and Copeland's label, which had, after all, taken them up to platinum status. But the collective mind had been made up. They had been unhappy with IRS for a long while now, and were determined to move on. Boberg believed that what it came down to in the final reckoning was sheer commercial pragmatism: "I felt that their analysis was that when it came to taking that act from one million to three million units, there were probably companies that did it better than IRS."

Bertis Downs sums it up from the band's perspective, rather more succinctly: "We felt we had reached the turning point."

Despite their many affirmations that hit singles didn't matter to them, given the top ten placing achieved by 'The One I Love', R.E.M. must have experienced some feelings of disappointment – or at least bafflement – when the next single floundered. It was a powerful track, well recorded with a strong chorus. Coming off the back of a hit, it should have done very well indeed. If it too had gone into the top ten, R.E.M. would have been in a very powerful position in negotiations with major labels for their next deal. Instead, it stalled at No 69.

R.E.M. did what they usually did in times of crisis. They buckled down and got on with business. While Bertis Downs and Jefferson Holt worked out strategies for negotiating with the bigger record companies, the band members kept themselves busy.

First they went into Cheshire Sound Studios, in Atlanta, with Scott Litt on January 9th, to record The Uptown Horns for a re-mix of 'Finest Worksong', intended to enhance the upcoming single version of the track. "When we first recorded it," explained Mills later, "we thought about using horns on it, but we couldn't quite get it together."

Another of the many alternative titles for *Document* had been *Last Train To Disneyland*. It was suggested by Peter Buck, who had also gone on record in 1987 bewailing the fact that, for him, America under the presidency of former actor Ronald Reagan had turned into Disneyland.

Insulting as that comment was meant to be, there exists in almost every human being alive a certain amount of affection for the products of the Disney organization; Michael Stipe is evidently no exception. Still in Cheshire Sound Studios, on January 10th, he and Natalie Merchant contributed their vocals to a version of the song 'Little April Showers' from the movie *Bambi*, for the Disney tribute album, *Stay Awake*, being put together by veteran producer Hal Willner.

The band also made use of the month to get on with the job of writing more songs and, in so doing, they got to grips with some of the more esoteric musical instruments they'd picked up over the years, notably accordion and mandolin.

Just as they'd developed the chaos technique for songs on *Document*, they now realized that playing unfamiliar instruments also forced them into new ways of writing. "The mandolin is tuned like an upside-down bass," explained Peter. "You have all these fifths bunched together, and I end up writing in keys I tend to avoid on guitar."

Berry recalls how, when Peter came up with the mandolin phrase that eventually became 'You Are The Everything', "I picked up the bass and Mike picked up the accordion and, in about twenty minutes, we had the song." With every member of the band playing the wrong instrument, it was virtually inevitable that the music they played would turn out different from anything they'd done before. As well as 'You Are The Everything', the January jams produced what has been described as a "rudimentary doodle" for 'Hairshirt', which would also end up on *Green*.

What a beautiful situation, to have a platinum album and be free of contract

Shortly after the confirmation of *Document*'s platinum status, in the last week of January, Bertis Downs and Jefferson Holt began sounding out Warner Brothers, A&M, Columbia and Arista Records. "What a beautiful situation," points out Miles Copeland, "to have a platinum album and be free of contract."

Interestingly, as has been confirmed by Warner Brothers' President Lenny Waronker, R.E.M. were not talking about money at this point. They were simply deciding which company they liked best in terms of what each one could do for the band. Just as importantly, they wanted to be happy with the relationship between artist and label. It seemed that control over their own destinies mattered more to them than megabucks, but perhaps to R.E.M. the assumption was that the one would be the inevitable outcome of the other. If they could control their own destinies within the context of a massively powerful record conglomerate, then the megabucks would follow as a matter of course.

"We were suddenly in this great position," said Bill Berry, "where we were telling labels that we wouldn't sign unless they'd give us complete artistic freedom, and a lot of them were willing to give us that." With the negotiations happily underway, R.E.M. headed for John Keane's studio again, where they spent much of February demo-ing new material for *Green*.

Described by Stipe as "a complete pisstake" and with a fairly undisguised lyrical debt to The Doors' 'Hello, I Love You', 'Pop Song 89' would become the album's opening track.

It had first been performed as an encore, without lyrics, on October 27th, 1987, during the Work tour, at Elliot Hall in Purdue University, West Lafayette, Indiana. After Stipe had come up with some words, Buck was intrigued by the title. "I said to Michael, 'Why are you calling it that?' And he said, 'I don't know: it's a pop song, it'll probably come out in 1989, so let's call it '89.'"

The subject of 'Get Up' seems to be dreams, one of Michael's favourite themes, so it's generally assumed to be about him but "apparently it's about me", Mike Mills revealed to *Uncut* magazine in late 2003. "I wasn't aware of this until the 1999 tour, when Michael told me and several thousand other people in an arena, on stage." It's certainly a well-known fact that Mills was the likeliest R.E.M. member to be found in bed in the late morning around that time.

The lyrical and musical roots of the bittersweet 'You Are The Everything', which was also put to tape during the Keane sessions, have already been covered, but perhaps I'll just mention here that it makes for a startling contrast, placed on *Green* between two much more dynamically powerful tracks, 'Get Up' and 'Stand'.

"I'd actually played the chorus of 'Stand' on guitar, just goofing around," Buck told me. "Then Mike started playing along. He kind of came up with the chords and the verse, then Bill just fell in. We had the song finished in about three minutes. It was really quick."

Having got the structure together, they felt it needed something more. Buck recalls, "We thought, 'Well, this is one of those big, stupid pop songs. Probably what we should do is modulate upwards at least once.' Well, we did it twice, it was complete overkill, kind of tongue in cheek. It's kind of a song that we would never have written in a serious manner. I still like it."

'Stand' is representative of several R.E.M. songs written around this time that Buck categorises as "big, dumb pop songs". But why would a band of four decidedly intelligent young men go out of their way to write this kind of material? "If you go back to my childhood," Stipe told me, "some of the best music on the radio was really 'throwaway' pop music. One of Peter's favourite bands in the world was The Monkees. I grew up with the Banana Splits. I loved The Archies, and we had all grown up with Bubblegum pop as a great influence.

"We wrote 'Stand' in a period of our lives where we were kind of challenging ourselves, and our musical abilities, to write really simple, really dumb, really catchy pop songs ... kind of for children, the kind of stuff we grew up with. Those kinds of songs really influenced us as musicians, probably to a greater level than people might realise. If you dig deep, there is something in the lyric but it's really just a song that you can shake your butt to and sing along to."

Stipe is alluding to the fact that, despite its throwaway pop feel, the words of 'Stand' are far from trite. "These are not just stupid lyrics," says Mills. "There is a thought there. You know, it says take a look at yourself and question why you do what you do, why you're where you are, and try to be aware of your motivations and your surroundings. I think that's a fairly weighty thing to contemplate in the middle of this fun pop song."

'Orange Crush', a significantly more weighty piece of work, had made its debut as far back as August 19th, 1987, at The 40 Watt Club. "It was a soundcheck thing we were working on and then all of a sudden it was in the set," explains Buck. "We played that and 'Pop Song 89' for the whole tour in the year before we recorded them."

It's natural to assume, when hearing lyrics that seem to relate to a wartime situation, with the words 'orange' and 'agent' in close proximity to the word 'whirlybird', that this one is about Vietnam. Stipe's father, of course, served in the Helicopter Corps in Vietnam, but Peter Buck has gone out of his way in the past to stress that the song is not about Mr Stipe Senior.

When I asked Michael if he could clarify the song's meaning a little more, he said, "When the draft came up under Jimmy Carter, I was draft age. I had to go to the post office and sign my name for the draft. I felt, at the age of 18, that I'd already served my time as an army brat. My father was gone at war in Vietnam and in Korea during my childhood. That didn't affect our relationship at all as father and son, but it was always difficult when he came back, and it was hard on him and hard on us, obviously, to have him gone for that long. Does that inform 'Orange Crush?' I think it does on some level. I mean the song has been taken by a lot of people to mean different things. It's certainly about war and, from my point of view, it's about what it is to become someone who can endure war and part of the military training and then the decompression that comes after that."

The sound of Peter Buck's recently acquired mandolin is prominent on 'Hairshirt', but it's played by the versatile Bill Berry. "I was out of the studio one day and Bill picked up the mandolin and came up with the chord changes and the melody," explained Buck. So, once again, the roles of the three R.E.M. instrumentalists took a topsy-turvy turn, with Bill on mandolin, Mike on organ and Peter on bass.

Although 'I Remember California' is shot through with nostalgia and a sense of love lost, Stipe is inclined to explain it more in terms of a travelogue. "The music and the words really capture for me everything that California is," he said in 1989. "I have this whole theory that people move west until they get to the end of the continent, when they can't move any more, so they essentially set up a lemming camp. Rather than jumping into the ocean, they created Los Angeles."

It was also during these sessions that Peter Buck settled in behind Bill's drum kit and knocked out a slightly wonky drum pattern that became the basis of a nameless track which would appear, completely uncredited, at the end of 'Green'. For the sake of having a way to refer to it, some R.E.M. buffs call it '11th Untitled Song', and that's good enough for me. "I'm the world's worst drummer," reckons Buck. "I was trying to teach Bill a drum beat and the reason I couldn't was because it just didn't work. But as I was teaching him this drum beat he started playing this guitar part that turned out to be 'Untitled'. Mike walked in and started playing it. We couldn't learn each other's parts, so we cut it that way. It was a struggle, because I can't keep a drum beat to save my life."

Not long after R.E.M. had completed their demos at John Keane's, an event took place on the other side of the continent that signalled the birth of a new musical force that owed a great deal to R.E.M. and would go on to establish the dominant rock style of the 1990s. It was on March 19th, 1988, that an early line-up of Nirvana played at the Community World Theater in Tacoma, Washington.

Looking back on those early days in a *Rolling Stone* interview some years later, Nirvana's leader Kurt Cobain, would say, "I was heavily into pop. I really like R.E.M., and I was into all kinds of old Sixties stuff."

IRS released 'Finest Worksong', complete with its funky horn section, as a single in the US on March 22nd. But saddled, like its predecessor, with a decidedly left-field video, it was doomed to miss the Top 40 by a country mile.

Buck took himself off on something of a busman's holiday throughout March and April, touring coast to coast as a guest guitarist with eccentric English psychedelic rocker Robyn Hitchcock and his band The Egyptians. He had first run into Hitchcock during the *Fables* recording sessions in London, and the pair had immediately struck up a rapport. "His guitar style meshes quite well with mine," said Hitchcock. "You can't really tell who's playing what, we both have that sort of picking, you know, the easiest word for it is folk rock, but it's basically sort of picking on an electric guitar."

By the time Buck returned to Athens in the middle of April, the new contract negotiations were drawing to a close. "There was a battle between me, A&M and Warners," says Miles Copeland, "and finally Warners said, 'Whatever Miles offers you, we'll double it.' The band came and told me. I gave them some advice, 'Go over there and sign! It's a brilliant deal. I'm proud of you.' Of course, after that, they started appearing in their videos, which meant they sold millions of records."

A $6m contract with Warner Bros Records, guaranteeing them complete artistic freedom, was signed in Athens on April 20th, 1988. "From day one," pointed out Buck, "every record contract we've signed has contained the stipulation that we can make the records when we want to make them, and that we tour when we want to."

After years of frustration because IRS couldn't break them outside of the US, a significant part of the attraction of Warners was that its European arm, WEA, had everything that IRS didn't. "The reason we joined up with them, actually," said Stipe, "is because they have the best distribution in Europe. It's great to be an American phenomenon, but I think that as a band we have a lot more to offer than that. I think what we have to offer surpasses, you know, cultural and even language barriers - that's why we're so great!"

On April 29th, Peter Buck and his new girlfriend, 40 Watt Club owner Barrie Green, took themselves down to Mexico and got married. The following day, 'Finest Worksong' entered the UK singles chart, where it would peak at an undistinguished No 50, confirming again how right they had been to move from IRS to Warners.

With work on the next album due to start again at the end of May, Buck, Mills and Berry managed to squeeze in another re-union with Roger McGuinn, backing him under the pseudonym of The Southern Gentlemen during a concert at the Uptown lounge in Athens on the 11th, playing a set that consisted largely of classic Byrds covers.

From late May until early July, R.E.M. and Scott Litt were resident in Memphis, Tennessee, working at the legendary Ardent Studios, best-known as the recording venue of choice for cult janglemeisters Big Star. "We'd go in about noon and work through until dinner," recalls Scott Litt. "There was a Mexican restaurant next door, which we soon learned served pretty sublime Margaritas."

They arrived with a clutch of songs from the John Keane sessions, but there was still much to be done to knock those demos into shape. 'Hairshirt', for example, had no lyrics. Amazingly, Stipe told them just to record six minutes worth of the backing, which they did, and then, after familiarising himself with the tape by playing it through a few times, he walked into the studio and improvised six minutes worth of vocals to fit it. "He filled up every second of it," said Buck, "and I didn't even see it coming."

Two new songs for *Green* also emerged during the Ardent sessions, the first of which was 'The Wrong Child'. Because he felt that the Bill Berry mandolin melody on which the song was based had a classical feel, Stipe was originally intending to call it 'Beethoven', but as the lyric developed into a heart-rending description of the life of a child horribly disfigured by burns, another title had to be found. Stipe has said that the song was influenced by "hanging out with Mimi Goese (vocalist with experimental, arty New York band Hugo Largo). Watching the way that she used her voice made me want to move out of character and try out someone else's skin to sing. Not just in the lyric, but in the voice."

The second new song was 'World Leader Pretend', whose sombre lyric stands in sharp contrast to the bright Mike Mills backing which was its genesis. "'World Leader Pretend'," says Stipe, "was actually one of those one-take songs. I sang it once, and I was so moved by the song when I performed it in the studio that I refused to sing it again. Scott Litt didn't have a choice."

Michael's influence in the studio seemed to be growing with his confidence. In the early days, the musical shape of R.E.M. songs tended to be dictated by Buck, Mills and Berry, who would present Stipe with a backing track to which he would then add vocals. Although this system continued, Scott Litt noticed that there were now more occasions when the others would "present virtually finished songs to Michael and he'd say, 'I'm not so keen on this.' Then he'd hear one of them messing around on a mandolin drone or something and say, 'That's great. What is that?' So we started building songs around soundscapes rather than chord sequences." Perhaps more significantly, though, it meant that Stipe was becoming involved in the creation of the music at a much earlier stage.

Although they didn't produce enough completed material for an entire album, the Memphis sessions were deemed successful, and R.E.M. returned home to celebrate with a low-key gig at The 40 Watt on July 8th. The plan now was to finish the album off at Bearsville Studios, Woodstock, in upstate New York.

As well as *Green*, R.E.M. had to contend with the release of another album in 1988. They had agreed to IRS re-packaging a compilation of their earlier material, which was to be called *Eponymous*. The first single to be lifted from *Eponymous* would be 'Talk About The Passion' so, in early July, a stark, black and white, heavily anti-military promo video was shot in New York. This was the first project of Michael Stipe's newly established company, C-00 Film Corps.

The second batch of *Green* recording sessions started at Bearsville on July 25th with the only totally new song produced being the funky-rocky, Neil Young-influenced 'Turn You Inside Out'. "It's about manipulation and power," explained Stipe. "It had a great deal to do, emotionally, with what a performer can do to an audience." In this context, he added, the term 'performer' could apply to people as diverse as Martin Luther King, Adolf Hitler and himself.

Highly respected percussionist Keith LeBlanc (Tackhead, On-U Sound) was called in to augment the band on this track, and he remembers, "They wanted a different vibe, so they had all switched instruments, which I thought was pretty 'out there' for a band of that stature. I think Michael was on drums, and it was a little out of time, so they wanted me to do some percussion to knit it all together."

On August 2nd, they turned their attention back to 'Get Up', which was felt to be lacking a certain something in its middle section. Bill Berry provided the answer via a dream in which he realised that the section needed 12 music boxes playing simultaneously. "We had all the people who work in the studio call up their grandmothers in Memphis to get all of them we could," he says. "We wound them up and turned them on, and that's what you hear."

The next day they were working on 'Orange Crush' which, explains Buck, "never had super-finalised lyrics. Michael was kind of mumbling the chorus, and Mike would sing whatever he wanted to in the back-up. I didn't really have a chord pattern. I was just making noises. That's a perfectly valid way to write songs. So it's kind of like a live take. We just went in the studio and did an approximation of what we did on stage. If we were going to sit down and write a song we might have tightened it up a little more, but I like those things that just come off the top of your head, and they are what they are."

Just as 'Orange Crush' was enhanced during these sessions with wartime sound effects, 'You

Are The Everything' benefited from the addition of the sound of crickets chirping. "There's no shortage of crickets in Bearsville," pointed out Berry. "The studio is just surrounded by mountains and woods. And it is deafening at night."

August 7th was the first of three days of working on 'Stand' which, like 'Get Up', had something of a hole in the middle. "We played it a couple of times," Buck told me, "and realised that because it lacked a bridge, there had to be a guitar solo, so I did a stupid guitar solo. To me, guitar solos are essentially unfashionable, but we needed a solo there. I went out and bought a wah-wah which is the stupidest effects pedal available, and did it in one pass. Played it once, everybody thought it was funny, which was kind of the point, and so we just left it the way it was. No heavy deep foresight or thought went into it. I didn't own a wah-wah pedal at the time, and I would never use one, if it wasn't for 'Stand'."

Michael's friend Georgina Falzarano claims that the lyric of 'Stand' was inspired by her terrible sense of direction. "The left / right thing is very difficult for me," she says. "Michael was really intrigued with how I remember direction and asked me exactly what it

I was so moved that I refused to sing it again

was I do. I told him I visualise I'm standing in front of my house, because when I'm looking at my house I can tell that's north, then I can tell where east and west and south are in relationship to where I am."

When the Bearsville sessions ended in early September, a promo for 'Stand' was filmed in Ithaca, New York. The video is memorable mainly for introducing the world at large to a fact that fans of R.E.M.'s live shows had long been aware of – Michael Stipe sure can do some weird dance moves. As Peter recalls, "When we started doing the video, Michael said, 'I've got this dance I've kind of invented, and we're gonna use it in the video and I swear people are gonna really do it.' And I said, 'That's garbage, no-one's going to do it.'" Nevertheless, Michael got his way.

Later that month, Adrian Deevoy of *Q* magazine visited Athens to interview R.E.M. about the upcoming release of *Green*. While in the rehearsal room below their offices, he poked around on the shelves and found a master tape marked "R.E.M. – Live Demo – Whole Lotta Love", sitting beside a packet of mandolin strings, a plastic dinosaur and a discarded bicycle part. There was also a pile of ancient 45s including singles by, "Love, The Beatles, Kenny Rogers, The Rolling Stones, Isley Brothers, Nashville Teens, Free, Peter and Gordon, Tommy James & The Shondells and Buffalo Springfield". He was told that these singles had been played for inspiration during the Green sessions.

During Deevoy's visit, Stipe took him to a 40 Watt Club gig by singer-songwriter Vic

Chesnutt, whose career would shortly be given a huge boost by R.E.M.'s involvement in his debut album. "Michael Stipe claps," wrote Deevoy, "cheers, drinks some more beer, squats on the floor with his arms over his head, writes things on a piece of paper and generally has a fine time."

On September 25th, Stipe played with Athens-based duo Indigo Girls at the Athens Music Festival. "At that time," remembers Indigo Girl Amy Ray, "Michael would take people under his wing a little bit and be like a mentor." He had, earlier in the year, written a song with them, 'I'll Give You My Skin', for a PETA (People For The Ethical Treatment Of Animals) charity benefit album. He would go on to help out with their debut album, and R.E.M. would take Indigo Girls out on tour with them in 1989. Around the same time, a video for 'Orange Crush' was shot in New York, featuring evocative images of a young man preparing to go off to war. A memorable piece of work, it was eventually listed in *Rolling Stone* magazine's "top 100 videos of all time".

The big event of October for R.E.M. was the Live *Green* Presentation on the 13th. This was a live performance in Athens of tracks from the album, relayed by satellite to the annual Warners Convention in New Orleans, in hopes of firing up the staff in advance of the biggest promotional onslaught yet launched on R.E.M.'s behalf. Other than this, it was a relatively quiet month for the band, a deceptive calm before the storm. Stipe did manage, however, to take Vic Chesnutt into John Keane's studio, where they recorded his debut album in a session that lasted one day and is reputed to have cost $100.

At the age of 18, Chesnutt had got himself seriously drunk and swallowed several Demerols. Given that Demerol is a powerful narcotic, similar to morphine or heroin, it's no surprise that he then crashed his car, breaking his neck, paralysing both legs and rendering his right arm largely useless. Medical science being what it is, Chesnutt's life was saved and he was condemned to an existence that he regarded as a living hell. On the other hand, the human spirit being what it is, Chesnutt superglued a plectrum to his plaster cast and taught himself to strum a guitar while recuperating.

He became good enough to get himself gigs around Athens, singing his bitterly humorous songs, and that's where he ran into Michael Stipe. "He was fun to be with, always ready to do something crazy like run around naked," says Chesnutt. "Michael once told me he wanted to record me before I died," says Chesnutt. "Then one night, after I finished playing a gig at The 40 Watt Club, he came up and asked me right there and then, 'Wanna go into the studio tomorrow?' I was kinda drunk, but I said, 'Sure.'"

Stipe says that, once in the studio, "When I told the guy to sit down and play, he literally sat down and started playing until the pizza came. Then, when we finished eating, he played again." The resulting album, *Little*, set Chesnutt off on a career as acclaimed as it is eccentric, and he continues performing to this day.

On the 14th, Stipe could be found producing another local band, Hetch Hetchy, in Cheshire

Sound Studios. The IRS compilation, *Eponymous*, was released in the UK on the 17th, followed by its US release one day later. There were fears that releasing the compilation so close to the launch of *Green* might detract from the latter's impact but, in the event, Warners did such a sterling job of plugging their first R.E.M. product that any such worries were quickly washed away.

Stipe flew to London in early November to kick off the promo interviews for *Green*, which was released in the UK on the 7th, and in the US one day later. On November 26th it entered the US album chart, where it would peak at No 10, and the following day entered the UK chart, where it would peak at No 27.

Much was made of the album's title, with the general assumption being that it was an attempt to focus attention on matters ecological. While it's true to say that green issues were high on R.E.M.'s agenda, there's little doubt that they chose the one-word title precisely because of its many possible interpretations. Buck was quick to point out a few, saying, "Green is everything that you want," he said. "Youth, maturity, growth, strength, and it's also money and the other kinda nasty grubby things."

Some observers noted that, for the first time, almost all of the album's songs were written in the first person, amplifying the illusion that all of the characters in those songs are Stipe, and thus all of their thoughts and actions are his too. Although Buck stated that he felt the songs on *Green* were more personal, Stipe might well deny it. "I couldn't possibly be all the characters I've written songs about," he has said. "I'd be utterly schizophrenic and a lot more interesting than I am. But I do think about things, and I guess I've developed the ability to put that into a character or into the mood of a song and try to raise a question or comment on something."

Michael summed up *Green*'s musical direction as "pretty much *Murmur* revisited" but whereas the lyrics on *Murmur* were all but inaudible, his voice was now upfront, clear and strong. Another sign of Stipe's increasing confidence in the value of his wordsmithery to others was that *Green* even took the unprecedented step of printing the lyric of 'World Leader Pretend' on its sleeve. "Something I was really stressing on *Green*," said Stipe, "was that the individual has a great power and strength. People have to realise that to tap it. 'World Leader Pretend' is exactly about that. You have to overcome yourself before you can overcome what's outside of yourself."

The critics loved it. *Q* magazine plumped for "their best album yet", *NME* hailed "a sound, a resonance, that is old and new, irrational and clear-headed, full of stated beauty and suggested beauty", and *Sounds* opined that it was "R.E.M. at their confusing best".

Michael Azerrad of *Rolling Stone* agreed that it was "damn good", but also sounded a note of caution that was in many minds when he suggested that R.E.M. might now be "dangerously close to becoming a conventional rock and roll band".

The American release date of *Green*, it must be noted, was chosen to coincide with the American election day, and the band made full use of their high profile in the preceding days to attack the Republican candidate George Bush and applaud his Democratic opponent Michael Dukakis. Stipe, for example, declared himself terrified by a recent poll which suggested that 80 per cent of men in Georgia intended to vote for Bush. He even took out newspaper ads urging voters to choose Dukakis.

When Bush convincingly whacked Dukakis, the normally laid-back Buck erupted, declaring himself disgusted with his nation because "if Adolf Hitler came back and said 'I won't raise taxes', he'd win by a landslide ... We're essentially a nation of fat-assed used-car salesmen that want to protect our pile." By now, fortunately, he could afford to buy his cars brand new.

The Green World Tour would kick off in Japan at the end of the coming January but, in the interim, Michael Stipe kept himself occupied by handling production chores for another of his protégé bands, Hetchy Hetchy, in Atlanta's Cheshire Sound Studios.

And, with 'Pop Song '89' scheduled as a single, he began a two day video shoot in New York City on December 8th, during which he was shown dancing with three bare-bosomed women. Some might have dared to point out that, having just sold their souls to a massive multi-national entertainment conglomerate, the right-on, politically correct R.E.M. were now resorting to exactly the same kind of sexual titillation that they had so often pilloried in the past.

Stipe anticipated that, however. He took pains to point out that the video was actually a pro-feminist statement – because he too had his shirt-off. "I was totally digging being the shirtless, long-haired rock star shimmying with three naked women," he said, adding that, "At the same time, it was a commentary on that whole scene. So you can be cynical and groove at the same time." Or, to put it another way, you can have your bread buttered on both sides if you're as rich and smart as Michael Stipe.

They were, undeniably, on the way to becoming disgracefully rich, but they were also quietly contributing to worldwide environmental charities like Greenpeace and humanitarian organisations like Amnesty. And, in their own back yard, as Peter pointed out, "We go to city council meetings, we give money to certain candidates, we vote, we sign petitions, we've done benefits for local food banks and AIDS organisations."

Earlier in the year, Bill Berry had been the one who best explained why R.E.M. was committed to supporting and promoting these kinds of concerns. "You don't have anything if you don't have your health," he said, "and if the Earth isn't going to support us because of negligence, we're in a lot of trouble." Then he distilled the essence of eco-fear into something that every adult on the planet could understand when he voiced a chilling confession: "I'm afraid to have a child. It's that simple."

Chapter Thirteen

World Champions

"The very first time we played after the record came out, the lights went down and these screams went up. And they were, like, a full octave higher than they had been in the past."
PETER BUCK ■

R.E.M. did not release an album in 1989. Looming ahead of them as the year opened was what would be the biggest tour they'd ever undertaken, their first bona fide world-spanning jaunt, encompassing Japan, Australia, New Zealand, Europe and America. They would be on the road solidly for nearly eight months of the year.

Before the Green World Tour started, however, there were a few other matters to attend to. On January 19th, for example, they took time out of their busy rehearsal schedule to help out The Basement, an Atlanta teen club with a problem. The club had been initiated by well-meaning citizens, in the hope of keeping under-age kids away from the temptations of drink, drugs and mindless vandalism by giving them somewhere cool to hang out and listen to music. The problem? It wasn't cool.

The solution, the organisers hoped, was that if R.E.M. dropped by, the resulting media coverage would attract kids; if the place was cool enough for R.E.M., it would have to be cool enough for them.

Speaking with the teenagers, Bill Berry was intrigued to note that they, just like the world's media, were expressing strong opinions about the band signing to Warners. It seemed to him that they saw Warners as "literally like a monster, just something that consumes and spits out. I think a lot of kids wonder how we fit."

Like every R.E.M. tour before it, Green was unsponsored, but this was not because nobody wanted to sponsor it. Unlike such rock rebels as the Rolling Stones, Pete Townshend and Eric Clapton, R.E.M. steadfastly turned down every offer. In Jim Greer's 1993 book, *Behind The Mask*, Mike Mills explained their thinking: "All the old science fiction novels used to say corporations would take over everything in the future. Now it's true. I don't care what bands say, 'Oh we can't tour without corporate sponsorship.' I'm here to tell you that's bullshit."

This may sound a tad two-faced, given that R.E.M. were now in bed with Warners, one of the biggest multi-national conglomerates on the planet. It's worth taking a moment to look back, though, at the way in which R.E.M. had moved from the street-credible indie to the megacorp.

From the time of *Fables Of The Reconstruction*, R.E.M. were being approached by major record labels offering to buy them out of their IRS contract. It was pointed out to them that, technically speaking, IRS was in breach of certain contractual obligations which big-money lawyers could exploit to end the deal without financial loss to R.E.M. That the band turned down all of those offers despite the fact that they didn't care for Miles Copeland, and despite the fact that they knew IRS could not break them in Europe, speaks volumes for their integrity. They chose to let the contract run its full term, as they had agreed to do when they signed it.

They were fair and honest in their dealings with IRS, alerting the company well in advance to the fact that they intended to leave. "IRS's distribution had gone as far as it could," Stipe told the *Observer Magazine*, "and it was time to move on to someone who could get the records out worldwide."

For a band of R.E.M.'s political stripe, their choice of a multi-national company to replace IRS would, inevitably, be a case of selecting the lesser of several evils, but the personal politics of Warner President Lenny Waronker were probably closer to R.E.M.'s left-of-centre outlook than Miles Copeland's had ever been. In short, with the safeguards written in to preserve their creative freedom, Warners was a better home for R.E.M. in almost every way imaginable.

Also, the difference between signing to WEA and accepting corporate sponsorship is vast. Companies sponsor rock tours for just one reason. The fans of well-established rock bands have significant amounts of disposable income. They also feel ties of loyalty and admiration towards those bands. Consciously or unconsciously, over the years, they build up a trust in the band that is no different than the trust exhibited by the buyer of a particular brand of soap powder, coffee or newspaper. If the Rolling Stones are seen juxtaposed next to a Volkswagen, or if Britney Spears is seen fondling a Pepsi, it doesn't mean that the entire audience will go out the next day and buy those products, but the association of a trusted artist with a particular product has been made. And ultimately, that's one significant element in the immensely complex global marketing strategies that sell those products.

This is all fine and dandy if we assume that the manufacturers of those products are utterly honourable, but it's hard these days to find, for example, a bank that doesn't have connections somewhere along the line with arms manufacturers, or a major clothing brand that doesn't make use of sweat shop labour in the hovels of the third world, or a petroleum company that isn't spewing toxic effluent into the rivers, lakes and oceans of the world.

By signing a sponsorship deal with any of those organisations, a band is publicly endorsing its behaviour. Signing a record deal with Warners, however, was little different for R.E.M. than a member of the public accepting that if you want your car to take you from place to place, you've got to buy fuel. You can make the best of a bad job by having a car that runs on unleaded fuel, or diesel, or some other marginally greener alternative, but you've still got to line the pockets of the big oil companies. In an ideal world, of course, we'd all live just down the road from our place of work, and we'd walk or cycle there, but the world R.E.M. live in is no more ideal than the one we live in.

It's a well-established irony of the music industry that, in order to get anti-establishment, anti-greed, anti-whatever messages across to the biggest number of people possible, an artist with a conscience must be distributed by a company whose daily business practices embody just about everything the artist despises. Still, the clothes you wear can only be cut according to the cloth you have available and, with that in mind, Warners suited R.E.M. just fine.

On January 23rd, the band filmed a video for 'Turn You Inside-Out' at The 40 Watt Club. This was the closest they had come yet to a performance video, inasmuch as that they all appeared playing instruments in a live setting. But Stipe's former art tutor, James Herbert, was directing again, so naturally, there was no thought of lip-synching, or such tiresome conventional clichés as beginning-middle-end; and Stipe sang through a megaphone during the entire thing. One day later, they were in Japan.

When R.E.M. took the stage at Tokyo's MZA Stadium on the 26th, it was their first live gig (other than a couple of unannounced 40 Watt club bashes) for more than a year. Augmenting them onstage with keyboards and guitar was old friend Peter Holsapple.

Having supported them on many previous shows, Holsapple was very conscious of that the transition to ever-larger venues was having an effect on how the music was performed. "The hard thing is, you're trying to present something that originally had been this intimate kind of music," he said. "Suddenly, you find yourself having to do this in a coliseum. How are you going to do that? To their credit, I think they did a great job presenting it as a larger deal."

As soon as they started playing live again, Buck was able to measure the extent to which their popularity had surged since the previous tour. "I could tell, the very first time we played after the record came out," he said. "The lights went down, and these screams went up, and they were, like, a full octave higher than they had been in the past. " He also noted that when R.E.M. started, their fans had been kids of their own age, but now the band was old enough to have fathered a fair sprinkling of their audience.

And while R.E.M. trekked around the world, the business as usual of releasing singles and servicing the media continued in their absence. They were at the Logan Campbell Centre in Auckland, New Zealand, on February 4th, when 'Stand' entered the UK singles chart, where it would peak at No 51.

Green had given R.E.M. another gold disc in early January and, on February 14th, while they were in Brisbane, Australia, it was certified as their second platinum album. "I'm thrilled and terrified that this album has been so warmly received," said Stipe. "This album establishes R.E.M. as real fossil fuel ... I know that if I die tomorrow, my voice will be there on record, and no-one could do anything about it."

They were back home in the US on February 25th when 'Stand', propelled by Stipe's wacky dancing in the video, entered the US Top 40, going on to bring them their highest chart placing yet, peaking at No 6.

The American leg of Green World opened on March 1st, at Louisville Gardens, Kentucky, with Robyn Hitchcock and the Egyptians as support for most of the first month. Fans entering the venues each night were confronted by stalls for several environment-related organizations, most notably Greenpeace. On stage, at some point during the performance, Stipe would make a point of asking the audience to drop by these stalls and learn a little about their work. By the middle of the tour it was estimated that Greenpeace had added 30,000 new members. "The environment is one of the few things we can save in America," pointed out Buck. "After all, democracy is dead."

As the tour threaded its way across the States, Mike Mills was bemused to find that, despite their earlier cynicism, Michael's crazy dance from the 'Stand' video had indeed had its effect. He fondly recalls one show where "I had a whole row of these really cute little 11-year-old girls in front of me, all doing the dance."

Now a month into the planet-wide road trip, their enthusiasm for clambering on stage was, as yet, undiminished. Even on nights off they'd find a way to get out there and do something. They arrived in Chicago on March 5th, for example, a day before the scheduled gig at the Rosemont Horizon. Instead of slobbing out in the hotel, with a pizza in front of the TV, Buck and Holsapple threw a band together with Robyn Hitchcock and his Egyptians, dubbed it Worst Case Scenario and rocked out at a local club called Cubby Bear. "It was a sort of accident," admitted Hitchcock. "Holsapple was doing a benefit, and we all got up and played with him. We were basically covering ourselves and covering other people, doing old Soft Boys songs … basically just pop rock."

Marty Perez of *Bucketful Of Brains* magazine was there, and reported: "They opened with 'I Wanna Destroy You', proceeding into half The Beatles' songbook, a glorious Byrds medley, possibly a dB's song or two, and maybe an R.E.M. number. A dynamo of a show, both in presence and spontaneous combustibility."

Just three days later, after playing a full-scale R.E.M. gig at the Met Center, Minneapolis, the same quintet plus Mike Mills went on to the First Avenue club and played again, this time calling themselves Nigel And The Crosses.

Buck has since revealed that moonlighting with other bands was one of the things that made him appreciate R.E.M. all the more. "I play with other people all the time and I realize how fucked-up other bands are," he said. "There's one guy making decisions, the other guys don't like it. I wouldn't want to do that."

Hitchcock and Co had dropped out when the tour arrived at the Hirsch Memorial Coliseum, Shreveport, on March 25th, to be replaced by the very grateful Indigo Girls. "They took us out on tour with them," says Amy Ray, "and that was our big break after years of playing indie clubs. I don't know where we'd be if that hadn't happened. We were very close for a while, and musically tied together."

The tour swung briefly through the home turf of Georgia when they played the first two nights of April at the Omni in Atlanta, a venue four times the size of the city's Fox Theater where they'd ended the last tour. Appropriately for an April Fools Day show, the curtain rose on five full-size cardboard replicas of the band (including Holsapple) while a recording of 'Radio Free Europe' blasted over the PA system. After a minute or so, Mike Mills bounded out and yelled "April Fool", followed by the rest of the band, as they launched into their current smash, 'Stand'.

They rolled into Cobo Arena, Detroit, on April 5th. Michael Stipe remembers that "Whenever R.E.M. used to play Detroit, I always dedicated a song to Patti Smith, hoping she might be there. She wasn't." That night they offered a prototype of a new song entitled 'Belong' for public consumption. This was the first sign of new material emerging that would be used for the next album, *Out Of Time*.

One of the highlights of this first American leg was their debut gig at the historic Madison Square Garden in New York City, playing to 17,000 people, on April 10th. "R.E.M. emerged undiminished by the weight of their surroundings," said the *NME*, "still messing, still subverting, still blissfully out of step with expectations."

Undiminished, yes, but certainly not unchanged. Former R.E.M roadie (and Drivin'n'Cryin' guitarist) Buren Fowler was well-placed to spot how much more organized and formalized the entourage had become on this tour. "They had a production manager," he recalls, "and everyone had walkie-talkies and was dressed in black. And nobody was allowed on stage."

This feeling that taking care of business were getting out of hand was not confined to outside observers. Berry was very conscious that, "Now, we have meetings every three months to plot our being somewhere at a specific time for rehearsal, and plan the time we'll set aside for press. It's become a little more corporate than I ever imagined it would be, which is kind of a drag."

The baggage of success was clearly beginning to weigh them down and Michael Stipe was later to own up that, "With the Green World tour, ticket prices were so astronomical that I felt guilty that people were paying that much money to sit in the back row and not see a show."

The band was also offering a much more contrived set, with virtually no room for deviations or improvisations. The days of throwing in an oldie on a whim just for the hell of it seemed to have gone. Once again, this was simply because of the mechanics of playing a bigger show, and specifically because of the lighting and the use of back-projection movies. "As loath as they were to do a set-list," remembers Holsapple, "Peter Buck would sit there every night for two hours before the show and figure out the order. You have to keep in with the lighting cues."

Another new track, 'Low', took its first bow at the War Memorial, Syracuse, New York, on April 11th. This too would find itself a place on *Out Of Time*, and it also inspired Stipe to think of a theme for the album – love songs in all their diversity. Jon Savage of the UK's *Observer Magazine* was there that night, and Stipe offered him a little insight into his songwriting technique. "Some songs are written in one stroke but others are prepared for months and months. I have these notebooks: I'll pick a topic and run through the notes and say, 'This applies and this applies.' The moment of inspiration is extemporaneous but it's all been prepared before."

By the time they arrived at Toronto's Maple Leaf Gardens on April 12th, there were signs that perhaps they were becoming a little road weary. "Unfortunately, the group faltered now and again," wrote Bob Thompson of the *Toronto Sun*. "The discordant 'Feeling Gravity's Pull' came across just a little bit disjointed, and the hilariously cynical 'It's The End Of The World As We Know It (And I Feel Fine)' failed from what seemed to be Stipe's lack of interest." Thompson allowed, however, that they improved as the show went on, and was clearly amused by the performance of 'Pretty Persuasion'. "That's when he stripped – first his boots, then pants – to reveal bicycle racing shorts underneath ... Only R.E.M. could get away with making the scene seem important and enjoyable at the same time."

The environment is one of the few things we can save in America. After all, democracy is dead

On the afternoon of April 16th, before playing another massive stadium gig in the Boston Garden, R.E.M. turned out to play a low-key acoustic show for a 'Born On the Fourth Of July' benefit event at the Green Street Grill in the neighbouring town of Cambridge, just across the River Charles, a legendary spawning ground for folk music talent. "Michael told jokes," recalled Buck. "There were babies running around. This little girl was tugging at my foot while I was trying to play my mandolin solo. I like the idea of sitting around playing acoustic for families. That's what we'll end up doing, I guess."

This first US leg of the Green World tour came to an end on May 3rd with a show at Von Braun Arena, Huntsville, Alabama, supported by Drivin'N'Cryin'. There was hardly time for a breath before the European leg started at Phillipshalle, Dusseldorf, West Germany, on the 9th.

In those few days off, however, R.E.M. quickly nipped home and Bill soothed his frazzled nerves with a bit of gardening, during which he hacked down some vines that were beginning to overrun one of his trees. He didn't realize it at the time, but he must have been bitten by a tick. As Holsapple recalls, on the second day in Europe, "Bill got Rocky Mountain Spotted Fever and we were holed up in Munich for what seemed like for ever."

Rocky Mountain Spotted Fever is brought on by the bite of one particular type of tick and, while it would have been diagnosed immediately by any doctor in Georgia, it was a complete mystery to the medical profession in Germany. Despite its eminently daft name, the illness brought Bill Berry closer to death's door than he'd ever been before. "The first doctor that saw me," says Berry, "thought it was some kind of viral thing and prescribed tetracycline."

Overcome by fever, vomiting and diarrhoea, covered in spots and suffering hallucinations, the drummer was immediately hospitalized. "It was so incredibly touch and go," says Holsapple.

"I passed Bill in a hallway, did a classic double take, and thought I'd seen a ghost." The "viral thing" diagnosis was completely wrong, but good fortune must have been smiling on Berry because, by complete coincidence, tetracycline was also the recommended treatment for Rocky Mountain Spotted Fever. Buck has confirmed, "if they hadn't given him the right antibiotic, he might have died".

Bill was back behind the kit by May 17th, when the British leg of the tour set off from the De Montfort Hall in Leicester, with support from The Blue Aeroplanes. "We didn't even have a deal," remembers their leader Gerard Langley. "We arrived in a little Transit van, 11 of us and all our gear. And there, backstage, were two articulated lorries, one for R.E.M.'s PA, one for the lights, and three double-decker buses, one just for Michael as he keeps different hours from the rest."

NME, by the way, rated that Leicester show as "breathtaking", while *Melody Maker* assessed the Portsmouth Guild Hall gig two nights later as, "profoundly inspiring".

The Blue Aeroplanes, meanwhile, refused to let themselves be intimidated by the superior firepower of the headliners. Langley recalls how, at Newport Leisure Centre in Wales on the 18th, "Michael said, 'Thanks to the Blue Aeroplanes, whose star is waxing as ours is waning.' Michael is very good about giving credit to the support bands." Langley has also mentioned that Stipe was often to be seen in the wings to catch their set: "You'd look up and he'd be there with Morrissey or someone, pointing and dancing."

Stipe had long been an admirer of Morrissey, who told *Details* magazine that during this tour they "went on these extensive walks in which we would just keep walking in huge circles around London and through Hyde Park. We just walked and talked and that's always been very difficult for me. Michael is a very generous, very kind person."

Just before the UK leg ended with two shows at London's Hammersmith Odeon, Nigel and The Crosses made a triumphant re-appearance at the tiny Borderline Club in the heart of Soho, on the 28th. Jon Storey, yet another *Bucketful Of Brains* stalwart, was in attendance to capture the excitement. "There was enough fine music in the 90 minute/20 song set to satisfy anyone," he wrote. "Except, maybe, for the pain-in-the-ass R.E.M. diehards continually yelling for their heroes' stuff."?

'Orange Crush', the latest single from *Green*, entered the UK singles chart on June 3rd, where it would peak two weeks later at a disappointing No 28. In that intervening fortnight, however, R.E.M. were winning over thousands of new converts as the show swaggered on through Finland to Sweden, to Norway, and on into Denmark, Germany, Switzerland and Italy.

By the time 'Pop Song 89' was peaking at No 86 in the US Top 100 singles chart seven days later, they'd ripped through France, returned to England again for another big night out at Wembley Arena and crossed the Irish Sea to take the stage at RDS Simmons Court, Dublin, where the audience included schoolboy Neil Hannon, who would later found his own successful group, Divine Comedy. "The sight and sound of this brilliant band playing at the height of their powers had a profound effect on me," says Hannon. "The most obvious sign of that was the complete mess I made of my A Levels (school examinations) that followed shortly afterwards. In the long term it proved to me that music can be both inclusive and cutting edge; that popularity and art don't have to cancel each other out." Also out front that day was Bono of U2, who is said to have found the performance so powerful that it inspired him to get his band back out on tour again.

With a couple of further forays back into mainland Europe, playing in Germany and Belgium, another leg of the tour came to an end. R.E.M. returned to Athens to recover. Stipe by now had made his move out of town and was occupying a new home, said to be the plainest of the properties owned by R.E.M. members. Although the precise location was kept secret, he did reveal that it was a farm outside Athens where he was quite happy with not much more than his dogs, his silos and his creek. "Well, I wouldn't call it a creek," he told Details. "It's more like an underground spring that goes into a pond where the cattle go and shit."

Stipe's farm stood in some contrast to Buck Mansions. Friends had conferred this jokey title on Peter's Queen Anne residence, complete with elegantly tall windows, porch and widow's tower. Berry's home, dating back to 1864, was a desirable property in the Greek Revival style.

Intriguingly, the finest house of all seemed to be the one belonging to Jefferson Holt, which was described by visiting musician Nikki Sudden as "this really opulent house that he had spent so much money on. The house had ornate glass everywhere so you could see from one floor to the next. It must have cost him millions."

Around this time, Michael Stipe was interviewed by Jack Barron of the *NME*, who noted that the singer was wearing a men's disposable shaving razor and the ring-pull from an aluminum drinks can around his neck. Stipe explained that this was another of his ways to draw attention to an ecological issue that had come to his attention. ""If you take a single disposable razor and throw it in the trashcan, you don't think about it," he said. "But if you think how many disposable razors have been thrown away since 1971 and imagine them all in one place, and how many mountains of disposable razors you might have … well, that's kinda frightening."

Worn out though they must have been by months of touring, it wasn't long before they were itching to get back to work. On July 31st, Buck was in John Keane's studio producing the third album by Minneapolis band Run Westy Run. Asked about his work with this kind of act, Buck said, "If I like a band, I'll take them in the studio and work for free. I don't go in and say, 'Let's make a hit single.' It's more like, 'What's this band about?' I did a record with Charlie Pickett (*John The Revelator*, 1985). It was this kind of deranged Johnny Thunders blues band. And they'd worry about something being out of tune. I'd just say, 'Don't worry about it. It sounds fine. You're not the Doobie Brothers. I guarantee you, nobody is going to return this record and say the guitar is out of tune.'"

A week after the Run Westy Run sessions, he and Mills could be found back in the same studio working on Kevin Kinney's album *MacDougal Blues*. Mills also found time to score a movie for his friend Howard Libov.

Stipe, meanwhile, was gainfully occupied producing *White Dirt*, the debut album by local roots-blues duo Chickasaw Mud Puppies (Ben Reynolds and Brant Slay), with whom he'd formed a bond by playing with them at their informal weekly all-night music-making sessions. "It was just a group of people sitting around on a bed with candles lit and the windows open," he said. "What came out of this was a bunch of really good songs. At first, Ben was not a very good guitar player and Brant was not very good on the harmonica. But they've become incredibly proficient and their songwriting is excellent."

It had taken Stipe many years to overcome his inhibitions about singing and lyric writing, but producing other artists seemed to be something that fitted him like a glove. "I never intended to be a producer," he told *Q* magazine, "but I'm a fucking good one. I think I've got fairly great taste, and I would say that if a record has my production credit on it, you should buy it, because it's good."

Unfortunately there was by now enough of a backlash against R.E.M. for Stipe's endorsement to act as a double-edged sword, cutting both ways for any aspiring artist who became associated with him. "They said we were riding his wave. That's a buncha crap," said the Mud Puppies' guitarist, Ben Reynolds. "Others say R.E.M. got us this deal, got us that ... but we're grateful for what he did. He didn't impose his taste, because he's a good enough producer and friend to let our character come through. He didn't try and make us R.E.M. clones or mould us in any way."

On September 4th, Stipe had replaced Buck in John Keane's studio, working on the Indigo Girls' album. "The problem with Michael," says the band's Amy Ray, "is that he throws himself into one particular situation for a while, then he just moves on to the next one ... Maybe it's something where he just doesn't want to get too close to people." Stipe certainly did seem to be hitting his stride as a talent-finder and producer. In the next couple of years he would act as producer for Swell, Opal Fox Society, The Beggarweeds and for his sister Lynda's band, Hetch Hetchy, who were, he said, "writing these pop songs that sound like the New Christy Minstrels, but very industrial".

Despite the reservations that the members of R.E.M. felt about external groups re-locating to Athens to ride their coat-tails, Stipe still considered the scene to be healthy and vibrant. "There's this whole coterie of people who all play together, and it is very incestuous," he explained. "All these ideas are traded around – I get as much out of it as anyone else. It's inspiring to work with all these people."

As if all of that plus R.E.M. wasn't enough to keep him occupied, he would also open his own vegetarian restaurant, The Grit, this year.

With the latest single, 'Get Up', just hitting the shops in America, the next US leg of the Green World tour set off from the Market Square Arena in Indianapolis on September 8th. It would now run remorselessly until November 13th, when it would stagger to a halt with a benefit show for L.E.A.F. at the Fox Theater in Atlanta. Another of R.E.M.'s environmental beneficiaries, L.E.A.F. was the Legal Environmental Assistance Foundation, which had been set up to tackle "bureaucracies, corporations and individuals who disregard environmental health". It included Jefferson Holt as one of its chief executives.

"When we finished in '89," Buck has said, "we were just dead."

"It was a tough thing," confirms Holsapple. "When we were done with a year of touring, it was like, 'Man, next time we go out, we need to do six or seven nights at a theatre.' Just to change it up like that."

Looking back from the vantage point of 2003, Stipe told *Q* magazine, "I spent much of the 1980s feeling depressed and disillusioned. I would drink myself into stupors, and then I started in on drugs. I was very keen to experiment, and I went through every narcotic except maybe mescaline. But it was just a phase …"

Even so, R.E.M. had come out of the decade on top. The critics loved them, the money was rolling in, and they had more control over their artistic output than almost any rock band on the planet. The reason why they were still around and still apparently in such great shape, said Buck, was,"We have a real socialist democracy. We sit around and vote just about as much as we write songs. We vote on where we're going to play, where we're gonna make the records, who's gonna produce it. We each have equal say and input when we bring songs into the studio. Everything is a total compromise between the four of us."

He was willing to admit, however that the system didn't always go smoothly. "Me and Mike have wrestled on the ground before. We've thrown things at each other and cursed and broken things."

For Bill Berry though, the benefits of the band's internal democracy were being negated by the need to conform to the pressures of success. "It's getting to the point where we have to make a lot of decisions every day," he grumbled, "whether we want to play the game or do what we think is right."

The decision to have Don Gehman as their producer had made them players, and the decision to ally themselves with Warner Brothers had increased the stakes in the game, but now they were finding that the rules of that game increasingly worked against their natural instincts.

It would get worse before it got better.

Chapter Fourteen

Imitation Crabmeat

"I like baroque-sounding records. I think it helped that we were on the road a whole year, because we were so sick of electric guitars, drums and bass."

PETER BUCK

String-driven: R.E.M. at the time of Out of Time, 1990

R.E.M. were effectively off the road for the bulk of 1990. "We really felt the last tour was a kind of peak, playing the biggest places we ever played," rationalised Buck. "But if we were to do it again this year, it would be just the same. For our own sanity we thought it would be a good idea to take time off."

Thus began a period during which Bill Berry was finally able to confront the demons that had been haunting him since 1984. "I stopped drinking long enough to learn that I don't really need it," he has since recalled. "Things started coming into focus. My marriage improved. I'd been married since 1985 but it wasn't really a marriage until I got off the road and realised that I have other attributes apart from being a reasonably OK drummer with a very good group. I started respecting myself more and things just took care of themselves."

The absence of touring would take some of the pressure off Berry, but even so, his ongoing disenchantment with R.E.M. was evident to the others. "He'd been disappearing mentally and emotionally for eight or nine years," is how Buck described it. "He had become uncomfortable with the whole process, even before the brain haemorrhage. He didn't enjoy being successful and seemed to resent the fact that we wanted this to work so much and he didn't."

Stipe, however, was said to be the one who had been most adversely affected by the massive arena shows, with the months of living out of suitcases, living virtually on top of each other. A plan was drawn up whereby the four members of R.E.M. agreed not to see each other until the beginning of April 1990. But, admitted Peter, "We ended up rehearsing on January 6th. That's just what we do."

So Bill, Mike and Peter met up at their facility beneath the West Clayton Street office, with the object of producing new material for the next album. Only two new songs, 'Belong' and 'Low', had emerged during the Green tour, so they had entered the 1990s with a seriously depleted stockpile.Fortunately, the rehearsals went well and, according to Peter, "After a week we had ten songs. It was one of the few times I've felt like we had a pretty concentrated period of being right on it."

Among the first songs to surface at these sessions would have been the one known at first as 'Shiney People'. It started life as a delicate little four-chord acoustic guitar sequence that Mike had been playing around with on the Green tour. But when they played it to Michael, he immediately visualised the sequence as something much more upbeat and positively jolly. Mike was aghast, but it was not unknown for Michael to apply this kind of radical revision to an idea.

"Michael will come in and we'll play a two-chord riff," explained Buck. "And he'll go, 'That's great. Now, speed it up twice as fast, and get rid of that second chord change and, hey, while you're about it, why don't you change the key?' And then we go, 'Hey, wait a minute! What you're saying is write another song.' And he'll go, 'Well … uh, yeah.'"

In fact, the frequency with which this had happened in the past was given as the reason why Michael had been excluded from the earliest of these rehearsals – to enable the band to get their ideas into a solid form before he started adding his melodies and lyrics.

'Nightswimming' also showed up fairly early in the year, albeit in a very rudimentary form, bearing the title 'Night Swim'. It has been said that, somewhat unusually, Stipe brought the lyric to the others and asked them to provide music. When I had the opportunity of asking him, he shook his head. "I don't remember it that way. I have done that, over and over again, and I don't know that it ever worked, but I remember writing the thing and it just kind of fell out of me. It was a very easy song to write." The final version of the song, of course, would not appear until the release of *Automatic For The People* in 1992.

As before, they were pursuing the principle of switching instruments in hopes of finding new avenues of expression. "Most of the songs were written with me on bass, Pete on mandolin and Mike on the keyboards," said Berry.

While they were no doubt still congratulating themselves on being so prolific, they were brought down to earth with a bump when it was announced on January 23rd that a demolition order had been passed on St Mary's Church. R.E.M.'s first home was scheduled to be torn down at the beginning of March.

Peter Buck began another two-month long moonlighting gig when he played with Kevin Kinney at Atlanta CD in Atlanta, on February 8th. The Kinney tour would include a return to McCabe's in Santa Monica, on March 9th, where they would be joined by Nikki Sudden plus T-Bone Burnette and others. The following day would see Buck and Kinney unpack their guitars on a Los Angeles sidewalk and play a show for the passers-by.

Back in Athens, right on schedule, St Mary's had been demolished on March 1st. Given how much work R.E.M. had been doing to preserve the original character and architecture of Athens, it seems ironic that only the distinctive steeple of St Mary's was left standing. It became a feature to enhance the Steeplechase Condominiums and their parking lot, the new development that replaced the cradle of the town's most celebrated international ambassadors.

It was during 1990, indeed, that R.E.M. collected an award from the Athens-Clarke Heritage Foundation. This was, according to Bertis Downs, "a general recognition for their support of historic preservation in the town. The big issue at that time was the proposed destruction of the warehouse district to make way for a civic center. We all worked hard to improve the overall scenario, successfully, I might add."

Speaking to *Rolling Stone* magazine, Peter Buck stressed some of the other civic improvements that the band had a hand in. "We have kerb-side paper recycling, which is pretty cool.

Members of the city council whom we have involved ourselves with have been very good about trying to protect what is nice about the town. You try to do what you can locally, and do the food-bank stuff. All the things that make a small town."

Considering the band had started out so opposed to videos, it was as if R.E.M. wanted to make up for lost time when they released another compilation, *Pop Screen*, on March 6th. Running to 32 minutes, it included all of the videos made since the chart-topping *Succumbs*.

Towards the end of the Kevin Kinney-Peter Buck tour, Nikki Sudden had become a regular feature of the shows. He and Buck struck up a friendship which led, on April 5th, to Buck starting work on Sudden's album, *The Jewel Thief*, in John Keane's studio. Recalling the sessions, Sudden noted that, "Peter said, 'Don't worry, I'll get us a bass player and a drummer.' And obviously the people he tends to phone when he needs a bass player and a drummer are Mike Mills and Bill Berry."

On the same night that those sessions started, R.E.M. celebrated their 10th anniversary with a show at The 40 Watt Club, during which they supported two upcoming local bands, Beast Penis and Jarvik 8.

When Michael Stipe, Natalie Merchant and Billy Bragg played at the 9:30 Club, Washington, DC, on April 20th, it was the start of a series of events that would see British socio-political rocker Bragg teaming up with R.E.M. members in a variety of different contexts.

The 9:30 club gig was, effectively, just a warm-up for a major event two days later, the first Earth Day concert at Merriweather Post Pavilion in Washington. Billy Bragg told me: "I'd shared bills with R.E.M before, but I didn't really get to know Michael and Peter until we played together at the Earth Day Concert. While we were there, Michael was asking me what I was doing next, and I said I was going to play some shows in East Germany. He was really fascinated by that, so I invited him along and he was really keen. In the end, he and Natalie came along with me."

With a line-up that also featured 10,000 Maniacs and the Indigo Girls, the Earth Day concert was almost an R.E.M. extended family show, and raised $60,000 for a variety of environmental groups.

So it was that when Bragg played at the Big Day Festival in Glasgow, on June 3rd, Stipe and Merchant were there with him. Just a few days later, they set off as Bragg's guests on his tour through East Germany, the Czech Republic and Slovakia. "There we were, riding in the bus, sharing a hotel room, singing onstage together," says Bragg, "and no-one clocked who Michael was. He really enjoyed that."

Bragg points out that this was at the time of Vaclav Havel's non-violent Velvet Revolution, which brought communism to an end in Czechoslovakia. "There was a real sense that change was coming," he says. "Michael and Nat liked it so much they stayed when I left. They got into the whole vibe of what was happening. Michael got very emotional about the whole thing."

Stipe later confirmed that it had been "one of the most educational and inspiring trips that

I've ever taken. Billy is an incredible, incredible performer, and he's a really intelligent and very politically wise person. I learned a great deal."

Having produced a batch of workable backing tracks at the rehearsal stage, it was now time to think about making demos. Before starting work, however, they made a decision about one direction they wanted to move in. "I'd been pushing to do a string-laden record for years," said Buck. "I like baroque-sounding records. I think it helped that we were on the road a whole year, because we were so sick of electric guitars, drums and bass."

So they hired string arranger Mark Bingham, whom Stipe had met while recording 'Little April Showers' for the Disney tribute album. "We told him what we were looking for," says Buck.

It kind of fell out of me, a
very easy song to write

"A four to eight person string section, lots of cellos – kind of stark. We didn't want it syrupy."

The first five days of demoing the new *Out Of Time* material started at John Keane's Studios on Monday, July 16th, and the band would continue working regular five-day weeks for the next month.

One song that is said to have appeared during this demo stage was 'Country Feedback'. "I didn't even write that song down," said Michael later. "I just had a piece of paper with a few words. I sang it and then walked out." Returning the next day for a playback, they decided that the hastily improvised take was so good that there was no need to re-record it.

The demo recording sessions at Keane's ended on August 17th, and Buck felt that the results were more than satisfactory. "It's the most finished album we've done as far as going in with ideas is concerned. The demos were pretty concrete."

For the start of recording at Bearsville's Studio A in Woodstock on September 3rd, Scott Litt was again behind the desk, and the band was once again augmented by Peter Holsapple. "I was not privy to any sort of inner mental workings of the band," he states. "The decisions of R.E.M. came from the four of them, Jefferson and Bertis. I'm not quite sure why they got me involved, but it's safe to say that, at the time, Peter probably considered me a better guitarist technically. Otherwise, input was not requested, nor was it proffered."

Just as they had decided to go for a very string-intensive sound, so Stipe had set himself some new parameters for the writing of lyrics. "For me, *Out Of Time* is a record of challenges," he explained.

"A lot of them are real clear cut. One: I would write love songs. Two: they would not be political songs. Three: I would use the first person singular instead of the first person plural. I felt I'd pushed the plural as far as I could on *Life's Rich Pageant* and *Document*. Everything was sounding anthemic, because we were saying 'we' all the time instead of 'I' or 'me' or 'you'. With this record I wanted to move toward more of a personal politic."

He also made it very clear, however, that "When I sing 'I' in a song, that doesn't necessarily mean 'Michael Stipe, the singer'. It means I'm taking a lot of creative liberties with the idea of writing characters and, as a lyricist, trying to hurl myself into situations I may or may not have ever been in before."

The first day of recording at Bearsville focused on two songs, 'Texarkana' and 'Near Wild Heaven'. Stipe had been having problems for weeks with finding a lyric for 'Texarkana', so Mike who had originated the music, decided to step in. "I just came up with the melody line," he remembers. "Then I wrote the first line and sang it. The song was written and sung inside 30 minutes."

There's a definite Beach Boys flavour to the joyful 'Near Wild Heaven' whose lyric was co-written by Michael and Mike, and once again Mills takes the vocal lead with Stipe providing the backup. "It's very inward," reckons Mills now. "It probably could have stood another vocal line against the chorus besides the one that I put on there, but I think it's a really beautiful song. I like Peter's playing against the bassline."

On the 5th, they turned their attention to 'Me In Honey' and 'Half A World Away'. The first

I'd been pushing to do a string-laden record for years. We were sick of guitars, drums and bass

of this pair had grabbed Stipe's attention when it was nothing more than 30 seconds of a one-chord guitar riff. With the addition of a second chord for the chorus, it was virtually complete. Lyrically, says Stipe, it is "an answer to 10,000 Maniacs' 'Eat For Two'. It's a male perspective on pregnancy, which I don't think has really been dealt with. There's a real push me/pull you issue, saying, 'I had nothing to do with it', yet on the other hand saying, 'Wait, I have feelings about this.'"

It's odd that the folksy 'Half A World Away', which is perhaps Stipe's most evocatively sorrowful lyric on *Out Of Time*, stems not from any real experience but from something he saw on TV. He says it is "about someone who thinks they're in love, but they're possibly not".

'Shiny Happy People', formerly 'Shiney People', was recorded on the 8th. "We did a series of songs that were our version of the Archies," Stipe has explained. "It included 'Shiny Happy People' and 'Stand', and 'Get Up' and 'Pop Song 89', and it was us just trying to be a cartoon band, like Gorillaz."

It's possible that they achieved their aim almost too well. When he spoke about it at the time, Stipe seemed almost proud of the level of care and attention he'd lavished on the lyric. "I was very cautious with that song to make it as sincere as possible," he said. "You can't sing along without smiling. You literally can't, because the vowels that you have to form make your mouth go up. That was intentional."

Despite being such a light-hearted piece of inoffensive fluff, and despite featuring one of Buck's most deliriously melodic guitar lines, it has gone on to become a thorn in the flesh of the band, all of whom seem to hate it violently, except for Buck, of which more later.

On the 10th, work started on 'Losing My Religion', a song born out of a Peter Buck mandolin riff. "I really don't like television," he told me, " but occasionally, if I'm writing, it's really nice to have something going on in the room, so I'll turn on the Nature Channel or a baseball game with the sound off, and I'll play and watch it.

"I'd bought the mandolin just a couple of weeks prior, so it was still new to me. So, I had this little tape recorder running, and I was taping while I was playing the mandolin, and when I listened back to it the next day, there was a bunch of stuff that was really just me learning how to play mandolin, and then there's what became 'Losing My Religion', and then a whole bunch more of me learning to play mandolin."

When Buck had fleshed out his mandolin riff a little more, he took it to Mike Mills, who admits, "I couldn't come up with a bass line so I went to my default setting which is, 'What would John McVie do?' Because I really respect his bass playing and in a song like that – sort of a mid tempo song – that's what I was thinking when I came up with that line. I would prefer to have something spring from the deep well of my unconscious but sometime it just doesn't happen."

When I asked Stipe what he'd been trying to achieve with that song's lyric, he replied, "There is a grand tradition in pop music of obsessive love songs, and love songs that are so achingly emotional that they are almost creepy. I didn't want to write a creepy love song – I'd already done that with 'The One I Love' – but I wanted to write something obsessive. Where the person whose voice you're hearing is so inside their head with their attraction that they have lost touch with reality. Someone who is trying and trying to make that one gesture that is going to clue in the object of his obsession that he is crazy about them.

"The lyric is my contribution: the phrase 'losing my religion' comes from an actual phrase, 'lost my religion', which is a southern term that means something has pushed you so far that it has challenged your faith. So in that song I was trying to write something that is just incredibly obsessive and deeply internal and has nothing to do with the external or reality. I certainly succeeded in writing a very popular song!"

Buck claims never to have heard anyone other than Stipe utter the expression 'losing my religion' until a year after the record came out. "I thought it was something he made up. Then I was in New Orleans having shots of whisky with this 75-year-old lady, and she said, 'Oh, you did that "Losing My Religion". I haven't heard that saying since I was a little girl.' I guess Michael probably picked it up from his grandmother."

During what was mainly mixing sessions on the 14th, the band launched into 'Radio Song'. Stipe being a fan of hip-hop act Boogie Down Productions, asked their rapper, KRS-One, to contribute to a track that was decidedly funkier than anything R.E.M. had attempted before. Stipe's lyric is a blast against the lack of imagination shown by radio programmers who play the same tracks again and again. "I hope people have enough of a sense of humour," said Stipe, "to realize I'm kind of taking the piss of everyone, myself included. Hopefully, they'll get the humorous intent of the song, with my opening plea about the world collapsing and KRS-One's closing rap, which I find really funny and thought-provoking."

The involvement of KRS-One in Radio Song was a radical move, probably the first time a major white rock act had invited a hip-hop artist to collaborate in their music but, as Buck has since pointed out, "I don't think people noticed what we'd done in getting KRS-One in. That's partly because radio stations wouldn't play it, because it had rapping on it." So, if nothing else, they're consistent.

The Bearsville sessions ended on the 22nd with mixing sessions for 'Texarkana' and, two days later, the longform live concert video *Tourfilm* was premiered at the TriBeCa Bar And Grill in Manhattan, prior to US release on the 25th. Filmed on the last five nights of the Green World tour, it was directed by Declan Quinn and captures the band in celebratory mood as the gigs bring them ever closer to Atlanta, and their own beds again, for the first time in two and a half months.

The early part of October was devoted to further overdubbing for *Out Of Time* in John Keane's Athens studio, before moving to Atlanta's Soundscape Studios, where members of the Atlanta Symphony Orchestra added Mark Bingham's string parts to 'Losing My Religion', 'Radio Song', 'Low', 'Near Wild Heaven', 'Shiny Happy People', 'Half A World Away' and 'Texarkana'.

The strings for the album's only instrumental, 'Endgame', were recorded at the same time but largely under Michael Stipe's direction. The musical backing had been written with the intention of adding a vocal part, and Michael did sing some nonsense syllables over it. But, in the end, he liked the music so much that he felt decipherable words would only detract from its impact. "What I basically did was take my vocal line and replace it, except for the first verse, with instruments that I thought sounded like my voice."

The finishing touches for *Out Of Time* were done during November at Prince's Paisley Park studios, Minneapolis, Minnesota. This location, almost snowbound at the time, was chosen, said Mills, because "It's out in the middle of nowhere, there's not many distractions out here, which is a good thing."

Much of the time was spent on mixing, but also Kate Pierson of The B-52s flew in from California to add her vocals parts to 'Shiny Happy People', 'Country Feedback' and 'Me In Honey'. As the band that had first put Athens on the map, The B-52s can be seen as having paved the way for R.E.M., and Stipe has declared Kate to be his favourite singer because "I just love that nasal, adenoidal thing. It moves me."

The pair had discussed the possibility of singing together many times but the opportunity never arose until they passed each other one night on the stairs of Radio City Music Hall in New York. According to Kate, the negotiations were simple. "He said, 'Hey, do you want to sing on our new record?' And I said, 'Yeah, I sure do.' And that was that."

She remembers the sessions fondly. "I have a picture of Michael and I in front of Paisley Park, holding snow shovels and laughing," she says in Rob Jovanovic and Tim Abbott's book *Adventures In Hi-Fi*. "We were trying to meet Prince and every time we heard someone go by, we all looked to see if it was him, but we never even saw so much as his shadow."

Bill Berry has said that when 'Shiny Happy People' was being written, "Michael heard her part straight away. It wasn't an afterthought. He wrote it with her in mind."

"Musically," says Pierson, "it was a very good vibe and fun and free and easy. They heard what I had in mind and liked it, so I just went for it."

It was also at Paisley Park that the album finally got a name. Once again, the printable suggestions had been numerous and often extremely fanciful, from Imitation Crabmeat to The Return Of Mumbles. *Out Of Time* was chosen, says Stipe, for the prosaic but pragmatic reason that "We were literally out of time. We had to pick a title."

At the end of the month, with the album now firmly out of the way, *Tourfilm* became the second R.E.M. video to get a US gold certification. By December 5th, Stipe was producing the nine-strong Opal Foxx Quartet in John Keane's Studio and, three days later, the Hindu Love Gods album finally went into the shops. Regrettably, its release generated some bad blood. Shortly afterwards, Buck said, "I think the record's really great, but Warren's people had some unrealistic ideas about us promoting it or doing a tour or video for it, and I think we feel a little bummed about the whole thing."

Berry explained that the band felt they were being exploited by Zevon's record company and management who "kept begging us to support it with publicity and a tour or something. But we can't just drop what we're doing. It was just one fun drunken night long ago."

'Losing My Religion' had its first public performance on December 19th when Stipe, Mills and Buck re-united with Hitchcock and Kinney for a show at The 40 Watt. Just days later, Buck and Stipe were in John Keane's again, recording material for Hitchcock's album *Perspex Island*.

Hitchcock was still around to attend the band's annual Christmas party, held this year in Berry's house with guests ranging from the wondrously named Gwen O'Looney (the new R.E.M.-endorsed mayor of Athens) to Bill's mother.

As the first year of the 1990s wound down, Buck still felt that, despite the band's enormous success, the pressures of celebrity status fell squarely on Stipe alone. "I can go anywhere in the world and no-one knows who I am, really. If I go to rock'n'roll shows, sure, people come talk to me. I don't mind that. I kind of enjoy it sometimes."

And Stipe, although he acknowledged that celebrity was an unwelcome intrusion into his privacy, declared, "I'm optimistic about the 1990s. I think a lot of people will spend the next decade educating themselves and finding out how the world is run."

'Losing My Religion' was released in the US on February 19th, as the first single off the new album, accompanied by the first R.E.M. video to feature Michael Stipe lip-synching. "I've always taken a strong stand against lip-synching for its falseness," he explained. "In the last year I've realized that, yes, lip-synching is fake, videos are fake, television is fake, film is fake, the experience of watching it is fake.

"Everything about it is not real. The realness involved is the emotion that comes through and the message that gets across. I think we pushed video as far as we could without lip-synching. So the natural step was for me to try it."

He also felt that this particular video marked a turning point for the band. Previously he had been the only one with any real enthusiasm for the medium but "when the others saw how well it turned out, they got more excited about doing other videos".

A UK release for 'Losing My Religion' followed on February 27th, by which time Michael was talking in public about the song. "I hate to make this comparison," he said, "but 'Religion' is similar in theme to 'Every Breath You Take' by the Police. It's just a classic obsession pop song. I've always felt the best kinds of songs are the ones where anybody can listen to it, put themselves in it and say, 'Yeah, that's me.'"

Before long, the promotional bandwagon was steaming ahead, with journalists were being flown into Athens from all over the globe. One interview revealed that Stipe was now driving a grey Volvo station wagon, the first car he'd ever owned. By compiling information from a couple of other sources, it's possible to build up a picture which reveals how much their office – "the key to the core of the organization", according to Stipe – mirrored the band's philosophies at the time.

You wouldn't notice it as you approached the two-storey wooden structure, but the building's exterior was varnished, at Stipe's insistence, with a biodegradable shellac. A sign stuck to one of the windows read, "War is bad."

Alongside the standard wall hangings of framed gold discs were awards from various environmentally active organisations, and the office PA, Brooke Johnson proudly told one visiting journalist that everything in the office, from "computer paper to toilet paper", was made from recycled products. Instead of one wastepaper bin, there were several, specifically designated for different types of recyclable material.

Early in March, R.E.M. flew to Europe for a promotional visit that included TV and radio shows in Ireland, Germany, Holland and Luxembourg. It also meant that they were out of the US when *Out Of Time* was released on March 11th, but they did arrive in the UK just as 'Losing My Religion' was making its way up the singles chart, where it would peak at No 19.

The band had been genuinely uncertain of how their new album would be received: the first with love songs, the first with lots of strings, the first with an instrumental track. But the British press took to it immediately. *Melody Maker* loved its "stunning baroque beauty"; *Q* was bowled over by how "reflective, challenging and intriguing" it was; and *Sounds* hailed it as "a moral victory for independence and self-sufficiency", referring, of course, to the band's relationship with Warners. *Out Of Time* entered the UK chart at No 1, another first.

One of R.E.M.'s most celebrated alter egos, Bingo Hand Job, were unveiled during two "secret" gigs at the tiny Borderline Club in central London, the first of which was on March 14th. The name, as everybody else involved was quick to point out, had been dreamed up by Stipe. "When I came up with Bingo Hand Job," he admitted, "Bertis Downs, our lawyer and sixth member, was depressed for three days. He wanted us to be called after a river in Virginia or something." Despite the veil of "secrecy" surrounding the shows, black market tickets were said to be changing hands at £150 a pair.

The band was augmented by Peter Holsapple, Billy Bragg and Robyn Hitchcock, who told me, "I got involved with this particular gig because R.E.M. were intending to do a show that April for Mountain Stage, a radio show in a tiny venue that holds about 600 people, based out in the backwoods in Charleston, West Virginia. My agent was rung up and asked if I'd like to be on that show with them. Then they decided to do a kind of European version of Mountain Stage, but in the end, it actually happened first."

The Borderline seemed a logical venue because it had been the scene of a Nigel And The Crosses gig, back in May 1989. "They rang up and asked if I'd like to join them for a low-key show," remembers Billy Bragg, "which was originally intended for the fan club only, and then they added a second night for media and music business people."

There was also a practical reason for the gig. "You can't get a work permit to come to Britain unless you're making money," Stipe explained. "Doing some television shows isn't good enough. I think they're worried you'll get your permit to go on *Top Of The Pops* and then slip on down to Spud-U-Like to work as a dish washer, taking valuable jobs from Englishmen."

As Bragg remembers it, "Rehearsal consisted of the soundcheck at the Borderline on the afternoon of the gig, so the performances were pretty laid-back, but there was absolutely no pressure. The whole thing was completely relaxed because, despite R.E.M. being huge rock stars, they're not at all like rock stars to be around. Everybody who took part was given new names for the night, like we were the Bingo Hand Job gang. Robyn Hitchock was Violet, I was Conrad, Mike Mills was Ophelia, Stipe was Stinky, Peter was Raoul, Berry was The Doc and Peter Holsapple was Spanish Charlie."

The show was opened each night by Chickasaw Mud Puppies, followed by Billy Bragg. "There was one magical moment for me while I was watching Billy," says Hitchcock. "I was standing in the crowd with my arms round my girlfriend, Cynthia, who was in front of me. Then I suddenly felt another pair of arms slip round me from behind, and I became the filling in a sort of a human sandwich. When I turned round, it was Michael, who'd come over to say hello."

Bragg remembers that most of the audience left with a small souvenir that night, because "they'd had these promotional face flannels made up. They had the faces of American outlaw types, who were, I suppose, meant to be the original Bingo Hand Job Gang, with the names underneath, and the words 'Sanitized for your protection'. These were given out to the audience as souvenirs, rather than just being something for the media liggers."

Bingo Hand Job were back at the Borderline the next night, and Stipe joined the Chickasaw Mud Puppies for their closing number before the rest of R.E.M. strolled out to join him. Much of the set, especially the songs featuring guests, consisted of covers. But Bragg points out, "They didn't just play old stuff. They introduced quite a few new songs which people had never heard before, like 'Radio Song', 'Low' and 'Endgame'."

Bragg's favourite memory of the Bingo Hand Job shows happened that night. "After Robyn Hitchcock's set, Michael had just done a little waltz thing on the organ, then he went up to the mike, just goofing around, and sang the first couple of lines of the Suzanne Vega song 'Tom's Diner'. It might not have gone any further but I started doing boom-box kind of rhythms on my mike, and he picked up on it and we kept it going."

Robyn Hitchcock was by now out among the audience, and he remembers, "It looked great because Peter, who occasionally has these rare theatrical moments, was standing behind Michael, in an almost Christ-like pose, with his arms outstretched and his eyes closed. I don't know if Michael even knew he was there, but it looked wonderful."

The whole show ran for three and a half hours, climaxing with a marathon all-hands-to-the-pump rendition of Dylan's 'You Ain't Goin' Nowhere', after which, says Bragg, "It ended with Michael, Mike and Bill doing a lovely a capella version of 'Moon River'."

Returning to the US, they continued the media onslaught with an April Fools Day live session on *Rockline* in Los Angeles, followed by similarly high-profile-for-minimal-effort shows in Santa Monica and Toronto.

On April 10th, R.E.M. recorded an *MTV Unplugged* concert at Chelsea Studios in New York, during which director Joe Perota was given a unique opportunity to learn about Michael Stipe's creative processes.

While the band were going off to take a break, Stipe asked Perota to keep an eye on his lyric book – an artefact that was obviously irreplaceable and very precious. Perota was honoured but, predictably, couldn't resist taking a peek inside.

Hoping, no doubt, to find clues about the genesis of 'Losing My Religion' or 'Shiny Happy People', Perota was confronted instead with "a lot of shorthand that only he (Stipe) understood. I felt I was looking at James Bond's codebook." Along with what appeared to be songs were scraps of paper and grocery lists.

R.E.M.'s Mountain Stage concert at the Cultural Center Auditorium in Charleston, West

Virginia, on April 28th, was virtually a Bingo Hand Job re-union with Holsapple, Bragg and Hitchcock taking part, along with Clive Gregson & Christine Collister.

Bragg was touring the US at this time. When he turned up to play The 40 Watt Club on May 5th, Buck invited Billy round to celebrate Mexican Independence Day at Buck Mansions. The entertainment at the heart of this annual celebration is a piñata, a papier-mache donkey filled with sweets and treats, beaten by children until it falls apart and disgorges the goodies.

But there were no children at the Buck residence, and the heavens had opened up, giving Athens a drenching. The visiting Brits, Bragg and his companions, were sent out to ceremonially destroy the piñata but, as Bragg recalls, "It would not open up and give us the sweets. I can remem-

Peter was standing in an almost Christ-like pose. It looked wonderful

ber them all standing there in the porch, eating Mexican food, Michael skipping on the porch, everyone pissing themselves laughing at us while we stumbled about in the mud."

Buck and Stipe then helped Bragg with recordings of his songs 'Everywhere' and 'You Woke Up My Neighbourhood' at John Keane's Studio. But Bragg has also told me, "We did some recording at Peter's House. He had an upstairs room, like a library space, which was set up for recording with a little Portastudio in it, and a harmonium out on the landing. We did things like a version of 'Salt Of The Earth' to the tune of 'Tracks Of My Tears', and a version of the Jimmy Webb song 'P.F.Sloan', and Michael and I did the Eric Bogle song 'My Youngest Son Came Home Today'. I've still got the tapes."

Bragg was still in Athens on May 18th when *Out Of Time* reached No 1 on the US album charts. "I was really struck by just how casual they were about it," he says. "The only thing that really seemed to please them about it was that they'd bumped Mariah Carey off the No 1 position. They enjoyed that."

As well as being their first US No 1 album, *Out Of Time* was also the first by a rock band in more than a year. In due course, it would rack up quadruple platinum status. "I felt really weird that this record is really popular and other records just fell through the cracks," said Stipe. "Not just in this country but globally. We were No 1 in Israel for nine weeks. Israel! Go figure. It was the first non-Israeli act in five years to go to No 1. And that was right after the Gulf War."

If they'd been big before, they were now officially the biggest band in the world. And they were about to get bigger.

Chapter Fifteen

Ever-
Increasing
Fame

"Suddenly I realized
that we were part of
pop culture. And I
didn't mind at all."
MICHAEL STIPE ■

For the people: Michael Stipe on the 1992 Automatic tour

The *Out Of Time* album didn't just go to No 1. It went there twice. On June 1st, 1991, having briefly been replaced by Michael Bolton's *Time, Love And Tenderness*, *Out Of Time* returned to the US No 1 slot again. Then, on June 19th, it became a double-platinum album.

It was a moment of revelation for Stipe. "Suddenly I realized that we were part of pop culture," he says, "and I didn't mind at all. I have a feeling that, as a media figure or a singer, I have a lot more to offer than a lot of what goes down. Especially in America. Everything is so facile and ridiculous. We're pretty much a living surrealist novel. The whole continent breathes weirdness. Not that I'm the voice of rationality ..." How true.

A mere three days after the double-platinum news, 'Losing My Religion' peaked at No 4 on the US singles chart. "We were shocked that that song became our biggest hit," says Mills. "It doesn't have a chorus, the lead instrument is a mandolin, and it [the original version] is five and a half minutes long. So everything that could have been stacked against it was."

Stipe identifies the success of 'Religion' as "the moment when I went from being recognisable to a relatively small, predominantly white audience of 20 to 35-year-olds, to having everyone from old black men to young Hispanic kids, checking me as the guy who sang that funny song."

Another 48 hours further down the line and the RIAA announced gold certifications for both *Fables Of The Reconstruction* and *Reckoning*, which had evidently been given a new lease of life by the success of *Out Of Time*.

Despite the hurricane of success now howling around their ears, R.E.M. tried to carry on as before. In June, Buck and Stipe joined The Feelies onstage at The 40 Watt Club, and during the annual New Music Seminar at Tramps in New York City, Stipe hosted a Deep South music night featuring three bands he had produced: Daisy Group, Opal Foxx Quartet and The Beggar Weeds. As the month ended, Buck was in the final stages of mixing Nikki Sudden's album at John Keane's.

It was also during June that they started writing more songs, usually in the West Clayton Street rehearsal space, and were delighted to find the tap flowing freely. "We'd write one on Thursday," said Buck, "tape it that night and never play it again. Then, when we made the record, we had this list of about 25 songs."

Among the first fruits of these sessions was the idea for 'The Sidewinder Sleeps Tonite', closely followed by 'Man On The Moon'. Buck explained that song to me: "I think the chorus was something I was already working on. Then Bill had a C chord on the guitar and he picked up his beer and just slid the chord up while he was playing, and we thought, 'Yeah, that sounds good.' He did the C to D thing, and we helped him piece together the rest of the stuff. It's a complicated song, in that there's a fair amount of chords and parts, but it really flowed naturally."

'Ignoreland', the only real rocker that would appear on the next album, was the last track written before the end of this batch of rehearsals. Its title is intended to convey the fact that Americans ignore the rot and political corruption at the heart of their society. Buck feels that the song never got any better than that original take, and that when they re-recorded it later, they took most of the spirit out of it.

'Shiny Happy People' entered the US Top 40 singles chart on August 10th, and would peak at No 10. But ever since its release, foul-mouthed comic actor Denis Leary had repeatedly attacked it, using MTV as his platform. In one such attack, he ranted "Pull the bus over right now! Everybody off! I want the shiny people here and the happy people over there! I represent the angry, gun-toting, meat-eating people!" Galling as it may have been for R.E.M., the fact that Leary felt the need to attack them was just one more sure sign of their success.

When the travelling alternative rock tour Lollapalooza, featuring Pearl Jam and the Red Hot Chili Peppers, arrived in Atlanta on the 18th, Warner Brothers' staff member Bruce McGuire was pleasantly surprised when "I walked through a hallway and saw Michael standing there. He was like, 'I know you.' Michael can't go out in the crowd and watch a show like that, he almost has to hide out. He couldn't have any peace otherwise."

The 8th Annual MTV Awards ceremony was held in Universal Amphitheater, Universal City, California, on September 5th, with R.E.M. collecting no less than six awards including best group, best video and best alternative video. For each award, Michael Stipe took the stage in a different t-shirt, each bearing a message – Rainforest, Choice, Wear A Condom …

The record before sold a million, and that one sold ten million. And it changed us

It was nothing if not a diverse month because, on the 8th, Stipe was playing the role of an ice-cream vendor, Captain Scrummy, on the Nickelodeon cable channel's wacky kids show *The Adventures of Pete And Pete*. His performance aired in the episode entitled 'What We Did On Our Summer Vacation', and features Michael demonstrating the timeless quality of his thespian talents while delivering such memorable lines as, "You look like a bonafide Sludgesicle Man."

As connoisseurs of garage pop, R.E.M. had been fans of The Troggs, covering their songs since the very first gigs in Athens. In recent years, they'd been doing 'Love Is All Around', usually as an encore number, and had even mentioned in an interview that they thought it was a great song. Not long after, says Buck, "We got a fax from Larry Page, who produced and manages them, saying he's working on a record."

Reg Presley, The Troggs' songwriter, had barely heard of R.E.M. when Page suggested that maybe he and R.E.M. should work together. But by the time they met up in Athens to begin recording, on September 9th, Presley was up to speed. "We spent the first five minutes walking around one another, going, 'Wow'," he says. "With The Troggs it had always just been that you had a guitar so you had a sound. With them, you had a roomful of 65 guitars to get exactly the right sound."

Buck seems to have thoroughly enjoyed the experience, saying, "They got a little ribbing for The Troggs Tape (a legendary and hilarious tape of Troggs' recording sessions), which all of us know by heart, so we had to be really careful not to say anything like 'dub-a-chug'."

At the end of five days, they emerged from John Keane's studio with the classic Troggs' comeback album, *Athens Andover*, but returned to the studio almost immediately to work on the new R.E.M. material they'd been cranking out in their regular West Clayton Street meetings.

By this time, 'Losing My Religion' had been certified by the RIAA as yet another R.E.M. gold disc to hang on the office wall, assuming there was any space left.

When I asked Mike Mills how the success of *Out Of Time* and subsequent singles had changed things for the group, he replied, "The record before sold a million, and that one sold ten million! And it changed us in every way you can imagine. Fortunately for us, our arc of success had been gradual from record number one onwards. So it wasn't nearly as traumatic as [it would have been] for someone whose first, second or third album had become so successful. Because we had played all over the world before, and had a fair amount of success, we were able to deal with it."

'The One I Love' by R.E.M. entered the UK singles chart on September 21st, and would peak at No 16. The track had, of course, first been released four years earlier by IRS, who were now attempting to cash in on R.E.M.'s increased popularity. The label would also shortly release a *Best Of R.E.M.* compilation album in the UK.

Compilation albums featuring R.E.M. abounded that month, with *Tom's Album*, a 'various artists' compilation of covers of the Suzanne Vega song 'Tom's Diner', being released on the 24th. Among the versions was the one R.E.M. and Billy Bragg had improvised (and recorded) during the Bingo Hand Job gig in London. Speaking to *Song Talk* magazine, Suzanne Vega made it clear that the admiration was mutual. "I'm surprised by how much of my listening is done when I'm cooking or when I'm dancing around the apartment and I'm listening to R.E.M," she said. "And of course R.E.M. is classic because you can put in your own words, practically. They're still great songs."

Only a week passed before a Leonard Cohen tribute album, *I'm Your Fan*, was released, featuring R.E.M's version of Cohen's 'First We Take Manhattan'. Asked if he liked it, Cohen replied: "Very much. One of the things that I liked about them was their respect for the original arrangement, which I felt was very generous of them."

Touring in support of the *Nevermind* album, upcoming young band Nirvana played in Athens on October 5th. "The first time I ever sat down with Michael Stipe," recalls Nirvana drummer (and Foo Fighters leader) Dave Grohl, "was over breakfast at his vegetarian-friendly restaurant in Athens. He had come to see our band the night before at The 40 Watt Club. He turned me on to facon (veggie bacon) and soysage (veggie sausage)." Grohl also points out that, "We all looked up to them, not really as idols or pop stars, but more like the cool dudes that you bought weed from who dabble in photography and work at the local record shop."

By the time 'Radio Song' was released in the UK on November 4th, the English baggy scene was in full swing, with bands like Happy Mondays and Stone Roses combining rock with dance beats. "It's funny," remembers Buck. "When we came to the UK to do press, everyone said, 'Oh, it's totally baggy.' And I had no clue what baggy meant. I thought it was an insult, you know, the way an old man is baggy, or something."

Meanwhile, the regular sessions at John Keane's had been going swimmingly with basic tracks for 'Everybody Hurts', 'The Sidewinder Sleeps Tonite', 'Man On The Moon', 'Star Me Kitten', 'Try Not To Breathe', 'Find The River' and more being successfully demoed.

The musical backing for 'Find The River' was, says Buck, "done completely before we even went into the studio. Mike put almost every instrument on it and, after that, we just added vocals."

Speaking of which, Mills has chosen his backing vocals on this track as his favourite on any R.E.M. track. "I had the idea," he explains, "that Bill and I would go in and do some harmonies without listening to each other. It's great because mine is this incredibly angst-ridden, high, emotional thing, and Bill's is this really low-key sort of ambling part. They're two opposite ends of the spectrum but they're both on there and it's a beautiful song."

Intriguingly, when they came up with the instrumental parts for 'Star Me Kitten', they were convinced that Michael would have a hard time finding words to fit, and yet it was one of the first for which the singer found both words and melody.

It's hard to believe but 'Everybody Hurts', originated by Bill, was not taken at all seriously by the other two players at first. Early tapes reveal much laughter and fooling around, and the general consensus was that it would be doing well to get on a b-side. "In those days," recalls Buck, "at rehearsals and practices, Bill and I would show up on time, and everyone else would arrive an hour later. So Bill and I wrote a lot of things together. He had the verse and the chorus, but he didn't know which was which, or which order they should go in. He had two parts, and they just went around and around. It started out kind of a country and western song."

Nevertheless, they persevered with it. "I kind of hammered it out. I said, 'Let's make this the verse, make it three times the length of the chorus', and I think I wrote the bridge. Even at that point, it was still a country and western song. Then Mike came in. It took a few weeks of messing around, but we ended up with the template being one of those Otis Redding ballads with Steve Cropper doing an arpeggiated guitar part, something like 'Pain In My Heart', or 'I've Been Loving You Too Long', one of those kind of things."

To their surprise, the first time they ran through it with Michael in the room, he immediately heard a very pretty melody in his head and knew it would fit. By the time they'd played it through a few more times, Stipe had completed the lyric to what would become one of R.E.M.'s best-loved ballads. "I didn't even like the song all that much when I wrote it," confesses Stipe, "and yet I realised there was a universality to it. When I sang it and found the melody, it seemed very clear."

Among those who were hurting around this time was Peter Buck, whose marriage, sadly, was falling apart. One consequence of this was that he began to withdraw from the group sessions and work at home on his own, simultaneously taking refuge in wine and mind-numbing TV. As is often the case, his personal despair acted as a spur to his creativity, and he became prolific, turning out a song a day, although he admitted that most of them were "really awful".

Murmur was finally declared a US gold album by the R.I.A.A. on November 10th, followed by certification for *This Film Is On* as a US gold video on the 26th. The next day, R.E.M. performed 'Losing My Religion' for the MTV 10th anniversary special, in the Morgan Cultural Center, Madison, Georgia. On December 3rd, at the second annual Billboard Music Awards in California, they collected awards for modern rock artist and top world album.

It wasn't a bad way to end the year, but it seemed that the less R.E.M. played live and the less frequently they released albums, the more they had to attend award ceremonies. On February 11th, 1992, for example, Stipe and Mills were at the 11th Annual BRIT awards in London, collecting the best international group award, and on the 25th, with Peter Buck wearing his pyjamas, they were in Radio City Music Hall, New York, for the 34th annual Grammy awards, picking up the trophies for best pop performance by a duo or group, best alternative music album and best music video.

They returned to their core business, the making of music, late in February. For a change of scene, they opted to record their next batch of demos at Kingsway Studio, New Orleans, Louisiana, located in a house owned by musician-producer Daniel Lanois.

Here, they worked on 'Drive', which Stipe has called "an obvious homage to 'Rock On' by David Essex", plus another *Automatic For The People* track, 'Monty Got A Raw Deal'. "It's about [1950s screen idol] Montgomery Clift," explained Buck. "I wrote the main riff on my bouzouki in the hotel room in New Orleans. I don't know what the couple next door were doing – it sounded like an orgy."

Finally, towards the end of a fairly productive week in the Crescent City, they jammed out two late night instrumentals, one of which would end up on the album. Returning to Athens, Buck went into John Keane's studio with alt-country band Uncle Tupelo, who would eventually splinter into Wilco and Son Volt.

"That was a great studio and Peter Buck was very hospitable," says Uncle Tupelo drummer Mike Heidorn. "That was a pure acoustic record for us ... Peter Buck did put some feedback on a song with his Rickenbacker; the pedal steel was put on later by John Keane. But there was just beautiful acoustic moments that were happening."

The title of the resulting album, *March 16-20, 1992*, reveals the dates of the recordings, although on the 19th, Buck had to join the other members of R.E.M. to attend the first annual Coca-Cola Atlanta Music awards at the Fox Theater, because R.E.M. had won the awards for outstanding act of the year, outstanding rock album (*Out Of Time*) and outstanding video ('Losing My Religion').

It was decided to return to the familiar surroundings of Bearsville Studios with Scott Litt to create finished recordings for the upcoming album. The first track recorded, on March 30th, was entitled 'Wake Her Up', later to be known as 'The Sidewinder Sleeps Tonite'. As mentioned earlier, the starting point for the song is the old Tokens' hit, 'The Lion Sleeps Tonight', so I asked Stipe why he had changed a lion to a sidewinder. "It's a type of snake, the sidewinder, and I have no idea why it worked its way into the song," he said. "I have no idea what the song is about. It's a little bit of a cartoon song to me and it took place in a world of flat surfaces and clear delineation of no depth of field, it's all about cartoons. That's what I saw when I wrote it."

Buck, however, asserts that "there's no real elements of the original in Sidewinder, except when Michael does that 'dee dee dee' thing at the beginning." Nevertheless, the group felt there was enough of an influence that it should be acknowledged in some way. "We called up The Tokens to say, 'We think it's only fair that we should do something for you', and they were happy with the idea that we should put 'The Lion Sleeps Tonight' on the b-side of the single, which would earn them songwriting royalties."

The track features one of the most indistinct Stipe vocals on an R.E.M. song since the pre-Gehman days. He told me, "The beauty of music is that it's so open to the interpretation of the listener. I've said over and over again that the intent of the writer is so much less important than the interpretation of the listener. That's what music is for me, the passion of music. I have no idea what people like Cesara Evoria, Nusrah Fateh Ali Khan, Liz Fraser or the kid from Sigur Ros are singing about most of the time. It doesn't matter ... and do I lay awake at night worrying about it? No. When the songs are right, they are just right and you know it."

Work went ahead on 'Drive' and 'Bouzouki Song' (later re-titled 'Try Not To Breathe') on April 10th. The first of this pair was started by Peter, who was aiming to create a kind of folksy Appalachian-style ballad, but it ended up being a decidedly sinister-sounding political song with no chorus and a multi-tracked lead guitar solo. 'Try Not To Breathe' earned its name when

John Keane, who was rolling the tape, pointed out to Buck that his breathing was audible on the recording. When the guitarist responded, "OK, I'll try not to breathe," Michael's lyrical antenna twitched and a song title was born.

'Man On The Moon' was still called 'C To D Slide' when they started fleshing out their original demo on April 15th. "We were actually working on the record," says Buck, "and Michael just couldn't think of anything to do but we knew it just had to be on the record. We'd made a sequence for the record with that song on it with no lyrics, and we told Michael to go away for a week and write the lyrics."

By April 17th they were working on 'Hey Love', which would eventually be transformed into the overtly sexual 'Star Me Kitten'. What had started out as a bunch of Mike Mills chords, topped off with some Peter Buck tremolo guitar and knocked out in 10 minutes during the rehearsal stage, became a major production job in the studio. "I was talking to Scott Litt about 'I'm Not In Love'," says Mike Mills. "I'd always loved the song, and just the feeling of the background vocal sound; it was something we'd never tried. And Scott said, 'I bet we can do something which has that sound.'" Mills sang seven different notes into Litt's sampler, and then fed them through the channels of the mixing desk, with Mills operating the faders to bring individual notes in and out.

It was April 20th before they got round to 'Everybody Hurts' and, says rumour, the drums on the final version come courtesy of a $20 drum machine. Peter Buck is happy to admit that it's true. "I collect drum machines. I do try to play drums, but I can't keep any real kind of stick rhythm, so it's good for me to play along with something, then I can overdub stuff. I think that was a Realistic drum machine. In retrospect I might have had a little bit less of the ping-pong ball noise."

On the second last day at Bearsville, April 23rd, they recorded 'Sisters And Brothers', which would eventually appear as 'Sweetness Follows'. Buck seems dismissive when he describes it as "just an old blues song with some weird jazz chords thrown in", but it is one of the most affecting tracks on the album, sombre beauty contrasting with howling feedback guitars.

For Bill Berry, these sessions hadn't been everything he'd have liked. "We were just like, 'My God, this is the way Tom Scholz [of prog-rock band Boston] makes a record - this is ridiculous.' For four or five hours, there'd be recording going on when as many as three members of the band weren't even in the room."

And the album was still some way from completion. R.E.M. moved to the legendary Criteria Studios in Miami during May for further work on 'Everybody Hurts', 'The Sidewinder Sleeps Tonite', 'Try Not To Breathe' and 'Nightswimming'.

"The piano melody is mine," says Mike Mills, speaking of 'Nightswimming'. "I wrote it on the piano at Criteria studio, the same piano that Jim Gordon did the piano coda to Derek and the Dominoes' 'Layla' on. I often write these circular things, usually on piano, sometimes on guitar, that don't go 'verse chorus verse bridge verse chorus'. They just tend to go round and round and round and you can do whatever you want to with it. That one just happened to connect with Michael on a level that took him to a very, very good place."

For Peter Buck, 'Nightswimming' is very obviously autobiographical because "it reminds me of times we had, swimming naked at night. In Athens, people were real poor. Nobody had air conditioning, you'd go to a show and it'd be 105 in the club. You'd be completely soaked with sweat, dance the night away, and we'd all end up at this place. We were trespassing; it was called Ball Pond. There'd be fifty people from the show would go up there, take off all their clothes and go swimming."

When I asked Michael Stipe if he could confirm Peter's interpretation, he looked slightly bemused and replied, "No. It describes something that I touched on a lot later on the record 'Reveal', which was kind of the summer as an eternity and kind of an innocence that's either kind of desperately clung onto or obviously lost, and that's where that song goes. There are auto-biographical elements to it, there are some lines in that song that come from real experiences, but most of it is made up."

Although some of Michael's lyrics for this album have been discussed earlier, it's probable that most of them were not actually written until the Criteria sessions, because he had been suffering an extended period of writer's block, which manifested itself most obviously with 'Man On The Moon'.

Out Of Time was certified as a quadruple platinum disc in the US by the RIAA on June 5th and, shortly afterwards, R.E.M. were back inside a studio again. This time they were in Atlanta's Bosstown Studios, working once more with the Atlanta Symphony Orchestra on string parts for the album in progress.

Deciding on a string arranger for this album hadn't been easy. "We had a list of four people we might work with," says Buck. "We were looking for people who had worked with strings, but didn't do that typical big, swelling rock orchestration. Somebody who might have scored for an octet or something a bit more spiky."

The specific tracks they had in mind were 'Drive', 'The Sidewinder Sleeps Tonite', 'Everybody Hurts' and 'Nightswimming', and the man they chose was John Paul Jones, best known as the bass player in Led Zeppelin. "Scott Litt had heard some old string arrangements I did for Herman's Hermits in the 1960s, so they got in touch," says Jones. "They sent four songs over and a nice little hand-written letter from Michael. I just wrote the arrangements and turned up in Atlanta."

The session went very smoothly indeed. "John Paul Jones was great to work with," says Buck. "He knows his way backwards and forwards on just about every instrument, he's a great arranger and a super sweet guy."

After the tracks were in the can, recalls Jones, "We all swapped autographs, then went out to dinner, and for a few drinks, and a bit of old-style rock'n'roll behaviour. Not quite in the Led Zeppelin league, of course." The end was now almost in sight.

The final mixing sessions for the album were done during June and July at Bad Animals studio in Seattle. By this stage, 'Hey Love' had become 'Fuck Me Kitten', but a visit by Meg Ryan, who was in town filming *Sleepless In Seattle*, convinced them to change the title. Ryan pointed out that in the town where she'd grown up it would have been impossible to buy any album with the word 'fuck' appearing on the cover. Realising that it would at least earn the album a parental warning sticker, they switched to the euphemistic 'Star Me Kitten'.

Stipe's writing block, however, meant that 'Man On The Moon' still didn't have a lyric. "I was under immense pressure to finish this one piece of music that the band loved," he told me. "We had already recorded an album's worth of material and I had run dry. I didn't feel capable of writing another song, and I just told the band, 'Give me a couple of days walking round Seattle with my headphones on to see what comes.' I wrote a walking song really, which is 'Man On The Moon'. I didn't intend it to be about anything; it just happens to be about Andy Kaufman."

It was completed at the 11th hour, literally written and recorded on the same day that it was delivered to Warners. The album was done.

That summer of 1992, despite R.E.M.'s ever-increasing fame, it appeared to most Athens residents that the band were still able to function as members of the small-town community. Local photographer Rick Diamond said, "They don't have bodyguards. If someone recognises them in a club, they just go over and talk. They're just four regular guys who make great music. Mike Mills goes to a lot of Atlanta Braves games. He doesn't have a private box – he just sits out with his pals in the crowd."

But Dennis Greenia, then editor of *The Flagpole*, noted that Stipe had become "more guarded about his privacy because a lot of people have tried to violate it". Up until this summer, Stipe had indeed borne the brunt of the public's curiosity about R.E.M. He was the one singled out by obsessive fans, followed around by devotees, now known as Distiples, who probably knew more about his lyrics than he did. Following the theft of a tree from his porch, however, Peter Buck installed movement-activated lights outside his house. He would be the next to leave town.

One of R.E.M.'s favourite eateries in Athens was Weaver D's Delicious Fine Foods. Bill Berry has described it as "the best soul food restaurant, in my opinion, in the South". At Weaver D's, when given a food order, staff would always respond with the word "Automatic", because emblazoned on a sign outside the restaurant was Weaver D's motto: "Automatic For The People." R.E.M. liked the phrase so much, they decided to name the album after it. So, in August, Bertis Downs and Michael Stipe visited Weaver D and obtained his consent to make use of his slogan on the next album cover.

Although the album's official UK release date was October 5th, *Automatic For The People* started turning up in some UK music stores on September 30th, complete with album artwork that included a letter that purchasers could send to General Than Shwe of the Myanmar Defense Ministry, requesting the release of Nobel Peace Prize winner Aung Sung Suu Kyi, who had been held under house arrest for three years.

The album was released one day later in the US, and R.E.M. made use of a "listening party" for the album in The 40 Watt Club to raise funds for the Charity Community Connection. It entered the UK charts at No 1 on October 10th, and went on to log up a staggering 131 weeks on the chart. On October 24th, it debuted on the US album chart at No 2, held off the top by 'hat act' Garth Brooks' phenomenally successful album *The Chase*.

November brought a diverse range of activities that included Stipe joining 10,000 Maniacs onstage in Atlanta for a brief guest slot; a few days in John Keane Studios where they recorded, as promised, a b-side version of 'The Lion Sleeps Tonight'; the release of 'Man On the Moon' as a UK single; a live version of 'Drive' being recorded at special fan club only show in The 40 Watt Club for a Greenpeace benefit album; and the 'Everybody Hurts' video being filmed on Interstate 10 near San Antonio, Texas.

For Peter Buck, the disintegration of his marriage to Barrie meant that he could no longer face the thought of living in Athens, so around this time he bought himself a $100,000 home in Seattle. "If I was to sit down with a map and pick it out, you couldn't find a more different place from Athens, GA," he said later. "It's as far away as you can get in the continental United States, in weather, culture and everything. I think change is good, and I was at a point in my life where change … That was a good place and time to change."

The year ended, however, on a decidedly unpleasant note. Probably because of his gaunt appearance, a rumour began circulating that Michael Stipe had AIDS. "I was upset by it for about ten minutes," he said later, "and then I thought I realized where it came from and dismissed it. I decided not to answer it because I thought, number one, it was meaningless gossip and, number two, I really didn't want further to stigmatise AIDS by stepping forth and saying, 'I'm not in any way associated with this.'"

What he didn't say was that R.E.M. had in fact hired a private detective to find out where the rumours had started.

Compounding the issue, however, on December 11th, during a gig at the National Ballroom in Kilburn, in London, Nicky Wire of Welsh rock band the Manic Street Preachers told the 2,500-strong audience that he hoped Stipe would go "the same way as Freddie Mercury". This was the same Nicky Wire who had been so inspired by R.E.M. when he first saw them on UK TV show The Tube.

"How big a dickhead does someone have to be to say something that stupid?" asked Bob Mould of Sugar shortly after. The answer, if my sources are correct, is six feet two inches.

The new year didn't start off any better. Intensely depressed by the collapse of his marriage, Buck sold up and headed south. He went to Mexico and stayed there for almost six months, traveling around. "I grew this huge beard and hitchhiked around Mexico," he said, "and ate meals in places where you could see them killing the chicken out back."

Stipe and Mills, meanwhile had headed up to Washington DC to be on hand during the celebrations to mark the inauguration of President Clinton. This might seem odd, especially in the light of Stipe's assertions to *Rolling Stone* magazine in 1991 that he was "depoliticizing" himself. But the arrival of a democratic President was something that he'd not only been dreaming of for years, but actively working towards.

So, on January 18th, Stipe did a reading at the Lincoln Memorial, which included quotations from Woody Guthrie songs. Then, at the MTV Rock & Roll Inaugural Ball on the 20th, Stipe and Mills joined Adam Clayton and Larry Mullen of U2, under the joint name of Automatic Baby, to perform 'One'. "I was up there strumming my acoustic, thinking 'I hope Bono and Edge aren't pissed at us for doing this song with their guys'," revealed Mills afterwards. Stipe also joined 10,000 Maniacs for versions of 'To Sir With Love' and 'Give Them What They Want'.

When Stipe went off on an extended cross-country trip to visit various friends, Mike Mills stepped up to the plate to act as R.E.M.'s international ambassador. On February 13th, he read *The Three Billy Goats Gruff*, and sang a song based on the story, at the High Museum Of Arts in Atlanta. Then he hopped on a plane to London to be in time for the twelfth annual BRIT awards ceremony in Alexandra Palace, London, where he collected the best international group award on behalf of his absent colleagues. Days later he was in Denmark receiving a Danish Grammy for best international band.

On March 4th, the annual *Rolling Stone* magazine critics' awards selected *Automatic For The People* as the year's best album, and Michael Stipe as best male singer. Then, on April 14th, when R.E.M. was named international group of the year, and *Automatic For The People* chosen as international album at the IRMA awards ceremony in the National Concert Hall, Dublin, Eire, the ever-reliable Mike Mills was in attendance.

Meanwhile, despite the phenomenal success of the album, singles were being released that didn't perform as well as might have been expected. 'Man On The Moon' and 'The Sidewinder Sleeps Tonite', didn't exactly set the world alight, and even the glorious 'Everybody Hurts' peaked at No 7 in the UK and a very disappointing No 29 in the US. Stipe, however, didn't seem unduly surprised. "It was a strange choice to be a single," he has said. "I didn't see it the way everyone else saw it until the video was shot, and then it kind of made sense to me that this was a song that a lot of people wanted to hear."

Towards the end of April, R.E.M. held what has been described as a "summit meeting" in Acapulco, Mexico. The traditional view has always been that the band members were all keen to carry on, and they simply needed to map out a plan for the next few years. But there is no question that Bill Berry had serious reservations about carrying on in the band. To him, "R.E.M. had gotten to seem like a series of chores that I didn't want to do."

It's also widely accepted that as well as being a refuge from his broken marriage, Peter Buck's extended sojourn in Mexico was, at least in part, an escape from the other members of the band. It is said that he flatly refused to tour with the group again until he could be certain that some element of creativity was introduced to counter-balance the mind-numbing effects of month after month on the road.

As it had done at difficult times in the past, the democratic nature of R.E.M. assured their continued existence once more. Every function of being in the band – from touring to recording, flesh-pressing, plugging, video-making and beyond – was scrutinised in detail, and subjected to the acid test of the single member veto. No matter how much three members might want to do something, if one member couldn't stomach it, then it would not be done. Compromise, as they themselves have admitted, was the name of the game.

When it was over, Buck remained in Mexico, but the others were able to return to Athens as – if not a totally unified whole – at least a functioning unit. All four members had agreed to continue through the next tour and album, which they decided would be a seriously rocking affair. One of the major compromises made was that, to meet Buck's requirements, every show on the next tour would be recorded and the tapes sent by courier to Scott Litt. The idea was to bottle the lightning, to capture any moments of magic, little improvisations that might occur during gigs, or at rehearsals and soundchecks, which might be the spark of a new song idea. And who knows, if it went well, R.E.M. might even gain a live album consisting of new material.

The May 1993 schedule of events, to which Stipe, Mills and Berry returned, provides a fascinating picture of the way life had changed for the band who had once scraped a living by slogging from pizza parlour to gay bar to seedy club in a clapped-out van. Mills had the honour of throwing the ceremonial first pitch in a Baltimore Orioles game at Oriole Park in Baltimore, Maryland. Berry and Mills attended the wedding of powerful rock promoter Ted Mankin in Virginia Beach. While there, they got up and boogied with NRBQ on 'Woolly Bully', 'My Girl' and 'Double Shot (Of My Baby's Love)'. On the 19th, Berry, Mills and Stipe were given a tour of the White House, prior to attending the following day's front lawn reception in celebration of the signing of the National Voter Registration Act.

In June, Mills choose to work on the soundtrack album for the fictionalised Beatles movie, *Backbeat*, in Oceanway Studios, Hollywood, while Peter Buck started a six week safari holiday in Tanzania and Kenya.

In the second week of August, while rehearsing at John Keane's for an upcoming MTV Awards show appearance, R.E.M. found themselves moved to compose some new material. "When we got back together," Stipe told Robert Hilburn of the *Los Angeles Times*, "we were all in the same place. We all wanted to kick butt musically … get the energy back … But there's going to come a point where we get back together and the passion is gone. I hope we have the courage to stop."

Chapter Sixteen

Emotional Turmoil

"Our eyes were like
kaleidoscope whirly
things. All of us
were nuts."
MICHAEL STIPE ■

Into the storm: Stipe on the 1995 Monster tour

M ichael Stipe met River Phoenix in 1990. "His hair was completely covering his face," remembers Stipe, "and I was like, 'God, that was me at 22.'"

The young actor's side-project band, Aleka's Attic, had flown to Charlotte to record a track for a PETA benefit album. Stipe was involved in the same album, and the pair became good friends, hanging out together whenever their busy schedules permitted, and even writing songs together. Their bond was so strong that Stipe thought of River as "my little brother". Everything they had shared was about to be destroyed.

Michael Stipe had met Kurt Cobain on October 5th, 1991, when Nirvana played at The 40 Watt Club. "Kurt was a very, very intelligent guy," said Stipe. "Unbelievably inspiring. A great guy." He was also a long-term R.E.M. fan, and their relationship became so close that they were planning to make an album together. This too was about to be swept away.

R.E.M. performed a memorable version of 'Everybody Hurts' on September 2nd, at the tenth MTV Awards at Universal City in California. Meanwhile, on the other side of the continent, in the band's hometown of Athens, a house was being sawn in half.

The house, built in 1851, had been scheduled for demolition to make way for a new development. When Bill Berry heard about it, he became determined to save this historic building. So, as we'd like to imagine wealthy philanthropists do all the time, he bought the house and then hired the appropriate craftsmen, who removed the roof and sawed the house down the middle to create two sections that could be transported. The whole structure was then taken to Bill's farm, five miles south of town, where it was re-assembled and restored.

During the last week in September, Peter Buck had dinner with Kurt Cobain in Los Angeles and then, early in October, R.E.M. returned to Kingsway Studios in New Orleans. There they recorded about 20 new tracks over the next ten days, among them 'Star 69', 'Crush With Eyeliner', 'What's The Frequency, Kenneth', 'I Took Your Name' and 'Tongue'.

Around this time, Cobain and Courtney Love were at Triclops Studios, Atlanta, doing recording sessions for Hole's album *Live Through This*. Being in the area, they dropped by to hang out with Stipe in Athens. While they were there, Stipe took the opportunity to play them some of the New Orleans demos, which Cobain seemed to enjoy.

Shortly after 1am on October 31st, River Phoenix collapsed, shaking violently, outside the Viper Club in Los Angeles. His companion, bass player Flea of The Red Hot Chili Peppers, rode to Cedars Sinai hospital in the ambulance with him.

River was pronounced dead of a drug overdose at 1.51am. The autopsy found lethal levels of cocaine and morphine, plus Valium, marijuana and ephedrine – the main ingredient in crystal meth. He was 23.

Stipe was shaken to the core by the news. "River Phoenix was a very, very close friend of mine," he said later. "I've never suffered such a profound loss. I couldn't write for five months. We had started the record in September. I'd written two songs and then River died. And, having written *Automatic For The People*, I was not about to write another record about death and loss. So it took me five months to sit down and write again."

Setting aside the emotional turmoil in which Stipe now found himself, the practical effect of all this was that work on the next R.E.M. album ground to a halt. Buck returned to his new home in Seattle where, as he had always done in Athens, he had quickly made himself part of the fabric of the local music scene. He had already done some work on *Satisfied Mind*, the new album by local band The Walkabouts, and in November he joined them on stage.

"Peter had played mandolin and mountain dulcimer on our album, and he played with us several times that year," says Chris Eckman of The Walkabouts. "Ostensibly the Crocodile show was an album release party, but since the album had only been released in Europe, by Sub Pop, that part of it was something of a fiction."

He had also formed a friendship with Scott McCaughey of another local band, the Young Fresh Fellows. While working on what was supposed to be a McCaughey solo album, Buck and the other musicians (John Auer and Ken Stringfellow of the Posies and Chris Eckman and Carla Torgeson of The Walkabouts) gelled so well that McCaughey's album evolved in a new direction and was eventually released as the album *Old Liquidator* under a new band name, The Minus Five.

Stipe, back in Athens, was involved in singer/songwriter Kristin Hersh's video for her song *Your Ghost*, and when Nirvana played at The Omni in Atlanta, on November 29th, Stipe was there in the audience. On the same day, 'Find The River' was released as a single in the UK. It's worth noting that, despite many media references to the song being a response to the death of River Phoenix, it had been written before he died.

Peter Buck and Kevin Kinney ended the year with a joint gig at the Crocodile Café in Seattle, on December 28th. Intriguingly, having not long since suffered much misery at the end of his marriage to Barrie, owner of The 40 Watt Club, Buck was now romantically involved with Stephanie Dorgan, founder-owner of the Crocodile.

As the light of the old year dimmed, Stipe was still grieving and suffering from writer's block, Berry was maintaining his awkwardly low profile, and Buck had moved to the other side of the continent.

Only Mike Mills, the solid, reliable, workmanlike Mills, seemed to be bearing up under the pressure. Or was he? Mills had recently split from his longtime girlfriend Holli. Perhaps the break-up affected him deeply, perhaps he felt that his new high-profile position as roving R.E.M.

ambassador called for a makeover, or maybe it was just a classic mid-life crisis, but he had lately embarked on the process of changing his nerdy image. He was growing his hair long and striding around like a peacock in a Nudie suit – one of those garishly beautiful, embroidered, rhinestoned and sequinned cowboy outfits so beloved of country singers.

"I began making a series of decisions about three or four years ago," he told *Rolling Stone*. "There's a whole process of life called letting go. Clinging to things really makes it difficult to live, whether that's a love interest or a hairstyle. My decisions to stop worrying about things manifested themselves in big and small ways, from growing a little chin beard, to wearing an outrageous costume on stage, to renting a place in Los Angeles. You can call it growing, you can call it maturing, you can call it what you want, really."

Was Mills going off the rails? If the answer was yes, who would keep R.E.M. running smoothly? Even the backroom wizards, Jefferson Holt and Bertis Downs, seemed to be undergoing some sort of shift in their equilibrium. It was becoming noticeable that Downs' public profile, and his influence on the band, seemed to be waxing, while Holt's appeared to be waning in proportion.

The whole R.E.M. organization, which had run so smoothly for so long, was now in a state of flux. Superficially, it made no sense. This had been the year of their greatest triumphs – platinum discs, bucketloads of awards, overflowing bank accounts and entry into the highest echelons of American society. What more could they want?

They obviously had no desire to return to the days of scraping a living. Having decided to play the music industry game, they were reaping the benefits of success. Now, though, they were also learning that there were many different levels of success, and that once you moved into its most elevated regions, there were unforeseen drawbacks that came with the territory.

Peter Buck put into words one of the drawbacks that bothered R.E.M. most. "Once you're selling, like, nine million albums, you're attracting people who aren't really your fans. You start getting the psychos, the people who sit at home and the radio talks to them …"

What made it worse was that, as well as attracting those people, R.E.M. had also started to lose the core fans for whom they had done it all in the first place.

David Zwart, of young Stipe-produced Athens band The Daisy Group, summed it up nicely when he said: "Back when I was watching R.E.M., they were more into a punk rock thing. Back then our parents tried to keep us away from seeing R.E.M., and now I think our parents are coming to see them.

"It's not as much fun. It's kind of a thrill to my mom and dad that we worked with Michael Stipe of R.E.M. Different types of people come to see them now. It used to be the kind of thing that you weren't supposed to do, and now it's a very accepted thing."

In the classic teen equation of "us and them", R.E.M. were now being perceived as "them", and they didn't like it one little bit.

At the start of 1994, the extent of Michael Stipe's influence on Kurt Cobain became evident to the outside world when Cobain told *Rolling Stone* magazine that the next Nirvana album would be "ethereal, acoustic, like R.E.M.'s last album".

Buck spent much of January in John Keane's studio, recording with country singer-songwriter Nanci Griffith. But February found the whole band in Atlanta's Crossover Soundstage, working on new material that would become the album *Monster*. This would prove to be the start of a long, miserable process that would, once again, almost tear them apart.

"We recorded most of the tracks at a sound stage," Buck has recalled. "We had monitors and a PA system with the sound guy sitting in front of us. We recorded tracks there, which was a way to not make a record in a studio." The tracks they worked on were 'Strange Currencies', 'Bang And Blame', 'Circus Envy', 'I Don't Sleep', 'I Dream', 'Star 69', 'Revolution', 'Lucky Piece' and 'Pattern Shirt', but, for reasons that will shortly become clear, rather than attempt to detail their extremely complex evolution at this point, we'll look at them when we consider the release of the album.

Their objective, said Buck, was the creation of "an uptempo electric record but without using any elements of heavy metal, which none of us ever listened to".

The first hiccup in *Monster*'s evolution came at the end of the month when

You can call it growing, you can call it maturing, you can call it what you want, really

R.E.M. had to interrupt recording to fly to New York City. Stipe had been deeply affected the previous July when his friend, Patrick Lippert, had died of an AIDS-related illness. Lippert was also the president of Rock The Vote, an organization that encouraged young people to take an active part in politics. R.E.M. had long supported the organisation and now became the first recipients of the newly instituted Patrick Lippert Award at a Rock The Vote benefit party on February 28th.

They were barely back in Atlanta, working on 'What's The Frequency, Kenneth', when, remembers Buck, "Mike slowed down the pace and we all followed, and then I noticed he looked strange. It turned out he had appendicitis and we had to rush him to hospital." As a result, the song was left with a slower end-section than intended, and work on the album stopped again. In the tradition of all man-made monsters, this one already seemed to be turning on its creators.

Ten days later, following an appendectomy, Mills was only just back on his feet again when Bill Berry came down with a bout of 'flu that put him out of commission for the next fortnight.

Unable to get much work done, Stipe went to see Tori Amos at Center Stage in Atlanta on April 1st. He had met her on a number of occasions but, until now, had never seen her live. "I was completely mesmerized," he says. "And jealous. Seeing Tori made me want to perform again." Striking up an immediate rapport, they resolved to work together as soon as the opportunity arose.

Four days later, Kurt Cobain committed suicide in Seattle, Washington, but his body lay undiscovered until the 8th. Right up until the last days of Cobain's life, well aware that he was in a parlous mental state, Stipe had been ringing him regularly, encouraging him to leave the depressing circumstances that surrounded him in Seattle "so he wouldn't hurt himself or kill himself", and come to Athens where the two could work together. "It was all set up," Stipe has said. "He had a plane ticket. He had a car picking him up. And at the last minute he called and said, 'I can't come.'"

Stipe was still getting over the deaths of Patrick Lippert and River Phoenix, but this third blow had the unexpected effect of shaking him out of his writer's block. Within days of Kurt's death, Stipe had written 'Let Me In'. "I wrote that to Kurt, for Kurt and about him. I had just written an entire album about death, mortality and passage and really didn't want to repeat myself on this record, but his death profoundly affected me. I couldn't really ignore it much longer."

With Stipe seemingly back in the picture again, it was only to be expected that someone else would now find it impossible to carry on. As it happened, just a few days later Buck had to return to Seattle to be with girlfriend Stephanie Dorgan, who was about to give birth to their twin daughters, Zoe and Zelda.

Seeing Tori made me want to perform again

Still later in the month, R.E.M. attempted to carry on, moving to Criteria Studios in Miami again, but this session fared little better than other recent efforts, being disrupted by Michael suffering an agonizing tooth abcess which required medical attention.

Many chroniclers of R.E.M. have spoken of the "curse" of *Monster*, speculating that the album and subsequent tour were somehow jinxed or hoodooed, but if there was any discernible cause, other than the blind workings of coincidence, it was more likely to have been in the realms of self-fulfilling prophecy.

It's well documented that people under extreme stress will suffer physical distress, which can range from headaches to peeling skin to muscle pains to, well, almost anything. They are generally more susceptible to viral ailments, colds, flus and so on. R.E.M., having forced themselves to make another album when they knew they were unhappy about continuing, were prime candidates for the kind of problems (apart from Stephanie's pregnancy) that were delaying *Monster*. It seems that people who really don't want to do something are at the mercy of their own subconscious minds, which are perfectly prepared to make them ill if that's what it takes. The illnesses are not faked and not imagined but, under normal circumstances, they would very probably never have happened.

"We never changed a schedule in all of our years," Buck told *Rolling Stone*. "We'd do the schedule for a record – start on this day, end on this day – and if we went two days long, we'd be really over. This record, we changed the schedule 20 times."

It all came to a head in July when recording resumed yet again at Louie's Clubhouse, the Los Angeles home studio of Scott Litt. "We broke up," says Stipe. "We reached the point where none of us could speak to each other, and we were in a small room, and we just said 'Fuck off' and that was it. We were crazy, making the record. Our eyes were like kaleidoscope whirly things. All of us were nuts."

In classic R.E.M. style, they addressed the situation by having a band meeting, discussing it all rationally and deciding that they should just buckle down, ignore all the distractions, put petty (and not so petty) differences aside, and get back to work.

Things did improve, but even when the final mixing sessions took place at Oceanway Studios, Los Angeles, it still wasn't easy. "We would mix something for three days," said Buck, "and not even one of us would like it." And although this was, notionally, the final stage, Stipe was still writing lyrics and recording vocals. It was at Oceanway, for example, that the track known until then as 'Yes, I Am Fucking With You' finally became 'King Of Comedy'.

"At the end of the last phone call after the last mastering," Stipe was later to admit, "I fell on my knees and wept like a baby. I kissed the ground before me."

It's a cliché to say that becoming a father is the most profound change that most men have in their lives, but clichés tend to become clichés because they're true. Speaking of Zelda and Zoe, Buck was already saying, "They're a lot more important for me, in perspective, now than the band is … My important part of the day used to be coming into the studio. Now my important part of the day is going home."

On August 17th, *Green* was certified as having sold two million copies in the US, and on September 5th, 'What's The Frequency, Kenneth' was released as an album taster for *Monster* in the US. Three days later, Stipe collected awards for Best Direction, Editing, Cinematography and Breakthrough Video for the 'Everybody Hurts' video, at the 11th annual MTV video awards ceremony, in Radio City Music Hall, New York City. It was also in this month that Stipe formed another new film production company, Single Cell Films, this one with the express aim of producing full-blown movies.

When tickets for the Monster tour went on sale in the UK, they sold out in one day, a propitious sign for the album, which was released on the 26th (UK) and 27th (US) with a note on the sleeve that read, 'For River'.

"*Monster* is our punk rock album," declared Stipe, trotting out the party line. "Very in your face. And very sexy. Most of the songs are about sex and relationships." Mike, rather more revealingly, said, "We called this album *Monster* because it threatened to consume us all, both before and during its making."

The album opens loud and proud with 'What's The Frequency, Kenneth?' whose title, Buck explained to me, was a reference to US TV news anchor Dan Rather, who "was attacked in New York by two people who would intermittently beat him and then stop and say, 'What's the frequency, Kenneth?' Then they'd beat him again. It made headlines, but that's not really what the song is about."

Michael confirmed that the title was just a resonant and topical phrase that happened to make a good name for the song, which was "really about an older person looking at a younger person and their influences and trying to make sense of what it is that drives them and motivates them and having absolutely no clue".

'Crush With Eyeliner' features Thurston Moore of Sonic Youth on backing vocals and was, says Michael, "inspired by the New York Dolls. They knew how to exaggerate a song, to make

I've always been of questionable sexuality, or dubious sexuality

it sound really sleazy and over the top." It was also one of the first songs Stipe wrote when surfacing from the writer's block that plagued him after the death of River Phoenix.

Next up is one of Buck's least favourite R.E.M. tracks, the "Leonard Cohen rip-off", 'King Of Comedy', a heavily electronic-sounding track with a distorted Stipe vocal. The lyric includes the line "I'm straight, I'm queer, I'm bi", which, despite Michael's assertion that it was "extremely cynical", furthered speculation about the singer's sexual orientation. In the October 20th issue of *Rolling Stone*, when asked about the AIDS rumour, Stipe added further fuel to the fire when he said, "I've always been of questionable sexuality or dubious sexuality."

The mesmeric 'I Don't Sleep, I Dream' started life as "just a jam, a drumbeat and chord", according to Buck, but it evolved into one of the most fascinating songs on the album, with lyrics and music that attempt to create a musical equivalent of the dream state.

'Star 69' is another raucous guitar workout, this time on the subject of nuisance phone calls. Of all the songs on *Monster*, this probably evolved most from demo to finished track, having started out at six minutes long before having its bridge excised and its original chorus dumped, leaving it much more trim and dynamic.

R.E.M. are always keen to avoid repeating themselves, so 'Strange Currencies' nearly didn't make the grade because of its rhythmic similarities to 'Everybody Hurts'. It was felt, however, that Stipe's melody was too good to pass over, so the band set about subtly disguising the original rhythm. Stipe says that it's about "when somebody actually thinks that, through words, they're going to be able to convince somebody that they are their one and only".

The soul-music-inspired 'Tongue', featuring an unusual Stipe sortie into falsetto, started out, says Bill Berry, "as a weird drum track" played on what he describes as "Indian drums turned sideways".

The track, which Stipe says is "all about cunnilingus", is one of his personal favourites. He says it came about because he was "trying to think how it would be if Tori Amos wrote a Prince cover song".

'Bang And Blame', a song about domestic violence, has an almost reggae tinge to it, while 'I Took Your Name', built on a Bill Berry guitar riff, features more distorted vocal sounds, with Stipe's voice being recorded and played back through a Walkman, and backing vocals coming through a telephone.

As explained earlier, 'Let Me In', with its massively reverberating guitar, was a direct response to the death of Kurt Cobain. The title phrase, said Michael, "was me on the phone to him, desperately trying to get him out of the frame of mind he was in …"

'Circus Envy' is probably the source of the album's title, because the word "monster" appears twice in the lyric. A seriously fuzzed-up rocker, it features not only a fuzz-bassline from Mills, but a multiple fuzz effect on Peter's guitar, achieved by linking several different makes of fuzz box in series.

The closing track, 'You', is effectively a demo, with the music track having been recorded during the initial sessions at Crossover in Atlanta, although the lyric didn't come together until the final sessions at Louie's Clubhouse in Los Angeles. Stipe has categorized it as "a total obsession song".

Monster debuted at No 1 in the UK album chart on October 8th and at No 1 in the US on the 15th – the first time they'd gone straight to No 1 in the homeland. *Rolling Stone* found it to be "deeply felt, thematically coherent, consistently invigorating", but the British press reaction was curiously mixed. The music papers drooled, but the national newspapers were far from impressed, with *The Times* calling it "not as sure footed as the earlier work", the *Observer* rating it "all too routine" and the *Independent* concluding that it "doesn't really bear out their intentions of making a big, sexy rock record". Future British Prime Minister Tony Blair can't have been reading the papers that week because shortly afterwards he declared R.E.M. to be his favourite band. (This is presumably something he doesn't mention to George Bush.)

Stipe went to see Tori Amos again at the Civic Center in Madison, Wisconsin, on November 4th, then at the Riverside Theater, Milwaukee, 24 hours later. During both days, they were working on a song called 'It Might Hurt' for a Johnny Depp/Marlon Brando movie. The following extract from a hilarious joint interview in *Entertainment Weekly* reveals exactly how simpatico the pair were.

Are you enjoying working together?

Amos: With Michael it's almost like certain parts of my brain have been blown open. It's like you're in your own little buggy going down a dirt road, then all of a sudden you're in a briar patch. You didn't know you could drive in the briar patch, but he's shown me that you can.

Stipe: It's like you wake up from a nap and a total stranger is standing there, saying don't stretch like that, stretch like this.

So no fights so far?

Stipe: No, we're on the same page. I mean, we both write with invisible ink. It's like *The Name of the Rose*. You gotta have lemon juice to be able to read it.

Amos: You kind of just dig the way each other smells, or you don't. I love the way he smells.

Stipe: It's like two satellites eclipsing each other.

Amos: And a bit of shoe trading.

Stipe: And lots of snake oil.

Michael Goldberg, a senior writer at *Rolling Stone* magazine, was trying to float an ambitious new concept around this time – a rock music website, an electronic rock newspaper, to be called *Addicted To Noise*. To attract web-surfers, he needed big name acts, so, says Goldberg, "I called R.E.M.'s co-manager, Jefferson Holt, who I had a relationship with." While Goldberg was pitching his idea to Holt, Stipe happened to be in the R.E.M. office. He was so enthused by the idea that he immediately agreed to have Goldberg interview them in Australia for the new website. "Getting one of the three biggest bands in the world to agree to be interviewed and participate in this new thing was a very big deal," said Goldberg.

At the halfway mark of the 1990s, R.E.M. were about to take to the road again. It was five years since they'd trekked the world on the Green tour, at the end of which, Bill Berry now admitted he had been "almost suicidal, because I'd spent ten years looking at a bottle. You have to get out of that".

In those five years he'd re-structured his life, become a farmer, and fallen in love with his wife all over again. He was still, officially, a member of R.E.M., but it didn't sound much like it when he was saying in interviews that "at 36, I don't really want to be a rock'n'roll star on stage and make all the gestures. I have to say the success of *Out Of Time* and *Automatic For The People* had a lot to do with what's kept me going today." Buck and Mills both claimed to be looking forward to the tour, but Stipe said, "I'm dreading it … I love performing and I love travelling, but the two combined are pretty poisonous." How right he was.

The first gig of the Monster tour was set for, believe it or not, Friday the 13th of January at the Entertainment Centre in Perth, Western Australia. For Buck, even getting to Australia proved to be a whole new learning experience. "Having never traveled with children, I never had a grasp of the baggage situation. When I toured for the whole of 1989, I had a little road case that had two pairs of pants, four pairs of socks, my shoes and a coat. I also carried a little handbag with another pair of socks and a T-shirt and that was it.

"The first day of this tour was like the myth of Sisyphus retold - huge bags, all seemingly on my shoulders. And of course they got mis-shipped in Los Angeles, so I had 22 bags a mile and a half from where they were meant to be and only 20 minutes to get them there. I had to hire an off-duty guy who stole me two carts, and we're running through the airport with huge bags full of diapers and straight away my life is just chaos. I feel like the Joad family in *The Grapes Of Wrath*. I mean, all I need is a chicken and a goat and I can move to California."

At that point, any sane man would have turned round and gone home, but Buck was not a sane man. He was a rock musician. And besides, he had anoth-

I was almost suicidal. I'd spent 10 years looking at a bottle. You have to get out of that

er little matter to attend to in Perth. He was getting married. "The sun was setting over the Indian Ocean," he recalls. "There were these orange and red clouds and, later that night, there was this incredible lightning storm behind us. We got married in this incredible old white house with a lawn down to the ocean. There was a pub inside, just like you'd build in your own house. Grant Lee Buffalo played … it was certainly the most fun party I've been to."

The honeymoon ended the next night in the Entertainment Centre. How would R.E.M. cope after five years in mothballs? "As soon as we played the first soundcheck, we knew we were going to be OK," said the eternally optimistic Mike Mills. " I know it's a worn-out analogy, but it was like riding a bicycle for us. We didn't forget how to do it."

Stipe still wasn't so sure. "This is only our fourth gig," he said of the first night in Sydney, "and we haven't played in five years and I'm having to concentrate on what I'm doing just so I don't fall on something. I'm trying to remember the words without looking at them. I'm a little too much in my head right now."

By February 9th, when *Automatic For The People* was certified as having sold four million copies in the US, the band had cruised across Australia, then on through New Zealand, Japan, Taiwan, Hong Kong and Singapore.

The plan they'd outlined back in Acapulco called for them to spice up the drudgery of touring by using soundchecks, and any other opportunity that presented itself, to write songs. The first fruits of that policy blossomed on February 15th. Inspired by the sight of an electrical storm they'd seen beneath their plane on the night flight from Singapore, Stipe wrote 'Departure' during rehearsals for a show at the Velodrome in Anoeta, near San Sebastian in Spain. "It's a little Basque town," said Buck, "and they had a riot every night. Honestly, every night about seven o'clock, they would turn a car over, set it on fire and kick in a window. And you knew. You'd sit in a bar, and they'd go by, and you were able to time it."

Spain, France and Italy flashed past the windows of the six buses that made up R.E.M.'s fleet, and then it all fell apart in the Patinoire De Malley Auditorium in Lausanne, Switzerland, when Bill Berry collapsed onstage as the result of a burst blood-vessel in his brain. On March 6th, 1995, with Berry slowly recovering from his near-death experience, the remaining European dates of the Monster tour were cancelled.

The first date of the American leg of the tour was also pushed back by two weeks to ensure that Berry didn't return to active service too soon. The song 'Undertow' emerged during May, while the band was rehearsing in Athens. "We were rehearsing to make sure Bill could play," explains Buck. "He was like, 'Let's just start the tour tomorrow.' And we were like, 'Let's just do a week's rehearsal in San Francisco and hang out and not rush back into it. Just see how it goes.'"

The Monster tour resumed on May 15th at the Shoreline Amphitheater in Mountain View, San Jose, California, where Buck devised the track for 'Bittersweet Me'. Before long, though, there were beginning to be signs that all was not well in the R.E.M. camp. Sean O'Hagan, journalist and leader of the British pop band The High Llamas, caught an early June show at Rosemont Horizon, Chicago, Illinois, and reported, "That night's show was lame and uneven, the group floundering during one song when Stipe stumbled over a line, then forgot the next one altogether. I remember thinking that this was a group who were not having fun."

This leg of the tour trundled to a halt with three sold-out nights at New York's Madison Square Garden, on June 22nd, 23rd and 24th. The first night was made particularly memorable by Dan Rather, the unwitting inspiration for 'What's the Frequency, Kenneth?'

"We did the David Letterman show," Buck told me, "and they said that Dan Rather wanted to come and sing and dance to 'What's The Frequency, Kenneth?' So he came to Madison Square Garden. We made the point to him that the song wasn't about him; we'd just used the phrase because it was interesting, but he's a really nice guy. He's supposed to be serious, and here he is doing this weird dance and singing out of key with this rock band from Georgia. I thought it was great that he could poke fun at himself."

Mills rates it as "one of the strangest things we have ever done ... but I am glad we did it".

The third night at Madison Square, however, was an unmitigated disaster. "All my equipment broke," says Buck. "Every single thing I own, for some reason, broke in the one day – my amp was smoking, my guitar started crackling – the works." There was worse to come.

Chapter Seventeen

A Business Deal

"It's just a figure.
It's nothing to do
with why we make
music."
MIKE MILLS ■

Having cancelled many European dates because of Bill's illness, R.E.M. now had to return to Europe to honour their original obligations. So the Monster tour re-opened in Berlin on June 28th. Disastrously, following the gig in Cologne a few days later, Mike Mills was laid low with intestinal problems.

Adhesions, meaning scar tissue from an earlier operation, were causing trouble and needed immediate abdominal surgery. Once again, dates were cancelled. "Everybody started saying the band was cursed or something," recalls Mills, "but any of these things could and would have happened under any other circumstances. If I'd been sitting at home watching television, I would have got those adhesions anyway."

Then two teenage fans drowned in the Boyne River during the gig at Slane Castle in County Meath, Eire, on July 22nd. R.E.M. appeared dispirited by the time they reached the National Bowl in Milton Keynes, UK, at the end of the month.

"While there were moments of magic, for the most part it was hard to believe that this was what all the fuss was about," wrote David Cheal of the *Daily Telegraph*. "Two hours of sporadically inspired but mostly just decent guitar-rock, while strange images (naked people swimming, naked people throwing fish, naked fish swimming, ants crawling) flickered on the screen behind them."

Supporting R.E.M. for this portion of the tour were Radiohead, whose vocalist Thom Yorke was quite overcome by meeting Stipe. "I've never believed in hero worship but I have to admit to myself that I'm fighting for breath," he wrote in his tour diary.

Another new song, 'Wake Up Bomb' was played live for the first time at Spektrum in Oslo, Norway, on August 3rd. Speaking of the songs written on this tour, Buck has said, "One of the things we wanted to try to do was capture, in a lot of ways, what being on tour is like. That total dislocation of city to city. Not knowing anyone, flying all over the place."

A look at their schedule over the next few days underlines his point. The day after Oslo they were in Stockholm. Two days after that it was Sicily, and then Tel Aviv in Israel. On August 11th, when *Monster* was being awarded its next platinum award for passing the four million sales barrier in the US, they were in Prague, where Michael Stipe got his dose of Monster tour misery.

Diagnosed with an inguinal hernia, he was immediately flown back to Emory University Hospital, Atlanta, Georgia, where he went under the surgeon's knife the next day. "It made us realise how much we cared about each other," says Mills, looking for that little ray of sunshine. "It made us realise that the most important things to us regarding the band are, firstly, our friendship with each other and, secondly, the great things that we can do together musically. We've come through far too much to let illness break us up. We're not quitters."

The second US leg of the Monster tour began at Miami Arena, Florida, on September 8th; 'Binky The Doormat' was performed live for the first time at the Assembly Center, Baton Rouge, Louisiana on the 13th. As the miles were racked up, Peter Buck was able to put a positive spin on things, saying, "The crew gets really tired of the same set every night … but we were putting in new songs and the crew started showing up at soundcheck and cheering us on. Overall, it was a really great, positive, experience."

At the end of October, while the tour was snaking up the California Coast, Michael Stipe made a momentous decision. He had given up eating meat in 1980. Then he gave up fish in 1988, after reading a report about fish toxicity in the North Sea. But then, "I woke up one morning in a hotel in L.A., and there was no kitchen anywhere around, but I smelled it. And I thought, 'That's weird.' Later that day I got a menu for this amazing vegetarian restaurant, and there was a tunafish sandwich, kind of in the bottom corner. And my body needed it … is what it boils down to." So he started eating fish again.

As the tour wound to a close, new songs were coming thick and fast. 'Zither' was recorded during three nights at the Spectrum in Philadelphia in the middle of the month, with 'Departure' being taped at the Crisler Arena in Ann Arbor, Michigan, on the 22nd, and 'Binky The Doormat' at Desert Sky in Phoenix, Arizona, on November 4th.

Three days later, 'Bittersweet Me' was put in the can during a soundcheck at The Pyramid in Memphis, Tennessee; on the 15th, 'So Fast, So Numb' was recorded at Orlando Arena in Orlando, Florida. Even during the climactic final dates at the Omni in Atlanta, on November 19th, 20th and 21st, 'Leave' and 'Low Desert' were taped.

"Seven finished songs and 12 unfinished ones," was Buck's final tally. "We did something no one else has ever done in history. We wrote and recorded an entire record at soundcheck while on tour."

And if that wasn't enough of an achievement, the Monster tour was over, the 69 US dates had grossed $45m, and all four members of R.E.M. were still alive.

The new year of 1996 started out encouragingly, with R.E.M. being voted best band and best tour in the *Rolling Stone* readers' poll on January 25th, and best band in the critics' poll.

Sessions to turn the tracks they'd worked on during the tour into a finished album were initiated at John Keane's, but Peter Buck still found time to take a break in Hawaii and even to buy himself a holiday home out there.

Although the precise date is not known, it must also have been around this time that a female member of R.E.M.'s office staff is said to have filed a complaint against Jefferson Holt. She is said to have told Bertis Downs and the band that Holt had verbally harassed her with lewd remarks and demanded sexual favours. No doubt to the band's relief, she did not file a lawsuit or register a claim with the Equal Employment Opportunity Commission. This meant that the matter could be handled in-house and, they hoped, resolved to everyone's satisfaction without any of the attendant bad publicity that such claims can attract.

Holt denied the allegations, but in the interest of fair play, the band launched an investigation. Jefferson Holt had managed the band almost from the start, and had been so integral to transforming them from promising young bucks into a world-beating supergroup that he was often referred to as the fifth member of R.E.M. However the investigation turned out, it was going to be painful for all concerned.

While the inquiry got under way, R.E.M. tried to carry on with business as usual. On February 19th, Stipe and Laurie Anderson performed together at the Tibet House Annual Benefit Concert in Carnegie Hall, New York. In March, the album sessions transferred to Bad Animals studio in Seattle, before returning again to John Keane's studio in Athens in April.

We've come through far too much to let illness to break up. We're not quitters

At the end of the month, Stipe was in the Universal Amphitheater, Los Angeles, performing the Peter Gabriel song 'Red Rain' plus 'Last Day Of Our Acquaintance' with Natalie Merchant during the VH1 awards ceremony. Final sessions for the album – which would be their last under the current Warners contract – were completed early in May.

It was, no doubt, with heavy hearts that R.E.M. issued an official statement on June 13th. It read: "R.E.M. and Jefferson Holt have terminated their relationship by mutual agreement. The reasons for this decision and terms of the termination are private and confidential, and no further discussion of these matters will be made by any of the parties."

Both parties had agreed not to reveal the circumstances surrounding the sundering of their relationship. Inevitably, rumours spread like wildfire. "Sources" were reported as saying that the decision to dump Holt was made so fast that he had turned up for work one morning to find the doors locked and the locks changed.

Some commentators favoured the sexual harassment theory; others felt he had been ditched so the band could split the bonanza from their contract renewal five ways (including Bertis Downs) rather than six. Still others held that Holt had made a series of bad business decisions and was now paying for his mistakes.

One so-called "observer" talked to Barney Hoskyns of *Mojo* magazine in August of 1996: "We can surmise at this point that Bert Downs has actually been the business brains behind the whole operation for some time. Jefferson was a good figurehead, who had the ability to get a certain amount of work done, but, ultimately, I suspect that he was dispensable."

In truth, nobody outside of the R.E.M. office knew anything, but everybody had a theory and was willing to publish it. "It's all anonymous sources," grumbled Mills, "and making things up. I've got one thing to say to all those people who commented, and that's 'Mind your own fucking business.'"

One of the few relevant on-the-record comments came in a telephone interview with the *Los Angeles Times*, when Jefferson Holt denied having sexually harassed anyone and added, "15 years is a long time, and as time passed, our friendships have changed. I think we found as time passed that we have less and less in common. I've become more interested in other things in life and wanted to spend more time pursuing those interests. I'm happier than I have been in a long time."

Even though neither side would confirm the sexual harassment aspect of Holt's dismissal, a former Geffen Records secretary, Penny Muck, went on record, saying, "I commend R.E.M. for the thorough way in which they dealt with this. The example set by R.E.M. will only continue to help empower all employees throughout the industry." Muck had sued Geffen Records five years earlier on a sexual harassment claim, so her statement lent weight to the rumours.

"Sources close to the band", again, were reported as saying that Holt received a substantial severance package, and that Bertis Downs was now taking over most of his functions.

With the meticulous attention to detail that one would expect from a good lawyer, Downs took to carrying a laminated card in his wallet. On the many occasions when he was asked by journalists to comment on the unsavoury business, he would simply pull out the card and read the words written on it, which were identical to the statement released on June 13th.

In years to come, the unexplained bitterness would remain. Holt has consistently refused to mention R.E.M. by name, usually referring to them as "that band" or employing some similar phrase that makes his disgust evident. Buck went on record to say, "I can guarantee I'll never be in the same room with him again", but not much else.

Michael Stipe, presumably grateful to be removed from the scene, went off on tour through Italy and Spain with Patti Smith from between July 8th and 15th, but was back in time for filming of the 'Bittersweet Me' video at the Chapman Park Building in West Hollywood on the 26th.

Asked, in a break during filming, how he felt about becoming one of rock's elder statesmen, Peter Buck replied, "It's the one thing I think about more often than anything. I'm very cognizant of how old I am, that this is passing and that every year the opening bands get younger and younger. And the bands that I go see, I realize, 'My God, I was having sex with my girlfriend in the back of a car right around the time you were born, and your parents are maybe five years older than me.'"

As the media frenzy over Holt's departure subsided, thoughts turned to the Warners' contract renewal. Needless to say, other companies were sniffing around, most notably Dreamworks, so Warners' US vice president Jeff Gold was quick to make his feelings public. "We love these guys as people and as artists," he said. "It's been incredibly rewarding to be able to work with artists and an organization as impressive as R.E.M.'s, and we hope to be able to continue working with them long into the future."

Their concert film *Road Movie* debuted at the Edinburgh film festival in Scotland on August 16th, and three days later 'E-Bow The Letter' was released as a single. The big story everyone had been waiting for, however, came on August 24th when Warner Brothers announced that it had re-signed R.E.M. to a new five album contract which would net the band a cool, and record-breaking, $80m.

This put them into the megastar bracket and leapfrogged them over Janet Jackson, who had secured $70m from Virgin back in January. The likes of Michael Jackson, Madonna and Metallica were left in the dust with their paltry $60m deals of recent years.

Many lifelong R.E.M. fans were shocked by the new contract, feeling that it symbolised the band selling out. How could these multi-millionaires possibly be the same likeable guys who used to play around Athens for beer money? How could they identify with the ordinary people who had idolized them for their spiritually uplifting music, their integrity, and their commitment to ecology, to equality, to justice.

And, to get specific, how could their lawyer stand up in a Senate hearing and blast the concert ticket company Ticketmaster as an unacceptable monopoly, then allow the band to get into bed with Ticketmaster again, charging $50 a ticket for some shows on the Monster tour?

None of these questions seemed to trouble anybody at Warners, where the joy was apparently unconfined. "When we made the announcement, people – and a lot of them – actually broke down and cried," gushed the company chairman Russ Thyret. "For the first two days that I was talking about it, I actually got choked up, because I was so happy." Aw, bless.

"Making the deal, and the thought of continuing to work with R.E.M.," said president Steven Baker, "is the greatest thing in the world." Presumably he meant to add something along the lines of "apart from banishing starvation and disease around the globe" but it slipped his mind in the unbridled ecstasy of the moment.

R.E.M.'s responses were somewhat more considered. Mike Mills was keen to point out that $80m wasn't such a big deal as some people might imagine it to be. "Nobody sits down and writes us out a cheque for $80m," he explained. "The potential value of the deal, somewhere down the road, could approach $80m. But it's just a figure. It has nothing to do with why we make music. We won't make five records just because we have to. If we think we're starting to smell like dead fish as a band, then we'll certainly reconstruct the deal."

Buck seemed keen to put it into the context of value for money. "The reason we got a decent deal was that Warner Brothers heard *New Adventures In Hi-Fi* and they were like, 'Oh my God, there's four top ten singles on here!'" His use of the adjective "decent" in this context is either a masterpiece of understatement or else he was already so, shall we say, "comfortable" that $80m no longer jangled his chimes as it might have done on that freezing cold day when they first rehearsed in the back room at St Mary's on Oconee Street.

And Stipe managed to make a statement that recognized the financial realities of the situation without addressing any of the aspects that were obviously bothering the fans. "Obviously Warner Brothers would like us to make records that sell a lot," he said.

"We'd like to make records that sell a lot. We can't force that to happen. They knew what they were getting when they signed us again, and we knew what we were getting. It's a mutually real good thing."

Indeed it was. The only people who felt excluded were the people who'd been buying R.E.M. albums from day one and, possibly, Jefferson Holt. "The deal was Warners' business decision and, I think, a very good one," reasoned Downs. "Warners have had a ten-year relationship with R.E.M. and they've put out some of the great records of their time.

I'm happier than I have been in a long time

Warners have got six really nice records out of the deal, and they're likely to get a few more. We don't sit around looking at balance sheets."

Permit me to ask a few rhetorical questions. Did anybody — even those diehard fans — really expect R.E.M. to turn down the Warners deal? Was there any good reason why they should turn it down? What would they achieve by turning it down?

It was, as Bertis Downs said, a business deal. The $80m wasn't about whether R.E.M. still had integrity, and it wasn't a reward for suffering in the name of art on those grinding road trips. It was simply a reflection of how many records Warners thought the band would sell in the future, with a few millions thrown in to recognize the fact that their original deal — for a measly $6m, back in April 1988 — had worked out infinitely more profitable for Warners than had been forseen at the time.

Much as an army marches on its stomach, a record company marches on its back catalogue, and the R.E.M. catalogue was now enormously valuable.

It's a sad fact of life that successful bands will inevitably lose much of their original fan base, but isn't it better that the comforting message of a song like 'Everybody Hurts' should reach millions of people rather than just a clique of art students in Athens, Georgia? Until we live in a communist world, the band members who created that song will be rewarded for it in cash rather than in medals to pin on their hats.

And in whose pockets would we rather see that cash — Warners' or R.E.M.'s? Of those two vastly wealthy organizations, which one is likeliest to put some money towards renewal of rain-forests, protection of battered wives or research into AIDS?

R.E.M.'s longest album yet, *New Adventures In Hi-Fi*, was released in Europe and Australasia on September 9th., and in the US on the 10th. The band was, as ever, thrown back into another mind-numbing round of promotional appearances and press interviews designed to make the album seem more interesting than the one before.

"We recorded sound checks and we were just playing together and it was very loose," said Buck, explaining the genesis of the material. "We managed to capture good performances that didn't necessarily have to do so much with the right tempo and all that as with a really good interplay between the instruments.

"And that's what we're kind of looking for: a way to short-circuit the recording process. Studios are dull."

As was by now the custom, the origins of every track on the album were discussed.

'How The West Was Won And Where It Got Us': although it appears first, this was one of the last songs written for the album, and it was put together not on the road, but in Bad Animals studio, Seattle. "It's supposed to sound Ennio Morricone-ish," says Buck.

The arrangement features Buck on bass, guitar, mandolin, and bouzouki, but one of the most interesting elements is the meandering jazz piano in the middle. "We just didn't feel the need for a bridge and we didn't know what to do," admits Buck.

Why not play like Thelonious Monk?

"I just said, 'Why don't you play like Thelonious Monk?' And Mike fell off the piano stool. I mean, Mike's a really good piano player but he's not Thelonious Monk. I thought it really opened the song up a lot."

After the mellow, filmic opener, the second track, 'The Wake-Up Bomb', hits the listener like, well, a wake-up bomb. "Michael was in a club in New York where all the glam kids hang out," explained Buck, "and he thought it was really funny. They all dressed like we used to do 15 years ago.

Basically, it was written from the perspective of a character who's kind of hanging out and doing that, and it's like, 'What in the world am I doing?'" And, no, it has absolutely has nothing to do with Oasis.

'New Test Leper': Buck's description of this fairly conventional R.E.M.-u-like track as "kind of a weird folk-rock thing with surf guitar" is reasonably accurate. "That's something we only played at sound check like twice," he says. "For some reason, we just forgot about it and never really played it. Michael just happened to luckily enough have it on tape.

"He says, 'I've got this great stuff for that song and none of us even remember playing it.' So we cut it in Seattle when we did the record."

'Undertow' is a Sonic Youth-influenced rocker, featuring two of the Young Fresh Fellows, Scott McCaughey on ARP Odyssey and Nathan December on guitar. "Whether it is literally or metaphorically," muses Buck, "it's about someone drowning ... Being on tour seems like a drowning situation sometimes."

'E-Bow The Letter': On behalf of those who might be afraid to ask, I made sure that Peter Buck explained to me precisely what an E-bow is.

"An E-bow is just a magnet encased in a little plastic, uh ... thingamajig is the technical term," he elucidated, "and it makes the string resonate so you don't have to pick it with your right hand. So you hold it over the string with your right hand, and use your left hand to make notes. It has a sustained kind of cello-like tone."

The lyric originates from a letter written by Stipe, who says, "I grabbed one line and repeated it over and over again, but it is precisely what I wrote in the letter. I'm not a great letter writer, obviously, but it works really well as a song lyric."

R.E.M. had already built a friendship with Patti Smith by the time they wrote this track, so, says Stipe, "There was this kind of girl-group chorus part that we needed someone to sing, other than myself. So Patti was the most obvious choice because a lot of her music is inspired by the girl-group 'Be My Baby' kind of pop song."

Speaking of 'Leave', the seven-minute marathon that follows, featuring Scott McCaughey again on ARP, Buck has said, "It's a large, noisy, clanky, synthesiser-driven rock'n'roll song. It was the very last song that was written and recorded and mixed for the record. It also has the ARP synthesiser, which is so noisy and kind of discordant. I think there might be a little of Public Enemy influence in there somewhere."

'Departure' was inspired, as mentioned previously, by watching an electrical storm on a flight from Singapore to Spain. It is a nice, simple rock item, with, says Buck, "one good chord for the verse and two for the chorus. Anything more would be extraneous". This song is a good case for the argument that listeners should not read too much into the lyrics of rock songs. Asked why it mentions *Rolling Stone* magazine's political correspondent, William Greider, Stipe replied, "It rhymes with hang-glider and spider."

'Bittersweet Me', which follows, features an estimated 40 over-dubbed guitars, and some very fancy chord changes, this one has a lyric inspired by watching trashy TV in Italy while getting sozzled on red wine. "For me, it's all snapshots," explains Buck. "I remember coming up with the initial riff at the Shoreline Amphitheatre in San Francisco. It was the first show when Bill came back from his aneurysm."

It quickly became a live favourite and "we played it every day for eight months but Michael finished it really late in the recording process, so I never heard the melody and the lyrics until right before we were mixing".

If the lyrics of 'Be Mine', which comes next, have a strangely familiar ring, it could be because Michael Stipe found many of the phrases in the the heart shaped sweets, known as candy hearts, associated with Valentine's Day in the US (they are known as Love Hearts in the UK). The track originated in a piece Mills wrote on keyboards in the tour bus, and he originally intended it to be an instrumental.

Peter Buck recalls,"Scott Litt said, 'You know, if we produce this the right way, it'll be just like "I Will Always Love You", and it will be No 1 for 16 weeks.' And we said, 'Yeah, so let's not produce it the right way.'"

The title of 'Binky The Doormat' comes from a character in the movie *Shakes The Clown*, starring, written, and directed by standup comic Bobcat Goldthwait. "For some reason," recalls Buck, "Michael got really obsessed with that movie when we were making this record."

In the film, a depressed coke-snorting clown feels he's being abused and describes himself as Binky The Doormat, a phrase Michael found sufficiently fascinating to merit an entire song.

Zither, the album's sole instrumental, was recorded live to a DAT machine at the Spectrum in Philadelphia. "In a dressing room," recalls Mills. "I think Scott was actually in the bathroom with the autoharp. We like to do instrumentals."

"It's the kind of thing you do backstage," explains Buck. "It's not a great romantic moment – but it's an interesting little piece. And I like it that we can say, 'Yes, it was recorded live in a bathroom.'"

'So Fast, So Numb' was one of the first three or four that we started working on," says Buck of this song, begun in Rome. "It was the first day that we got the eight-track machine brought in and we had a three-hour sound check where we worked out the sounds."

Although it was played at virtually every soundcheck, Stipe didn't come up with lyrics until months later, so it wasn't played during the actual shows. To the suggestion that it might be a drug song, Buck has said, "I have never thought about that. That is something that doesn't occur around us a whole lot, but it seems like it is a warning to someone for behaviour, maybe just emotional behaviour."

'Low Desert' didn't originate on the Monster tour at all, but dates back to the studio sessions for that album, at which time it went by the name of 'Swamp'. The track was thoroughly worked out at numerous soundchecks, but for Stipe, "It wasn't a swamp song. I wrote the words and said it was a desert song. It's about the dislocation of travel."

'Electrolite': "That was written when my girlfriend was sharing a little apartment in Chicago. There was a piano there and I came up with it," Mills told me. "It didn't really have a theme. It just came out as you hear it. Sometimes you just sit down at a piano and you just play."

One of the more exotically scored tracks on the album, it includes banjo, violin and guiro. "As we were recording it at soundcheck," recounts Buck, "I had the sound of a guiro in my head, which is one of those Mexican instruments that looks like a big wooden-ridged fish. You play it with a stick and it gives that rippling Latin percussive effect.

"So we sent someone out to buy one and Nathan, who was playing guitar with us on that tour, he had to play the guiro on that song. And the box said on it "The Ultimate In Musical Usefulness", which is how we credited Nathan on the record. Because this guy is a really great guitar player, but we relegated him to whacking a stick on a Mexican fish."

Remaining with *New Adventures In Hi-Fi* for a moment longer, it should perhaps be noted that Mills has claimed, "The only consistent theme on this record is alien abduction. It's in several songs. You just have to look for it."

New Adventures entered the UK album chart at No 1 on September 21st, and the US chart at No 2 on the 28th, but overall it sold only five million copies, marking the beginning of a gradual slide in R.E.M. album sales. "We worked really hard on that record and it sold less than some," said Mills, "so that just means that you're free to do anything you want."

There were those within the industry who felt there might be a connection between the departure of Jefferson Holt and the subsequent decline in sales figures but, as any record company executive will confirm, it's hard to quantify exactly what makes one record sell and another not. There was certainly a feeling in the air that R.E.M. was no longer the people's band; maybe that was mirrored by the people no longer being R.E.M.'s people.

Buck certainly didn't seem downcast. He had long predicted that the time would inevitably come when R.E.M. would see a slump in popularity, and he was realistic enough to accept it when it happened. His take on it was this: "I felt really liberated that we made a record that we were proud of, and know is a strong record, that got pretty

He's a great guitar-player, but we relegated him to whacking a stick on a Mexican fish

much universally good reviews, and through some confluence of events it didn't sell. That's OK. I felt better than if we'd made a bad record that hadn't sold."

Mills, well aware that his band was at the start of a long-term contract, was in a similarly unrepentant frame of mind. "Unfortunately for Warners," he stated, "there's no way they can put pressure on us because we always have complete creative control over everything we do – whether it's cover art or the song selections or whether we tour. The fact is we've set it up pretty well where we do exactly what we want."

By the middle of October, with no tour on the cards, what Peter Buck wanted to do was start work with Mark Eitzel, formerly the leader of American Music Club, at Bernal Heights in San Francisco, on songs that would eventually appear on Eitzel's solo album *West*.

The pair had met when Eitzel was playing at the Crocodile and they got along famously. A month later, they were in Ironwood Studios, Seattle, recording the songs they'd written. "I just went up to Seattle and did the whole thing in about a week," recalls Eitzel. "In a lot of studios, artists are the scum of the earth. There, they're the most important people. It was like, 'Oh, let's have dinner. The engineer can wait.'"

The year was rounded off with the release of two more singles, 'Bittersweet Me' and 'Electrolite', but there was very little in the way of promotional activity to suggest that R.E.M. were throwing much of their weight behind either of them. It seemed more as if the band had gone on another of its little sabbaticals and, if by any chance one of those singles showed signs of taking off, then they'd come back and do the business.

"We used to just work 365 days a year," said Buck. "We couldn't be apart. Now we kind of tend to get together and work in long stretches of time, working 10 or 12 hours a day and then break apart."

Having ridden out the storm of Jefferson Holt's departure, signed the biggest recording contract in history and sold a few million more albums, everything in R.E.M.'s garden looked rosy at the end of 1996.

"It's great," commented Buck. "Bill's a farmer, literally a farmer. He rides a tractor and farms hay. Michael's doing his film stuff. I've got a family and I live out here (Seattle) and do some musical things on the side. Mike does some musical stuff.

He's moving around. All we have to do is just remember to get together about once a year and make a record. It's really not that hard."

It couldn't possibly last.

Chapter Eighteen

A Three-Legged Dog

"I was working on
what I thought
would be our last
will and testament."
MICHAEL STIPE ■

Happier times: Bill Berry in 1986

Towards the end of 1996, Michael Goldberg of Addicted To Noise asked Peter Buck an interesting question. Are you happy? "I don't know if happiness is something that's even relevant, you know," replied the guitarist.

"Some days I'm happy, some days I'm not. I don't know if that has anything to do with my environment or whatever. If I wanted to just have pleasure, that'd be easy. But I'm not sure pleasure is all that interesting. And being happy seems like kind of a mindless state."

Maybe that's one clue to why R.E.M. had remained together for so long. If, like Buck, the other members didn't assume that happiness was the goal, then not being happy in the band would almost certainly be perceived as a better option than not being happy without the band. For Bill Berry, however, this kind of logic was rapidly falling apart.

On January 24th, 1997, Michael Stipe was in the Claim Jumper bar in Park City, Utah. Noticing an unattended piano, he decided to tinkle the ivories but was immediately approached by a member of the bar staff who informed him that members of the public were not permitted to make use of the establishment's piano, thus depriving the bar's customers of an entertainment which would, in almost any other circumstances, have lightened their wallets considerably.

Playing piano was probably not uppermost in Stipe's mind that night, because he was not in Park City as a musician. He was there on behalf of his film production company, Single Cell, to attend the annual Sundance Film Festival.

His latest project was *Velvet Goldmine*, a movie about the glam-rock era, to be directed and written by Todd Haynes, whose *Safe* was a Stipe favourite.

Haynes had run into Stipe at a party in New York just before the start of the Monster tour in 1995. "He was dressed head-to-toe in 1971 glam," recalled Stipe. "Like, carrot hair sticking straight up and the tightest sparkly clothes. He looked ridiculous. He said, 'I'm writing the script for a movie about glam rock, do you want to be involved?' Right away I said, 'Yes.'"

Haynes and his partner, independent producer Christine Vachon, had been having a hard time drumming up finance until Stipe became involved. "He's been able to get us access to a whole lot of people," said Vachon. "His calls get returned – put it that way."

Far from just stumping up cash, Stipe's involvement was multi-faceted, especially on the musical front. It was Stipe who engineered a dinner meeting for Haynes with Roxy Music's frontmen Bryan Ferry and Brian Eno, and several Roxy songs were used in the film. It was also Stipe who put Haynes and Vachon in touch with Grant Lee Phillips, leader of Grant Lee Buffalo, knowing that his interest in glam would make him an ideal songwriter for the project.

Stipe even wrote some material for the soundtrack himself and, one way or another, *Velvet Goldmine* would occupy a fair chunk of his time during the upcoming months.

There was, of course, also the small matter of knocking out another R.E.M. album and, with that in mind, February saw the start of rehearsals in the West Clayton Street rehearsal facility. These preliminary sessions were productive, resulting in about 20 usable backing tracks so, as usual, thoughts turned to bringing in Scott Litt as producer. Scott, however, had made other plans. "He was starting his own record label," Buck has explained, "and he had lost interest in producing records."

Wagging tongues have suggested that Litt's departure was actually occasioned by his siding with Jefferson Holt during the unpleasantness of the previous year, but there's little to back up such a contention. The members of R.E.M. continued to speak highly of Litt, and he did indeed establish his own label, Outpost Records, shortly after leaving the nest.

When experimental guitarist Michael Brook released the soundtrack album *Albino Alligator* on February 11th, it included Michael Stipe duetting with jazz vocalist Jimmy Scott on the classic Harold Arlen/Ted Koehler song *Ill Wind*. "Originally Michael was going to write some lyrics for the opening credit music," says Brook, "but he just couldn't write. And he tried. I sent him some other things. He tried, spent about a week and said that he just felt dried up, and that maybe we should do a cover. He suggested *Ill Wind*."

Stipe spent some of the early part of March in London, scouting for talent to pull into his *Velvet Goldmine* project. He told one English journalist, "I came here and asked a lot of people to kind of recreate the glam era. Pretty much all I had to say was 'Todd Haynes' and 'glam rock' and great people lined up to help."

Later that month, R.E.M. moved to the idyllic surroundings of Peter Buck's home studio in Hawaii to put flesh on the bones of the 20 songs they'd started in Athens. Even in that dream setting, it became increasingly obvious that Bill Berry was just not interested.

Added to the reluctance he'd displayed towards touring for many years, there were several new factors that were profoundly affecting the way Berry felt. His collapse in Lausanne was never far from his thoughts. He was now also under increasing strain in his marriage to Mari, which would end in divorce before the year was over. And, of all the members of R.E.M., he'd suffered most from the departure of Jefferson Holt. "It was soul destroying for him," said Buck. "He was just shaking."

Nevertheless, the others settled down to work. Michael Stipe told Dave Di Martino of Yahoo! "We got together in March 1997 in Hawaii and put down about 40 songs on tape, all using drum machines and most written without guitar. So we'd already embarked on what would be a very experimental record." Bill, however, was too distracted to even think about it. "I found myself wandering out to the beach and looking at the waves and stuff," he recalled.

Buck remembers trying to advise Berry that perhaps he needed some kind of therapy or marriage counselling, but the drummer didn't see either of those as a viable solution, and they returned to mainland America with nothing resolved.

On May 1st, starting with a date at the Crocodile Café, Buck set off on one of his most ambitious side-projects – a travelling musical revue that billed itself as The Magnificent Seven Versus The United States.

In essence, this combo was actually three groups, all of which included Buck. The first of these was Tuatara, who tended to open the shows. "I sometimes play with a bunch of jazz guys, Tuatara," he told me, "and I get a songwriting credit because they're out front blowing away freeform, soloing like crazy, and I'm sitting there blocking out chords and picking out a three note melody and setting the tempo, so by the time we've got it all together, I've got a track together and they're playing to my track. Of course, they get credit if they write the horn parts or whatever, but quite often I find that if you're not the best player in the room, you're the one who decides where things go."

Music critic Bex Schwartz saw Tuatara on this tour and wrote about it for his website, *Zeek*, saying that they "completely shattered my expectations. I'd never heard rhythms like that before, and I'd certainly never heard a horn section worked in so many mysterious ways.

He said, I'm writing the script for a movie about glam rock. Do you want to be involved?

"At some point during the show, I realized that Buck was holding steady with a nice, pounding bassline. Peter Buck, the guitar guy – he was playing bass! And he was buried in back of what looked like dozens of wacky musicians. And it hit me – Tuatara wasn't about Peter Buck the rock star, it was about the music, and he was just a part of it."

In the context of Tuatara, Buck was probably the least accomplished musician, and Eastern-flavoured jazz is not his forte, but he was less of an odd man in with the second group on the tour, the pop collective Minus 5.

Their line up was fluid, but the core tended to be Buck with Scott McCaughey of Young Fresh Fellows (and Tuatara), Barrett Martin of Screaming Trees (and Tuatara), and Ken Stringfellow of The Posies.

Finally, there was Mark Eitzel, whose collaborative album with Buck, *West*, was now in the shops. He found playing live with Buck a refreshing change from gigs with his former band. "In American Music Club there'd always be someone who hated every show," he explained.

In The Magnificent Seven, whenever Eitzel despaired, he would find his spirits Bucked up.

"Every time I'd be saying, 'Oh man, this sucks,' he'd be going, 'Mark, this is great, continue.'"

According to Eitzel, Buck only lost his temper once on the whole tour, during a New York show towards the end of the month. "I pulled a bunch of girls up onstage to dance. Afterwards, he was, 'Mark, you're making a mockery of your music and I want nothing to do with it.'"

The final show of the tour, on May 31st, took place at the Variety Playhouse, Atlanta, Georgia, and, as might be expected, Stipe and Mills took the stage to join in the fun. Bill Berry was in the audience but mysteriously vanished before the end. "Bill phoned me after the show to tell me he'd loved it," said an evidently mystified Buck, "but he had to leave halfway through because he was scared he'd be asked to play. It had taken him two hours to drive there, he stayed for 40 minutes, and then drove home so he wouldn't be asked to play one R.E.M. song."

His calls get returned — put it that way

The rest of that summer passed in a flurry of activity, most of it not directly related to R.E.M. Stipe and Mills took part in the Tibetan Freedom Concert at Downing Stadium, Randall's Island, New York, on June 8th. Buck teamed up again with Robyn Hitchcock and others in yet another guise, The Popsycle Shoppe Incident (named after a Minus 5 song) on June 13th, in the Crocodile Café.

"The mess of musicians," reported Gil Kaufman of *Addicted To Noise*, "ended up crowding the stage near the end of the show to toss off ragged covers of The Soft Boys' 'Give It To the Soft Boys' and Bob Dylan's 'Tell Me Momma'." In the same week, Buck and Hitchcock were recording together, putting down five tracks towards the next Hitchcock album.

Less than a week later, Buck was in London helping out Mark Eitzel with the promo on *West*, and his contribution to Eitzel's live show at the intimate Union Chapel was underlined when he turned up a little late. According to *Mojo* magazine writer Sylvie Simmons, the show had been less than inspiring until Buck turned up, at which point, "things improved; Buck's cyclical guitar playing – solid but airy – and calm strength helped keep the music grounded".

During July, Mike Mills was in Toronto visiting the set of the 20th Century Fox movie *A Cool Dry Place*, for which he had just been commissioned to compose the soundtrack. Then on August 22nd, when Hootie and the Blowfish played at the Civic Center, Raleigh, North Carolina, Mills joined them on stage for five songs.

The band was to reconvene at West Clayton Street for more work on the next album during the early part of October but, late on the night of Sunday the 5th, Peter Buck was in his Athens hotel room, when the phone rang.

This was the call from Mike Mills, saying, "When you walk in to rehearsal tomorrow, I want you to be prepared. Bill's going to tell you something and you're not going to want to hear it."

What happened next, the announcement of Berry's departure and its immediate impact on the band, has been thoroughly discussed in the opening chapter of this book, but once the dust had settled, there would be a fairly urgent necessity to record another album.

R.E.M. had often maintained that the departure of any one member would signal the end of the band. But the departure of a member didn't negate their contract with Warners, which legally required them to create more product.

"We talked about splitting up for about five minutes when Bill left," revealed Mills subsequently. "We're such stubborn guys that the more things that push us to quit and retire the least likely we are to do it. Also, Bill said 'I'm not gonna quit if you break up.' He said, 'I'm not gonna be the guy who broke up R.E.M.'"

As well as the abandoned sessions in West Clayton Street, there had been time booked in John Keane's during October and November, but these were now cancelled. "Without Bill it was different, confusing," admitted Mills. "We didn't know exactly what to do. We couldn't rehearse without a drummer."

"It was as if someone pulled the floor out from under us," Stipe has said, "but we didn't want to hire a fake Bill."

Although his marital problems obviously hadn't disappeared, Berry didn't seem to have any problem about how to fill his time once there were no R.E.M. commitments. Farming is an exceptionally time-consuming business, and he had other little projects in mind.

"I'm going to get into the computer and figure that out," he said. "I'm not going to let the year 2000 get here without being somewhat friendly with a computer. I mean, it's ridiculous that I haven't done it yet."

On a more philosophical basis, he added, "It's like a feather takes a long time to hit the ground when it drops, and you don't know where it's going to land. I'll know when it happens." He certainly had no plans to leave Athens.

"My friends are here," he said. "And the thing is I'm going to feel distanced enough from R.E.M. after this anyway. I don't want to leave. I want to have at least that connection, so I can run over to Michael's house and pet his dog if I want to." (Legend has it that Berry is one of the few people that Stipe's dog doesn't bite.)

Although the reasons for Bill Berry leaving R.E.M. were many and various, and although they stretched way back before his aneurysm, that was the explanation the band chose to focus on as the main thrust of their PR exercise in the immediate wake of his departure.

As time went by, however, Stipe would offer other perspectives. "He was tired of being in a rock band ... The spark and the desire to go into the studio and work on one song and do this kind of press junket and do videos and go on tour had left. He didn't want to do that stuff any more. I think he's brave and courageous, and I really admire him. A man in his position with this band, with all the stuff that comes to us, the successes, the acclaim, everything, is walking away, saying, 'You know what? I've decided that I want to change my life.' If you knew Bill, it's a very Bill thing to do."

Mike Mills, because of their long friendship, was the R.E.M. member who probably felt most abandoned. But, in public at least, he was able to make the best of a bad deal. "I have to look for some perspective on it and when I do I say, well, he's not dead, he's still around, and that sort of shrinks this particular situation to a very small size. At the end of the day we still have the band, we still have Bill; just the two things are not conjoined."

"Are we still R.E.M.?" mused Stipe during one interview. "I guess a three-legged dog is still a dog. It just has to learn how to run differently."

At the Morton Theater in Athens, on December 13th, Bill drummed with a group of friends at a charity gig for sufferers of Tourette's Syndrome, the neurological disorder that can cause involuntary movements and uncontrollable verbal outbursts. As part of the show, he auctioned off his drum kit to raise money for the cause. It was, no doubt, a symbolic gesture, but it was certainly not the end of Bill Berry making music.

The three-legged dog had its first lessons in learning how to run differently on February 2nd, 1998, when R.E.M. fetched up at Toast Studios

You know what? I've decided to change my life. It's a very Bill thing to do

in San Francisco. They were about to begin recording their first album with Pat McCarthy in the producer's chair, where Scott Litt had sat for so many years. Known for his work with U2 and Counting Crows, McCarthy had also worked with R.E.M. as an engineer, and had just completed an album with Madonna before starting on the tracks that would become *Up*.

"Our secret weapon was Pat McCarthy," said Stipe, speaking of the difficult months that lay ahead. "He had a lot of ideas and they were really meshing well or interfering with the ideas we had in a really interesting way. He was really the mortar that kept us this really skewered unit, moving forward through the record-making process."

More significantly, though, it was their first album without Bill, and it rapidly became obvious that the man who had long regarded himself as the least-important member of R.E.M. had been undervaluing his contributions.

Buck, in particular, missed Bill's contributions as an arranger. "I remember showing him things I'd written and he'd say 'This verse is too long' and 'Where's the chorus, the chorus doesn't really strike me.' He really loved that kind of stuff which was all to the good for us. It really helped our arranging and writing and stuff."

Like an amputee who experiences phantom sensations from a missing limb, they often found hard to accept that he was really gone. "There was always a place where we'd look for that other opinion because usually we have four opinions and we only had three. We'd look around and go, 'Where's the dissenting voice on this one?' Bill wasn't there."

In Bill's place was Peter Buck's collection of drums machines and old friend Barrett Martin, who soon found out that standing in for Bill Berry wasn't going to be easy. "We just couldn't face having a drummer," says Buck, "so he ended up playing stand-up bass and vibes just so we didn't have to come to terms with the fact that things have changed."

Scott McCaughey was also roped in for these sessions and, like Peter Holsapple before him, he found that, much as his instrumental talents were appreciated, there were distinct limits to the creative endeavours required of him.

"They've got so many songs between Peter and Mike," he explained, "it's all that Michael can do to write enough lyrics to get an album put together. They don't need any writing assistance, but they let us add things in the arrangements. We all feel like we're pretty much part of the band."

One of the first songs to be completed was 'Airportman', which, says Stipe, "was written, recorded, sung and mixed by us all in one day. That was an auspicious start to the San

I want to have at least that connection, so I can run over to Michael's house and pet his dog

Francisco recording sessions, which ground to a screeching halt shortly afterwards, mostly due to me."

He's referring, of course, to the writer's block that plagued him in the wake of Berry's departure. It's worth noting, though, that writer's block is not uncommon with Stipe. He had it during *Life's Rich Pageant* and *Automatic For The People*; he got another dose after the death of River Phoenix; he had it again during the collaboration with Michael Brook on *Albino Alligator*.

Buck feels that, of the *Up* songs, 'Airportman', 'Daysleeper' and 'Hope' were all thematically similar in their lyrics, which feature "people doing jobs that they're not happy with and living lives which make them aspire to more than that". Maybe that would include drummers in famous rock bands who'd rather be farmers?

Buck had come to the sessions with a heavily synthesised track called 'Boomerang', which he and Scott McCaughey had worked on in Seattle, using a primitive sampling device known as, you've guessed it, a Boomerang. Stipe immediately cottoned on to it and, after changing the key to better suit his voice, quickly came up with a new title, 'Hope', and a lyric.

"He sang it and said 'What do you think?'" recalls Buck. "I went, 'It's great and it was great when it was 'Suzanne' by Leonard Cohen, too.' And he says 'Is it that close?' and I went, 'Well, I bet his publishers will think so.'" As a result, the album credits show 'Hope' as having been written by Cohen/Buck/Mills/Stipe, and the cheery Canuck songster could probably afford to buy himself a Himalayan retreat or two on the proceeds.

Another song that was already around when the sessions started was 'Daysleeper', which, Peter Buck told me, "was something Mike and I had been working on at the very end of *New Adventures In Hi Fi*, but it was too late to get on the record, because Michael didn't have lyrics. But we'd made a demo, and that was where we started the next time. Which is probably why it has a big chorus and sounds like a band playing it, whereas a lot of the other stuff on *Up* is more electronic and spacey."

It was also released as the first single from the album, a Warners decision that didn't impress either R.E.M. or Bertis Downs. "It's the most traditional-sounding, R.E.M.-sounding song on the record," says Mills, "which is of course why the record company picked it, but it's kind of a shame because it's not at all indicative of the album."

Presumably while in turmoil over Berry quitting the band, Stipe turned to Patti Smith for advice, and then turned her advice into the song 'Walk Unafraid'. "Patti Smith gave me kind of a talking to at the beginning of this record," he recalls, "and told me that I needed to be fearless … I wanted the song to be more universal than just me having to embark on the writing of an album. That's a little too specific and not that interesting, so I wrote this song."

Given that the Toast Studio sessions lasted nine weeks, it would not be unreasonable to imagine that the album would be almost completed by the end. In fact, Buck's contributions, the creation of basic tracks, were done early in the process and, before long, he found himself clicking his heels. "I sat there on the studio couch and read a book a day for, like, two months," he later revealed. "I'd go, 'Is there anything for me to do?' And they'd say, 'No, not really.' Mike and Michael are much more … they like little details. They'll sit and work over one little bar of music for, like, a day."

Mills has acknowledged that this was a problem, saying, "We found that different members of the band had certain ideas about how to go about making a record." It seems that whereas Buck visualises an entire song from the moment he starts writing it, Mills feels that the song has to be played several times before it begins to reveal its finer points. And yet this difference in approach must have existed for many years without causing undue conflict. The loss of Bill Berry was what had changed. It had upset the equilibrium they'd known for so long, and now they were having to find new ways to work together.

"I was working on what I thought would be our last will and testament," Stipe told John Harris of *Q*. "When you see relationships that are that important to you fold and collapse, and you can't find a solution to it. I'm really not overstating anything here. It was awful."

Bad as it obviously was, there were moments when chinks of light cut through the gloom. "We were in San Francisco, so we had people like Mark Eitzel and the High Llamas in town, so they came by," notes Buck. "And every one of them said, 'Jeez, this is great, it doesn't sound like anything you've ever done. These are really great tracks.' At that point, we had three vocals."

The decision to print all of the song lyrics in the album booklet was also taken at Toast. "We had a really great night in the studio in San Francisco," Stipe says. "I post the lyrics on the wall (using Post-It Notes) to keep myself writing new ones and so that these guys can see what's going on. Mike was reading them one day and said, 'These are really good; we should print them on the CD.' Me and Peter were like, 'Sure, O.K.'"

This was a radical break with R.E.M. tradition, but Stipe justified it as a simple case of what-the-hell, saying, "Everything else has been thrown out the window; why not throw that one out the window too?"

The sessions for the album, now tentatively called *Bombay*, moved back to John Keane's in Athens on May 10th, and continued there sporadically until the end of July, but Stipe took time out to attend the Cannes Film Festival in France on the 23rd, where he took part in the press conference for *Velvet Goldmine*, which was being entered in competition on that day. The *Toronto Sun* reported that Stipe was in good spirits as "the wildest-looking but softest-speaking person at the *Velvet Goldmine* press conference. Dusted in glitter, shaven bald, wearing an orange work shirt with his name emblazoned on a tag, and goofing around with a blue pig's nose that he popped on to his own for photographers."

There was also a *Velvet Goldmine* party on the same day, held in a palatial, marble-floored villa overlooking the Mediterranean. Said

> They've got so many songs between Peter and Mike, it's all Michael can do to write enough lyrics

to have been the Festival's most exclusive bash, it was attended by 300 or so guests, including Bono of U2, Winona Ryder, Sigourney Weaver and Bryan Ferry. The champagne flowed free all night and Stipe, complete with silver nail varnish and glitter, held court in the garden.

The event was a success for Stipe, because the film won the Special Jury Prize for Artistic Contribution, but the extent of the public's awareness of Stipe's involvement in movie-making was revealed to be minimal.

It was widely assumed, even by interviewers, that *Velvet Goldmine* was his first venture into cinema. As he explained to *Dazed & Confused* magazine, "It was the 12th. And this is the genius of the Internet – a lot of movies I worked on before were so under the radar, not only in

Hollywood but in independent New York film making ... that no-one's ever seen them other than on the film festival circuit." *No Alternative*, for example, was a compilation of music performances and short film subjects aimed at AIDS education for young people, which he had directed in 1993. It reached its target audience, but was never intended for national cinema release.

After *Velvet Goldmine*, however, Stipe's participation in the movie business began to enjoy a higher profile. For the record, he produced the acclaimed *Being John Malkovich* (1999), acted as co-producer of *American Movie* (1999) and *The Sleepy Time Gal* (2001), and was executive producer on *Spring Forward* (2000), *Our Song* (2001) and *Thirteen Conversations About One Thing* (2002).

The June recording sessions at John Keane's were also interrupted, this time by the Tibetan Freedom Concert at the Robert F. Kennedy Memorial Stadium in Washington DC. It was scheduled for the 13th but had to be delayed for one day because of appalling weather. The event, which also featured Pearl Jam, Red Hot Chili Peppers, Radiohead, The Beastie Boys and more, went ahead on the 14th. "It was weird getting up there without Bill," said Stipe. "He called us right before we went on, wished us the best of luck, and asked us to tell Joey (Waronker, tour drummer) not to play too well and make him look bad."

Having added string parts at Tree Sound Studio in Atlanta between the 18th and 20th, R.E.M. were coming towards the end of recording as the month closed, and most of the work that lay ahead – apart from a couple of Stipe vocals – was mixing.

'Diminished', which Stipe sees as a particularly good example of how totally non-autobiographical R.E.M. songs tend to be, was mixed at Tree Sound on the 16th. "There are writers I respect a great deal who I think do write very autobiographically," he says, "or who have created personas through which they write, supposedly, autobiographic work. I'm not that person."

'Diminished', he points out, is a courtroom drama, and "I've never been in a courtroom. I've never been accused of murder or thought that I may have murdered someone but blacked out and can't remember it."

Two days, the 21st and 22nd were devoted to the mixing of *Up*'s only real love song, 'At My Most Beautiful'. Buck told me, "'At My Most Beautiful' is perfectly realised. It's a great song ... a song that from the first time we played it, made sense as a band."

It wasn't that easy for Stipe, though. "It took a full year for me to write the verse to that song. I wrote 'I found the way to make you smile', that came very easily, and then I had to figure out what exactly it was that I found that would make you smile, and that took a full year. It happened one morning in my house, by myself and two cups of tea. I just wrote the whole thing in 45 minutes and I was so happy it was done and that it made sense and it wasn't a cliché."

'Falls To Climb' was one of the few tracks that still required further recording, and this was done towards the end of the month at Baby Monster Studios in New York. "I had the idea of writing a song about someone who was a very obvious scapegoat," said Stipe, "or kind of a whipping boy. And in the song it's the one who has a very slight physical form and is perhaps even some-what crippled and looked upon as a weak link but, through her actions, proves herself to be wiser and more benevolent and more giving than anyone in the group of people she's sacrificing herself for and, through that sacrifice, moves away from her physical form and on to something better."

In what looks like a frenzy of indecision, further mixing sessions were carried out in early August at both RPM Studios and The Hit Factory in New York, as well as at John Keane's. "When we were mixing *Up*, we decided that it was all over," says Stipe. "That record broke up the group."

It has to be to their credit, however, that despite languishing in their emotional trough, they got the work done, completing 'Lotus', 'Hope', 'The Apologist', 'Sad Professor' and 'Parakeet' in these final days.

Speaking of 'Lotus', another of the album's singles, Stipe told *Addicted To Noise*, "That lyric just kind of tumbled out of me. I didn't really think about it. I'm still not sure I've completely figured out what it's about. I like it. I think it's about someone who found a good place, lost it, and is trying to regain it. Floundering around a bit."

Asked if perhaps the lyric, "Thank you for listening, goodbye," from 'The Apologist', was a coded farewell from Stipe, Buck replied, "I don't know if it's a personal thing. I think it's about an individual, I don't know who. If we did break up after this one it might be suitable, but I wouldn't want to. We've already got a lot of stuff going for the next one."

Stipe claimed to have had the title stuck to his office wall with a Post-It Note for almost four years before he could come up with the lyric about "a guy that's been through some kind of a detox or 12-step program and, as part of his therapy, is going back to apologize to all the people from his former life, for the person he was. It becomes more and more evident, as the song goes on, that whatever he was, whatever monkey he had on his back, whatever his damage was before, is nothing compared to what he's become."

Summing up the album, Buck told me, "If there are 14 songs on that record, probably ten of those songs are just perfect the way they are. But there's a couple of things that seemed to me as if they just didn't really work, that were just done at the last minute, and maybe the sequence wasn't really right."

When the album was finally finished, it looked as if the band might also be. Recognizing that they had reached a crisis point, Bertis Downs suggested that it was time for a meeting, and arranged for them all to go away for a week together in a lodge in Idaho. "Michael and I were flying out there hoping it wasn't over," remembers Mills, "but thinking that it probably was."

Chapter Nineteen

Group Therapy

"We sat in a room
for several days and
vomited on each
other – and we
emerged much
stronger."
MICHAEL STIPE ■

Opening up: Stipe on the Reveal tour, 1999

daho. Some 83,557 square miles of Rocky Mountains, high desert and cow farms, with an average density of ten humans per square mile. Located in the north west of the United States, Idaho is famed for its potatoes. And its lentils. The state capital of Idaho is Boise – Jewel Of The West and City Of Trees – famed for its low crime rate.

"We just wanted to be somewhere where we could focus on what we were doing," said Mike Mills, explaining why R.E.M. chose Idaho as the location of their crisis meeting.

Good choice. In California, you'd be worrying about the San Andreas Fault. In Michigan, you'd be scared to go out at night in case you get mugged. The cops give longhairs a hard time anywhere in the mid-West. There are inbred weirdos in the swamps of Louisiana, and gun-totin' religious maniacs on every second ranch in Texas. But Idaho? Low crime rate, potatoes and lentils. Perfect.

The members of R.E.M., plus Bertis Downs, arrived at their remote lodge in Idaho fearing the worst – that the band was finished. "We sat in a room for several days and vomited on each other," is how Stipe describes it, "and we emerged much, much stronger."

The meeting was, essentially, a self-administered group therapy session, and the main lessons they learned were that they had been foolish to go back to work so quickly after Bill Berry had left; that they had not appreciated how different the group dynamic would be without him; that they had taken their frustrations out on each other during the making of the album; and that, all things considered, they still wanted to continue as R.E.M.

Mills has said that Idaho gave them the opportunity to "get together, clear the air, and re-learn how to communicate with one another".

"For the first time," said Stipe, "I was forced to imagine life without R.E.M and it was terrifying. As we talked, I think each of us realised just how much the band meant to us. Getting back together was like church."

A religious experience for Stipe then, but Buck's take on it seemed considerably more pragmatic. "I had to sit down and decide, 'Why do I do this? Is it worth the emotional turmoil?' And I came to the decision that it was." Then he added the spooky coda, "Even if we weren't friends."

Had it really come to this?

Early the following month, they were out and about again, filming a video for 'Daysleeper' in New York and, while there, taking the opportunity to talk to the media. Robert Crampton of *The Times* asked Buck if, now that he was living in Seattle, he missed the other band members?

"We're still good friends," replied Buck, adding, "We've all gone completely different directions in our lives."

Asked what his life now consisted of, Buck said, "I make music all the time and I have a family. I walk five miles a day and I read for three hours a night and I see bands once a week."

Stipe's life, as Buck had inferred, was radically different. He was unmarried, and as pre-occupied with his film projects as he was with making music. For example, while R.E.M. were in the UK during October to promote the release of *Up*, *Velvet Goldmine* also had its British premiere, and Stipe had to devote time to both.

When they played a live nationally broadcast show in the BBC Radio Theatre in London on October 25th, the *NME* reported with obvious relief that, despite Berry's absence, "little has really changed with R.E.M. Strip away the click and buzz of drum machines and samplers, place the new songs in the context of an unravelling pantheon that includes 'Man On The Moon', 'Country Feedback' and even 1983's 'Perfect Circle', and the idea of a radical shift suddenly seems utterly fanciful."

Up was released in all territories outside the US on October 26th, and one day later in their homeland. Sylvie Simmons of *Mojo* reckoned that it "could be the best they've done. It's surely their most accomplished. Past ones may have had more sing-along songs, but nowhere does their music have this depth." *The Times* declared it "brilliant".

The *Sunday Times*, however, was not so sure, lambasting it as "a series of ill-fitting and self-consciously experimental styles", and *Select* magazine seemed to agree, saying, "It lacks the sheer breathtaking sense of scale seen in R.E.M. landmarks like *Murmur* and *Green*."

The American reviewers were just as divided. *Entertainment Weekly* figured that *Up* was "the sound of the band trying to reshape its sound and vision". And the *Los Angeles Times* didn't seem entirely happy: "Peter

Michael and I were hoping it wasn't over, but thinking it probably was

Buck's once-assertive guitars mostly have gone all liquidy or simply disappeared; a layered array of pianos, organs, string adornments and mechanically ticking synthesizers and beat boxes supersedes the old guitar-band approach."

Rolling Stone, on the other hand, saw the new three-piece line-up as a stimulus to new inventions: "Losing Berry has allowed R.E.M. to literally think outside the rock box; the drum machines, shakers and congas that surface in his place are only the most obvious aspect of the group's expanded consciousness."

R.E.M. themselves clearly realised that they'd produced something that was sure to confuse a lot of people. "If somebody played me anything on this record 18 years ago, I would have thought, 'Jeez, I'm gonna go insane when I get older! Because this is really nutty!'" said Buck. "So much of the vocabulary of this record is so far away from what we were doing 15 years ago that I doubt very much I would recognize it."

They were also, as always, unrepentant. "We decide what we do and when we do it," asserted Mills. "We all know that *Up* was not the record that Warners wanted us to make, commercially, but we think it's a strong record. It's the record we wanted to make."

Fighting talk. But it probably also helped when Bill Berry stood up to be counted among *Up*'s fans. "I feel like a real chump," he said. "I leave and they go off and make their best record." Buck, obviously touched by Mills' words, admitted, "I wouldn't be nearly so nice if I'd left the band. I'd hope they'd make a shit record just to prove that I was the guy in charge. Bill is clearly a much nicer person than I am."

British critics were afforded another opportunity to see the band live when the UK TV show *Later With Jools Holland* devoted an entire edition to a live R.E.M. concert at BBC TV Centre in London. Gary Teratzo of MUSE came to the conclusion that "It is not, after all, the end of the band as we know it following Bill Berry's decision to swap his drum sticks for farming implements. In fact, R.E.M. have just gotten better."

I was forced to imagine life without R.E.M.

Having decided not to tour behind *Up*, R.E.M. were using such high profile TV shows as their means of getting the music across to the masses. Similar live sets were recorded for shows in Norway, Sweden, Germany, Spain, Austria and Italy, while American fans could catch them on a VH1 *Storytellers* special, and the usual round of Letterman, Conan O'Brien and Rosie O'Donnell chat shows.

Meanwhile, *Velvet Goldmine* had opened in six US cinemas on November 6th, where it ranked a disappointing 25th for the first three days of its run. At its peak, it played in 93 US cinemas. But, after 24 days, it dropped to 48th place, raking in significantly less than $1m. There would, of course, be further income from TV, cable and video releases, but it was some way from being the blockbuster for which Stipe must have been hoping.

Up entered the UK album chart at No 2 on November 7th, and the US chart at No 3 on the 14th, but it would ultimately fall a long way short of former sales achievements.On a brighter note, November 16th found R.E.M. notching up yet another unlikely achievement when they joined that elite group of rock artists who have appeared on *Sesame Street*. For Stipe, this TV studio recording date (not broadcast until February 1999) was no doubt as near as he could ever hope to get to being in an episode of *Banana Splits*. The band gave every appearance of thoroughly enjoying their re-hash of 'Shiny Happy People' as 'Furry Happy Monsters'.

Looking back on 1998, Bertis Downs described it as "the most fragile time we've all been through", but then suggested that they had triumphed in adversity by adding that the year had also been "a really positive one in re-forging the group's bonds, making them realise that what they do is what they really want to do, and that's the reason why they're doing it".

As the new year opened, *Up* had sold a meagre 500,000 copies in the US. In a curious inversion of the situation that had existed with IRS, R.E.M. were now much more popular in Europe than they were in America. In the UK alone, the album shifted 300,000 units, and the figure was 1.5m across Europe.

Putting the US sales into context, Buck told the *Washington Post*, "I'd feel bad if U2 and Pearl Jam and Smashing Pumpkins were selling ten million records and we weren't, but everyone kind of hit the same little skid. Maybe it's just not our turn. And that's fine. We've still got a lot of work to do and we feel strongly about it."

Now, out of the blue, it seemed as if that work might include a new tour. On February 1st, during an hour-long webchat on Disney's *ZoogDisney* website, Stipe mentioned live dates as a possibility. "We're having a band meeting next week to talk more," he said. "If we did so, it would be maybe for a month in the U.S. and a month in Europe. Maybe."

By the time the February 8th edition of *Rolling Stone* hit the streets, it was official. What they announced was a 15-country jaunt amounting to 45 performances in Europe and America. Scott McCaughey, drafted in as a supporting musician again, described the schedule as "long enough to cover a lot of ground, but not long enough to burn everybody out".

R.E.M. were quick to deny allegations that they were simply trying to prop up a dying album, and to assert that WEA hadn't put any pressure on them. "The record's dead in the water," Stipe would insist. "We're doing this because we want to do it."

The start of the tour, however, was still six months in the future, and R.E.M. had no shortage of things to do to pass the time. February 17th, for example, found them in the Palace Theater, Hollywood, filming a live concert appearance, parts of which were to be used in the popular Fox TV series *Party Of Five*. "I've always enjoyed the combination of the visual form [with music], in terms of movies or television," said Mills. "It goes all the way back to seeing Alice Cooper on *Diary Of A Mad Housewife*."

There was also the *Musique Plus* TV show in Montreal, another Tibet House benefit show in New York, and then a European promo trip to tie in with the release of 'At My Most Beautiful' as the latest single from *Up*. Probably the most interesting aspect of that trip was the recording of an *MTV Presents* show at Ladbroke Grove Tabernacle in London, on March 2nd. Despite a long wait outside in pouring rain, and despite the artificiality of a TV set, the *NME*'s reviewer was overcome by what he called "the unstoppable force of some of the most memorable music of the 20th century unleashed in a confined space".

There was still more to do before they could set off on that long-awaited tour. Their Andy

Kaufman song, 'Man On The Moon'', had snowballed into a film project. Buck has said that the idea came about after Kaufman's family heard the song, but when I asked Stipe, he said, "It was a huge hit, a lot of people heard it, including the guys [Scott Alexander and Larry Karaszewski] who decided to write a screen play about Andy Kaufman's life, and they named it after our song 'Man On The Moon'."

The reality seems to be that Alexander and Karaszewski did have the idea, but then abandoned it. Some while later, Kaufman's *Taxi* co-star Danny De Vito had the same idea independently, and the two scriptwriters were then asked to write a Kaufman movie.

However it happened, the upshot was that R.E.M. were approached to compose the soundtrack, which they did during April and May of 1999. "I've always said I'd really like to score a film," Buck told me, "but it'd be like a $100,000 low budget thing, done by some guy with a great artistic vision, not something where I have a committee leaning over my shoulder telling me how I should do it."

As it happened, *Man On the Moon* was a big budget, Hollywood project, with a top director, Milos Forman, and starring Jim Carrey, the hottest comedy actor in the world. "It's not real super-satisfying for me," Buck explained, "to have five people who really know nothing about music telling me what to do. There was one point where one person identified one thing which they didn't like – which was a minor chord – and suggested that possibly we shouldn't use minor chords. I said, 'You mean in this particular instance, or always?' But that's what happens when you're answering to people who don't understand music."

Michael Stipe had an entirely different kind of problem. "They wanted another song that was also about Andy Kaufman," he told me. "I had to come up with a song that was equal to or better than 'Man On The Moon', which is one of the best loved songs of our entire career, and my personal favourite song as a live performer."

Stipe also had strong doubts about Jim Carrey's ability to pull of the role of Kaufman, and went so far as to voice those doubts to Milos Forman. In the end, however, Stipe realised that the star had "left all the Carrey-isms in the dust for this role … his dedication to the role really astounded me".

The tour finally hit the road on June 17th, with a show for 16,000 fans at Pavilhao Atlantico in Lisbon, Portugal. "One of the main reasons for this tour," Buck told Tom Doyle of *Q*, "is to keep the band functioning." On the same day, R.E.M. finally opened up its own website: www.remhq.com. "We're officially the last band to join the electronic age," announced Bertis Downs. Asked what had finally prompted them to get on the web, Mills explained that there was too much misinformation out there, and they felt they should provide an authoritative source. "Things were popping up that we had no control over," he said. "It's better if we do it ourselves; that way we know what's going out."

The tour trundled on through Spain, briefly entering the UK where *Rolling Stone* unfavourably reviewed the first of two huge London shows, at Earls Court on June 22nd. "From the outset, the pacing was off. From generic rockers like 'Lotus' and 'Crush With Eyeliner' to the flaccid, vaguely lounge-y 'Suspicion' and banal and broodish 'The Apologist', R.E.M. weren't able to hit legitimate arena-rock stride until eight songs in, when they dropped the punishing 'Wake-Up Bomb'."

They redeemed themselves, however, with an acclaimed headlining slot at the Glastonbury Festival three days later, before moving on to Germany, Denmark, France, Belgium, Switzerland, Austria, Hungary and Italy.

Bertis Downs rates the show at Lansdowne Road in Dublin, Eire, on July 16th, as one of the five best on the tour. "During the second song," he says, "the kids were bopping up and down, like pogo dancing, all the way beyond the soundboard ... It was that way ... That was remarkable, that meant the crowd was really into it. It was a huge stadium, it was packed."

Three days later, Stirling Castle in Scotland provided them with an inspiring venue, a hilltop castle esplanade, a panoramic view of the surrounding countryside and, on a day that would otherwise have been too hot, constant cooling rain.

By the time the US leg of the tour opened at the Greek Theater in Los Angeles, on August 9th., worldwide sales of *Up* had reached about 2.5m copies. Even though reviews were generally favourable, Stipe felt that "The first couple of shows were a little wobbly. We were just all jet-lagged and back from 12 days of vacation, so the energy was definitely there, it was just a little wild; it wasn't terribly focused."

As the tour wound across America, R.E.M. were widely perceived to be back on form. At the New World Music Theatre, Tinley Park in Illinois, on the 20th, for example, Troy Carpenter of *Nude As The News* website reported that "The three (augmented by drummer Joey Waronker and multi-instrumentalists Scott McCaughey and Ken Stringfellow) showed more spunk than their audience in playing probably the coolest set of pop tunes to grace Tinley Park in quite some time. Under an elaborate system of Christmas light-objects, Stipe postured, preened, and paraded while Buck and Mills diligently stroked their instruments."

Jane Stevenson of the *Toronto Sun* was equally impressed by the August 24th show at Molson Amphitheater, in Toronto, Canada, saying, "R.E.M. showed they're a long way off from throwing in the towel, at least as a legendary live band."

The tour ended on September 11th at Woods Amphitheatre, in Mansfield, Massachusetts, but the show that meant the most to them came on August 31st, in Atlanta's Chastain Park Amphitheater. When Stipe dedicated the song 'Find the River' to Bill Berry, the audience was alerted to the fact that the former drummer was in the venue. To a chant of "Bill! Bill! Bill!" he took the stage, hugged all of the band members, and then walked off again. Asked, during a web chat, for his most magical musical memory of the last 20 years, Mike Mills chose this moment.

Summing the tour up, Bertis Downs said, "I guess we just got lucky this time. We got some good breaks, everybody stayed healthy, the band played very well ... The crowds were very enthusiastic and when the crowds like the show it really makes the band play better."

"At the end of that tour," reckoned Stipe, "it affirmed our confidence in wanting to work with each other and wanting to keep on doing this, which is what we set out to do by booking a summer tour. It also made it abundantly clear to all of us that none of us want to tour for a year at a time. It's just crazy.

"There is a time when we did that, there was a time when we did that for ten years, and that time has passed. A longer tour, I don't know, maybe a tour that goes to many more parts of the world than Western Europe and North America, yes."

Immediately after the tour, Stipe was off to Toronto international film festival, where he was promoting his latest movie projects, *American Movie* and *Spring Forward*, and a little over a month later, on November 23rd, the *Man On The Moon* soundtrack album was released, followed by the nationwide release of the movie, catapulting the band back into another round of appearances on high-profile TV shows including *Saturday Night Live*, *Letterman*, *Conan O'Brien*, *Queen Latifah* and *Charlie Rose*.

By all accounts, R.E.M. didn't place undue significance on the arrival of the new millennium. But, on January 4th, 2000, Michael Stipe turned 40 and admitted, "More and more, I think about getting old. I think it's part of my job as a pop star going on 20 years in the public eye to be really conscious of where I'm at. But I think this obsession with age and ageing is something that's increasingly insidious in our culture."

The energy was definitely there, but it was just a little wild. It wasn't terribly focused

Evidently his 40th birthday had given him pause to reflect. "To me the central question becomes, 'Why am I doing this at the age of 40? Am I doing it for money? Am I doing it for fun?' Clearly it has to be because I still love music.

"Life is exceptionally short. You have to do what you want to do and you have to know why you're doing it. I do it because making music is my first love. Which is just as well, because in early February, R.E.M. started once more the process that would lead to another album, with rehearsals in West Clayton Street. After further rehearsals during March in Royaltone Studios in Hollywood, they headed for Canada on May 1st.

"We started the record in Vancouver, BC, laying down the basic tracks," explains Stipe, "and then with a brief recording layover in Athens, we moved on to Dublin for most of the summer. I really wanted to work outside the U.S. It felt like the record we were trying to make was more at home away from home. I think it worked. Sometimes distance brings clarity, and I didn't want to fall into writer's block by being in familiar surroundings."

At the Warehouse Studio in Vancouver, they laid down basic tracks for more than 20 songs. "Some are super-embryonic, and others are completely self-realized," said Stipe. "It kind of picks up where *Up* left off. Some of it is pretty strange, and that's the stuff that appeals to me."

Bill Berry, meanwhile, was making a low-key return to recording and performing. On April 19th, he'd recorded contributions for the Tourette's Syndrome benefit CD, *Welcome Companions*, with Athens-based guitarist and audio engineer Rick Fowler, who suffers from the syndrome.

"Rick's goal is to heighten awareness and help fund more aggressive research into this frustrating ailment," stated Berry. "Becoming involved with the *Welcome Companions* project was alluring to me on two levels: it offered me the opportunity to contribute to a great cause as well as to challenge my musical capabilities after a three-year hiatus." On June 17th, when the CD was released, Berry appeared at the accompanying concert.

Buck returned to Seattle in June, leaving Stipe to work on lyrics. "The whole process unfolded very naturally," says Buck. "We didn't sit aound in the studio waiting for something to happen. When Michael was writing lyrics, I could be off recording or playing with my side project, Minus Five. We wanted the music to reflect exactly where we found ourselves at any given moment."

The trio were back working on the new album in West Clayton Street again during July, before moving on to Dalkey Lodge near Dublin, in Eire, where the bulk of the album was completed between August and October, with Pat McCarthy at the production helm again.

Stipe recalls how "Pat McCarthy and Jamie Candiloro (engineer) built a little nest in this 700 -year-old house, with a garden and foxes and ancient trees and the train in the backyard, and it was brilliant and liberating to work like that."

And, whenever he felt the old mental block coming over him, he had worked out a strategy, in the endearing way that multi-millionaire rock stars do. "I'd jump on a plane whenever I got stuck. I'd go to Israel or France, Italy or Denmark, then come back, put it together and sing it."

He has singled out 'Disappear' and 'All The Way To Reno' as songs that emerged from that process, but he has, more generally, proved reluctant to talk in any detail about the songs on *Reveal*. Stipe told Sean O'Hagan of the *Guardian*, "I really don't want to reveal anything about a character or a song because I can remember, as a teenager, a record falling into my lap, and how magical and mysterious and revolutionary and unbelievably life-altering even one song on a record like that can be. I would hate to diminish or be unfaithful to that notion."

Arranger Johnny Tate's string parts for *Reveal* were recorded on October 3rd and 4th in Windmill Lane Studios, Dublin, after which the final recording sessions took place back in Athens at John Keane's, before mixing began at the Hit Factory in Miami on October 31st.

They were still in Miami when the George Bush vote-counting fiasco erupted. After Bush's election as US President on November 7th, alarming anomalies in the registering and counting of the Florida votes were brought to light, which suggested compellingly that Bush had not in fact secured the majority he needed to take office. Of the three R.E.M. men, Mills was the most volubly anti-Bush, saying, "I despise him. He's our President for better or for worse, but he didn't get the most votes, so he's certainly got no mandate and I personally find him reprehensible."

On November 10th, Peter Buck and Bertis Downs marched in a Miami protest rally, led by the Rev Jesse Jackson. But Stipe, while making his dislike of Bush fairly evident, chose not to thump the tub.

"I've got in and out of the machine of celebrity activism," he explained. "I think I had a hand in creating it in the mid-1980s. I realised the power I have with what I do is alluring, whether it's music or photography or film, but I'm becoming more reluctant to be pushed onto a pedestal of politics – I'm tired of myself. That said, my own political drive hasn't diminished at all – it's just that my ability to be cynical about it has increased."

Stipe pointed out that he would continue to support certain causes and to campaign on specific issues, but he now preferred to participate in such activities "not so much as a celebrity, but as someone that has other means, so I can make contributions to and support stuff more locally or more privately, which I have done. So I am actually a little more comfortable with that."

After the mixing was completed, Stipe declared the making of *Reveal*, in direct contrast to the making of *Up*, to have been "incredibly happy … The whole experience has been very liberating. We've become acclimated to new conditions and potentials. That's a great place to be."

Buck was pleased with the way it sounded, which he described as "warm and layered and analogue, but [it] has a distance and breath to it that's modern and complete and liberating … like a beautiful vacuum".

That Idaho meeting was now paying dividends. "Having to re-evaluate the group and the reason we were together gave us a whole new perspective on what we were doing," concluded Buck. "I think what we discovered is why we started this in the first place – we love our job."

Just six weeks later, on January 13th, 2001, R.E.M. played their first show in 16 months, the Rock In Rio Festival in Rio de Janeiro, Brazil, to their biggest audience ever: 190,000. It was a massive undertaking, with Foo Fighters and Beck playing on the same day.

Bertis Downs said, "Our whole production crew worked ridiculously hard the whole time, and especially the lighting guys, under the able direction of Bruce Ramus – they started hanging the ropelights and assorted other bells and whistles after Sting's loadout early Saturday morning, some time around 4.30am. They finished in time for soundcheck at noon." At this point, there came an encouraging portent for the show when several hundred kids managed to gain entry to the arena early and were treated to an unexpected sound-check party.

The real set, which previewed 'She Just Wants To Be' and an unusually speedy version of 'The Lifting', from the upcoming album, delighted the evening's giant throng. John Harris of *Q* wrote of how, "Clearly relishing the show's mind-boggling size, he (Stipe) made several trips to within inches of the crowd, turned in some spectacularly swivel-hipped dancing, and infused more celebratory songs with the whoops and yelps of someone who was clearly in his element."

The first single scheduled from *Reveal* was 'Imitation Of Life'. To accompany it, one of the band's most ambitious videos was filmed over a fortnight at the end of February. Directed by Garth Jennings and featuring a cast of 76, it artfully played with time by looping individual activities contained within a single wideshot of a party around a pool.

"They asked me what I wanted to do in the video," said Buck, "and everything seemed to revolve round some kind of talent, like acting,

I do it because making music is my first love

none of which I had. So I thought, if they got a monkey, and sat the monkey in my lap, then the monkey could do all the work. And, in fact, the monkey was a better actor than me, and actually had more jobs than me to do. He didn't come the second day, 'cos he was doing *Planet Of The Apes*, so we got a stunt monkey. That's true."

Buck, having committed himself to a brief US tour with Minus Five, wasn't with Stipe and Mills when they arrived in Europe at the end of March for the inevitable pre-album promotional assault, but he more than made up for his absence when his plane touched down at Heathrow Airport on April 21st.

He was met on the tarmac by police officers who arrested him on charges of "air-rage", stemming from an incident during the flight in which he was alleged to have assaulted two members of the cabin crew and caused criminal damage to the plane while drunk.

"That whole thing was exactly as stupid as it sounded," he would later tell Jim de Rogatis of the *Chicago Sun-Times*. "A friend of mine gave me a sleeping pill, and I'd never taken one before. You'd think I would have, but I never did. He said, 'Have a cognac and just go right to sleep.' I just blacked out. I don't remember anything for like eight hours. Basically, I just staggered around like an idiot, bumping into things."

Stupid or not, when it hit the tabloids, the story would catapult Peter Buck to notoriety as a rock'n'roll hell raiser, making him a household name to people who'd never heard an R.E.M. song in their entire lives.

Chapter Twenty

The R.E.M. Way

"It's a sterling combination of stubbornness and creativity."
MICHAEL STIPE

Great southern band: R.E.M. in Australia, 2003

Crew members on flight BA 048 from Seattle to London told police that a drunken Peter Buck had torn up a written warning from the captain of the flight, thrown yoghurt over a male member of staff, pulled tight an air steward's tie and wrenched the arm of a female cabin crew member.

In classic R.E.M. fashion, Bertis Downs took hold of the reins and the matter was handled with the utmost efficiency and decorum.

Bail was set at £25,000 and immediately paid. The hearing was set for June 18th, allowing Buck time to complete the promotional tour for *Reveal*, and the guitarist immediately expressed his gratitude to the court. For the moment, other than making this brief, polite statement, Buck remained tight-lipped about the incident.

Had Buck been a member of, say, Oasis, not only would his responses have been dramatically different, but there would have been an immediate suspicion that the entire incident had been stage managed to provide headline-grabbing publicity for the new album. R.E.M., thankfully, are not Oasis.

The feeling in the music industry was that something wasn't quite adding up. Buck was, like all of the members of R.E.M., almost too polite and well behaved to be in a rock band at all. His generosity towards other musicians was legendary, his patience with irritatingly inquisitive journalists exemplary. Middle-aged, a responsible family man, father of twins, all round nice guy – it didn't make sense.

If Buck had thought about it long enough, maybe he'd have remembered that night in February 1985 when he'd drunk some beers, taken two Halcion sleeping pills and fallen asleep on Ken Fechtner's sofa, only to wake up the following morning and find the floor littered with shredded newspapers.

He'd obviously torn them up in the night and then forgotten doing it. Tests have shown that Halcion and alcohol can cause amnesia in certain people.

There wasn't much time for Buck to think about it though, because as soon as he left the court he was thrown into a non-stop round of rehearsals, interviews, TV and radio appearances and live shows, the highlight of which was the South Africa Day freedom concert in London's Trafalgar Square on April 29th. – the day before the UK release of 'Imitation Of Life'.

"When we were doing the '99 tour," Peter told me, "I think we recorded it backstage. It had these really bad synth trumpets on it. It was really slow, had this big hammering drum machine, but the chords and the arrangement were there. Like all demos, it was about six minutes long … To tell the truth, the demo was really draggy. By the time the third verse came along you just wanted to slit your wrists."

When it was being recorded again for *Reveal*, the band's approach was to speed it up and tighten the construction, making it more of a pop song. Even so, it was almost left off the album. "Although we were very happy with the song," remembers Buck, "it was a matter of not having finished it until very near the end of the process. I remember we were not really concentrating on it until some of the people from the record company said, 'You know, I love that song.' Everyone seemed to like it but it was not particularly in the running at that point. So we said, 'OK, we'll just buckle down and work on a chorus and come up with something.'"

Despite this resolve, inevitably, Stipe was very late in completing the lyrics. Buck says, "I remember driving to dinner one night and Michael said, 'Oh, I've got the chorus,' so we put the tape in the car and he started singing along to it and we said, 'That's great! We gotta do that tomorrow!'"

R.E.M. had completed a whirlwind tour of Italy, France, Spain and Germany by the time *Reveal* was released (May 14th in UK, 15th in US). It sold 33,000 copies in the UK on its day of release, which assured it of the No 1 position, although in the US it would peak at No 6.

The album opens with 'The Lifting', originally known as 'Tabla Demo'. The track was, however, deemed too similar to 'All The Way To Reno', so it was radically re-worked during the October sessions at John Keane's.

"We tried to make 'The Lifting' less of a similar groove to 'Reno'," says Scott McAughey, "and we finally got something that was pretty rocking." This new version was basically a live take with Mills, McCaughey, Ken Stringfellow and Jamie Candiloro all playing keyboards, to which Buck added a beautiful E-Bowed guitar solo.

The first of *Reveal*'s gorgeously atmospheric ballads, 'I've Been High', comes next. This is the song containing the line 'Have I missed the big reveal?' which Bertis Downs liked so much that he suggested *Reveal* as the album title. "It's about capturing the perfect moment," says Buck. "I honestly don't know if 'I've Been High' is a real capture-the-moment thing, or someone thinking they're capturing the moment. It's kind of a sad-sounding song, so maybe the sadness has to do with the fact that it's not. You're supposed to read it and be distanced from it. That's one of the things that I like about his [Stipe's] writing."

Having started life as a demo called 'Glockenspiel', 'All The Way To Reno (You're Gonna Be A Star)' was transformed into one of R.E.M.'s most lush and blatantly commercial pieces of work. "Another instance of buying an instrument," is how Buck explained it to me.

"I go to this shop in Seattle and they know that I'm interested in whatever little weird oddities come in. Actually, a glockenspiel isn't that odd. It's kind of like a vibraphone, it looks like an old-fashioned lyre, and you play it with little sticks.

"It was a marching band glockenspiel, and I bought it and put it on every demo I did for about six weeks, and it drove everyone completely batshit. It was completely insane."

When I asked Mike Mills if it had been deliberately constructed to be commercial, he was quick to deny the charge. "Once we finished it I said it should be a single, but I think it poisons your ability to write and record and play songs if you are thinking 'Single!' beforehand. The bass line is one of my favourites. It just started from Peter's guitar parts and the bass line came to me right away. It was the first thing I played and it just seemed perfect. I love what Michael did with it."

'She Just Wants To Be' was the first song recorded for the album during the May 2000 sessions in Vancouver, probably because Stipe had written lyrics for it shortly after hearing Buck's original demo. "It was me on acoustic guitar," explained Buck to David Cavanagh of *Q*, "Mike on bass, Joey on drums and Michael singing. In the afternoon I put overdubs on. At the end of the first day, we had what sounded like a good song." Asked what the lyric is about, Buck has said that the subject matter is "a person – someone I think we've met".

'Disappear', originally demoed as 'Underwater Acoustic', starts out much like 'Swan Swan H' from *Life's Rich Pageant*, and then gets bitter. "I think there's a little bit of Michael's trip to Israel in there," reckons Buck. "It's about self-effacement, obviously." Intriguingly, Buck has also revealed a little bit of horse-trading that went on between Stipe and Thom Yorke of Radiohead as a result of this song. Stipe had learned that the new Radiohead album, *Kid A*, included a track called 'Disappear'. Anxious not to be seen as stealing someone else's song idea, he asked Yorke about it. Yorke replied, "I stole some lines from something you told me, so if you take anything from me, it's OK.'"

Buck told me that the version of 'Saturn Return' that appears on *Reveal* is actually the original demo. "It was just a weird series of chord changes, and I didn't really want anybody to know them. I kinda played through them once, built a loop, said, 'OK, we're gonna do 'em, everyone get the weirdest sounds they can, and we played along to the loop.' We did it once and once only. That was it. Then I gave it to Pat and said, 'Here it is. It's finished.'"

'Beat A Drum' was written and demoed in a sparse version at Dalkey

By the third verse, you wanted to slit your wrists

Lodge, but it was not recorded, and fleshed out with its distinctively Beach Boys-like instrumental parts until the Athens sessions in October. 'Imitation Of Life' has been discussed earlier, and then it's back to those Beach Boys sounds for the heat-hazed melancholy of 'Summer Turns To High'.

"That was one I wasn't sure I was going to show the band. It had so many chords," says Buck. This fact is reflected in its working title, '32-Chord Song'. "I didn't think it was right for how this record was going. But I just played it once and the band just fell in and played it amazingly well. At that point it was in 6/4 time and had a real Irish feel. It was acoustic guitars, accordions, really kind of a sea-shanty type thing with a ton of chords.

"Michael loved it, but it was too busy for him. So we stripped everything off, brought it down to just drums and bass and one keyboard, and then Michael threw this melody on top that pushed it completely out to left field."

Where 'Beat A Drum' went through dramatic changes, 'Chorus & The Ring', written and recorded in Vancouver, is a case of what you hear is what they played. "Peter just started playing it and we all joined in," explains Scott McCaughey. "Mike came into the room literally just in time to pick up his bass.

None of us had any idea what this song was." For proof, discerning listeners might care to listen closely on headphones. It has been said that Peter's voice can be heard faintly calling out the chords for Mills to follow.

The achingly pretty 'I'll Take The Rain', says Stipe, was the odd one out on this album. "*Reveal* was our summer record," he explains, adding that this track was, "the winter song, the only one. I wanted to write a lyric that matched the tone of the music, but I felt that the record needed something to balance all that sunniness."

The album closes with 'Beachball', yet another Beach Boys-inspired outing, which, strangely enough, started off as a song about junkies on the streets of Vancouver.

"You can score any kind of drug you want," says Buck. "The studio just overlooks it. We'd look out the window and see people dealing drugs, and every time I'd walk to the studio, someone would be going, 'I got the rocks. Valium.' I'm like, 'No, thank you. I've got a bit of work to do. Maybe I'll check back later.' Michael wrote this song about drugs."

Then, apparently, he changed his mind and, retaining just the opening phrase, 'Foggy seaside town', wrote something much more optimistic. According to Buck, it's about "these people having fun at the beach. The 'well-tequilaed guys who smile at strangers.' I find that line kind of threatening, personally. But then it ends, 'You'll do fine.' And I like the record ending with 'You'll do fine.' I tend to take that song at face value, that it is kind of an expression of joy."

Summing the album up, Stipe has said, "I think all of us would agree it represents a turning point for us. With this one I think that we've proven to ourselves that as a trio we can be a successful creative unit." Mills saw it as "more focused than the last album because we didn't have an ongoing crisis to contend with as we made it. We were free to concentrate on having fun. We produced a great album."

Celebrity fans of the album included Bono of U2: "Reveal is extraordinary. I know it's extraordinary because I felt ill when I heard it. It's a very beautiful, awe-inspiring record."

The critics tended to agree. *Rolling Stone* hailed its "ceaselessly astonishing beauty"; *NME* declared that its "lightness of touch means that *Reveal* is initially underwhelming but in time, gracefully rewarding"; the *Mail On Sunday* loved its "wonderful atmosphere, warm and sunny". Among the few dissenting voices was the newly established *Blender* magazine, whose reviewer said, "R.E.M. undoubtedly deserve credit for trying to redefine their sound, but fans will have to wait a little longer for the band's new direction to become an audible reality."

Once again, no doubt to Warners' dismay, they chose not to tour in support of the album. "We talked about it and in our minds we felt like we just did it," said Buck. "And I talked to friends of mine and they said 'It was great to see you play last summer' and I said, 'Well, actually it was a year and a half ago that we played', but it just seemed like it was really recently."

An extraordinary example of how little the news media knows about what's going on emerged just as the album was hitting the streets. In an interview with *Time* magazine, Michael Stipe mentioned that he had been "in a relationship with an amazing man" for about three years. This revelation rocketed around the world, trumpeted as Michael Stipe's "coming out".

In fact, Stipe had directly referred to his sexuality on a number of previous occasions. In 1994, for example, he'd described himself to *Rolling Stone* magazine as "an equal opportunity lech", adding that he had enjoyed sex with both men and women. As recently as July 2000 he'd told *Dazed And Confused* magazine, "As long as I've been sexually active, I've always been attracted to, and slept with, men and women. Right now, I've met an incredible man who is an artist, who I have completely committed myself to. So that's great."

One thing the *Time* magazine piece did get right, however, was an admirably concise physical description of the trio. "Stipe's bald, Buck's a little paunchy," wrote Christopher John Farley, "and Mills has that unsettling Bob Costas thing going on where he appears both boyish and middle-aged."

By May 16th, R.E.M. were back in the US, filming a video for 'All The Way To Reno' at Bishop Ford High School in Brooklyn, New York, with director Michael Moore. "He had the idea of doing a video about high school," said Bertis Downs, "and then to take it one step further by having the camera-operators and essential crew all be high school students. So it had a real fun feel to it, with Peter, Mike and Michael back in the gym, the lunchroom, the chemistry lab, the principal's office, and so forth. Once we got over the initial shock and remembered it was just pretend, it was a fun and different sort of day."

Meanwhile, Buck's air-rage trial was ticking along, requiring him to make inconvenient visits to the UK to appear in court. On June 18th, for example, he appeared in Uxbridge Magistrates Court and was ordered to return and stand trial in Isleworth Crown Court on July 31st, at which point he pleaded not guilty. At the trial itself, on November 13th, the judge dismissed the jury during the second day, without giving a reason. The re-trial was pushed forward into 2002.

Grammies and platinum records are one means of measuring success in the music industry. But one of the best indications that the public at large loves you is an appearance on *The Simpsons*. R.E.M. got their shot at animated immortality in the middle of June, when they went to Los Angeles to record their voiceovers for the show. The episode, which aired in November, featured a classic scene in which, after being lied to by Homer, Stipe threatens him with a broken beer bottle. But he is held back by Buck, who declares, "That's not the R.E.M. way!"

Stipe was in his apartment in Greenwich Village, New York, on September 11th and suddenly became aware of the chaos that was erupting all around. He looked out in time to see the second terrorist-controlled plane hit the World Trade Center, and immediately took to the street with his mobile phone lending it to anyone who required it to call family and friends. The horrors of that day would soon provoke an unexpected reaction in Stipe.

When the latest Tom Cruise movie, *Vanilla Sky*, was released, on December 14th, the soundtrack was graced with a little known R.E.M. song called 'All the Right Friends'.

Peter Buck told me, "Michael and I wrote that back in 1979. In the summer of 1980, maybe September, we had a whole set of songs like 'All The Right Friends': kind of first person, kind of naïve, maybe too many parts, because you don't really know what to do when you're first writing songs.

"When we were asked to do the *Vanilla Sky* soundtrack, we got the call about eight days before they needed it, to ask if we had anything sitting around in the can. We did have a couple of things, but they wanted a rocker, and our manager Bertis had always loved 'All the Right Friends', so he suggested we record it."

In the early part of 2002, as ever, Peter Buck was keeping himself busy with side projects, working on the Tuatara album, *Cinematheque*, the Bambi Molesters' album, *Sonic Bullets: 13 From the Hip*, and a new Minus 5 album. Stipe, meanwhile, contributed vocals to the *1 Giant Leap* project, a multi-cultural film and CD venture dreamed up by Jamie Catto of Faithless and his colleague Duncan Bridgeman.

Although there was still no tour on the horizon, R.E.M. did play a couple of benefit gigs. The first was at Carnegie Hall, New York, for the Gay Men's Health Crisis, on January 31st, along with Sutton Foster, Sweet Honey In the Rock and Jewel. A fortnight later, they turned out at the Kodak Theater in Los Angeles for Love Rocks, another charity fundraiser that also honoured Bono of U2 as humanitarian of the year for his work on debt relief.

Highlight of the show was a duet with Cher on 'I Got You Babe', featuring Stipe in the Sonny Bono role. Buck's air-rage re-trial finally got under way on March 4th in London, and rumbled on into the beginning of April.

It emerged that while in his cell after the incident, Buck had felt as if he was hallucinating. "There were bright lights overhead," he said. "I wasn't really awake. I had this fear I had had a heart attack and was in a weird hospital in Disneyland."

On March 25th, Buck's old mate (and humanitarian of the year) Bono turned up at Isleworth Crown Court to testify as a character witness, and the same supporting role was played by Stipe and Mills the following day. After five and a half hours of deliberation, the jury cleared Buck of all charges on April 5th.

Asked by *Billboard* in May whether the band had knocked any material for their next album into a decent shape, Stipe's response was a definitive, "Yes. No, Well, yes. No."

Bertis Downs, thankfully, clarified the position later in the month, saying, "They're certainly in the early creative stages, but they're not actually going to start working on the record till later in the year, and I don't think we'll put it out until next year." They did, in fact, spend a week during June doing groundwork in Athens with Scott McCaughey and Pat McCarthy, but Peter spent much of the summer and early autumn out on tour with Minus 5 and others.

The most encouraging news R.E.M. fans had heard in a long while came on October 3rd, when Mike Mills took part in a fund-raising gig for Georgia state senator Doug Haines at The 40 Watt. Sharing drum duties on the night were former Pylon sticksman Curtis Crowe and a certain Bill Berry. There were no R.E.M. songs in the set of nine covers, but Michael Stipe joined the band for a romp through The Turtles' 'Happy Together'. Might this be the start of Bill's return to a higher profile? Later in the month, amid rumours that a greatest hits package might be on the cards, R.E.M. returned to The Warehouse in Vancouver, and the sessions spilled over into November.

The big news, however, was saved for the last month of the year. It was announced that R.E.M. would be touring in summer 2003, with European festival dates to set the ball rolling, followed by US dates. The dates would be tied to the release of the recently rumoured hits CD.

On December 15th, to the delight of an audience that had paid $10 each to see Minus 5 at Richard's On Richards, a small club in Vancouver, R.E.M. took the stage during the intermission. They played a short set that included a new uptempo song, under the working title of 'Weatherman', suggesting that the next album might be more rock-orientated than *Reveal*.

The early part of 2003 was dominated by rumblings of a potential war with Iraq, as President George Bush, under the guise of his war against terrorism, fanned the flames of America's grief over the World Trade Center tragedy into reasons why Saddam Hussein should be ousted as leader of Iraq, which he claimed was secretly building "weapons of mass destruction".

Michael Stipe, for all his avowed intentions of restricting his political activities within a more personal framework, was unable to contain himself. "I can't believe that we're going to war," he said. "I still can't believe that we're a democracy and the President was voted in, in a non-democratic way, by the Supreme Court who were put in place by his father ... It's shooting fish in a barrel, isn't it?"

Joint US/UK military operations against Iraq began on March 19th, and R.E.M. made their position clear on March 25th by posting an angry new anti-war song, 'The Final Straw', on their official website.

"We had to send something out there now," said Stipe. "We are praying and hoping for the lives of all people involved – the troops, the Iraqi civilians, refugees, POWs, families of troops, the innocents – that they are safe and okay. Safe home, all."

On March 28th, R.E.M. announced full details of the 26-show, six-week US tour, set to begin on September 1st at Seattle's Bumbershoot Festival and end in Atlanta's Philips Arena on October 11th. Ruminating on the dilemma of whether to play huge arenas or small venues, Peter Buck felt that the band was between a rock and a hard place. "When *Reveal* came out, we played a whole lot of things to 50 to 100 people. But then, no one can get into those shows, so people complain about those, too." The reality of the situation, he decided, was that "if we play small places, that means we're going to be out for like eight months. At my age, I can't be away from my kids for that long. It's more ergonomically sound for us to do bigger-size places."

It was also around this time that Stipe offered a progress report on the new album. "I think we've got half of it in the can, and the other half needs to be reckoned with and it might be a little bit of a wrestling match," he estimated. "My charge is to find the time to just work on some of the songs while I have the adrenaline (of touring) coursing through me. It'll take a couple months to drop and that's not a good time to write songs."

Shortly after the band started rehearsing for the tour, on June 11th, Bill Berry turned up to tell them that he was now a fully qualified sushi chef as well as a farmer. Three days later they moved on to Europe to begin preparations for the first leg of the tour.

The Tivoli, an ancient theater with a capacity of just 1000, in Utrecht,

There were bright lights overhead. I wasn't awake

Holland, was the setting for the first show. "Kicking off to the most rapturous applause possible, the band went straight into 'Begin the Begin'," reported Steve McCarron of the *stayfun* website. "It had been four years since I last saw them live and I had forgotten the flamboyance of Stipe; his dress sense; his dancing. As much as I was looking forward to this concert, I hadn't considered what I was actually going to witness. Only one song was necessary to remind me how much of a rock star he actually is."

Two joyous nights at London's Brixton Academy preceded another headlining appearance at the Glastonbury Festival, where the encore of 'It's The End Of the World As We Know It' united the huge crowd (including me) into one surging mass of delighted humanity. Similarly ecstatic responses awaited them in Belgium, Germany, Switzerland, Poland, France and Italy, and this time, the band was capable of enjoying it all.

"We each have our rituals," pointed out Stipe. "Peter has to be at the show several hours in advance of going onstage. He gets really nervous … and plays guitar a lot to warm up his fingers. I go crazy if I'm reminded of what I'm going to have to do, so I take off on my bicycle. And about 30 minutes before I go onstage is when I lock the door and pace around. I focus on dumb things, like, 'God, I need to replace these shoelaces,' then slap on some makeup, have a smoke, and walk out. But I don't do vocal exercises or spit at the moon three times or anything like that. I just do it."

Although it had originally been announced that the US tour would start on September 1st, it actually kicked off from Vancouver's Thunderbird Stadium on August 29th. "The show threw some curve balls," wrote Jake Kramer of Vancouver *Indiemedia*, "with Radiohead's Thom Yorke on vocals for two songs, and with 'World Leader Pretend' being played for the first time since the *Out of Time* promotional junket in 1991."

"Man, it looked lovely, it felt wonderful, it sounded great," raved Phil Oats of the *Terminal City* website, but Thunderbird Stadium, like several venues on this outing, was far from full.

In Las Vegas, later in the month, Stipe was asked how he felt the tour was going. "It's been great. I had so much fun in Europe, even though it was gruelling," he said. "There were certain festivals that we really wanted to be at, and there were certain places that we wanted to play that weren't the easy obvious paths or choices to make. And so we crammed them into this six-week time period and it was really, really hard, especially on our crew, but I had a fantastic time.

"Even the bad shows, I look back on them, and the shows where I had a horrible time were usually the ones where the audience members were completely over the moon about what they just experienced."

On September 11th, with the tour still under way, Stipe revealed that the World Trade Center attack had had an unexpected effect on him and, by extension, on the new material the band was writing. "I tried really hard after the attack in New York two years ago today, to not write political songs. I kept trying and trying, and they just kept coming. So I decided that I was being stupid and just allowed them to come. And a lot of the new stuff is informed by that. That kind of outrage, not necessarily about the attack in New York, but how it was handled."

The moment R.E.M. fans had dreamed of for years came to pass on the drizzly night of October 10th, at Alltell Pavilion in Raleigh, North Carolina. Bill Berry stepped onto the stage with them, and Mike Mills welcomed him with a kiss on the cheek.

"We were all excited that Bill was coming to the show," said Stipe, "but no-one, I think Bill included, expected that he would jump on stage for even a shout-out, much less to play and sing with us. It was great and raw and spontaneous and I'm happy he was up there. I think Raleigh was a spur-of-the-moment thing that will not happen again. It was great to see him step off the tractor for one night under the lights."

In Time – The Best Of R.E.M. was released on October 28th, bringing together what the band considered to be the best of their material from the Warners era. "We didn't want to call it Greatest Hits or Best Of or The Very Special Collection," Buck told me.

"Believe me, I have a bunch of those. I mean, *Abba Gold*, I was the first person to buy that in a non-ironic manner, but I just kind of like the idea that we have been out of time for so many years and our record was called *Out Of Time*, it was our first big hit, so possibly this record is just *In Time*."

When I asked Stipe how much involvement the band had in selecting material for the compilation, he told me, "The band had everything to do with putting this compilation together. We went to a lot of different sources, from fan sites to our own fan club, to our office, to our friends and family, to our record company, to our contemporaries in other bands and said 'What R.E.M. song or songs would you want to hear on a greatest hits starting in the year 1988?' It was fairly consistent throughout; there were about two or three songs where we got to choose between one song or the other. But for the most part, everyone pretty much agrees."

Of the two "new" songs on the compilation, 'Bad Day' had in fact been started back in 1986. I asked Buck why it had taken so long to come to fruition. "When we were starting to do this 'best of' thing, we wanted some extra songs, and we didn't really know which way to go," he explained. "We have leftover songs from *Reveal* that we could put on without expending an iota of effort, but we decided to pick something from the past that we really liked but never finished properly."

Given the opportunity to work on the lyric again, Stipe realised it could be updated to have contemporary resonance. "We wound up with a song that spans two generations of American politics and comments on both and also in a way is an indictment of the media and their approach to politics," he said.

"The idea of news as hard news or news as entertainment, and where those two kind of cross, which is where we are at in the year 2003. It's now become just entertainment and the people that are kind of looked at as the experts and the talking heads on the news channels are really just entertainers."

The other previously unheard track, 'Animal', was genuinely brand new, and is perhaps another indication of where R.E.M. might be headed on their next album. "It's a super high octane rock song with really weird, discordant background vocals and strange guitar textures," said Buck. "It's real spontaneous. We listened to the demo tape once, played it through three times, and the track just sounded great. There isn't much overdubbing on it except the vocals and the guitar solo. It sounded like a real track immediately."

Shortly afterwards, Stipe told the *NME* that good progress was still being made towards the next album. "We're going back into the studio in January, and we have seven songs to finish before mid-January to present as possibilities for the next album. And we have six that we've already done. And there are another 13 I want to work on."

Bertis Downs has described some of the newer songs being worked on in Athens at the start of 2004 as "lush and atmospheric", and even revealed a few tentative titles, including 'Magnetic North', 'I Wanted to Be Wrong', 'Around the Sun' and 'Wanderlust'.

There are many ways to measure a band's popularity – record sales, platinum discs, their cars, their designer suits, their country mansions, the women around them. With R.E.M., however, popularity has never been the right word, because that's not what they've courted.

Maybe the word should be impact, or influence, because R.E.M. are one of the few bands who can genuinely claim to have affected the lives of their listeners. On one very simple level, in a review of *Dead Letter Office* on the *epinions* website, the reviewer recalls how, "Every time they mentioned an artist in an interview, they turned out to be terrific. I got Jason and the Scorchers and Pylon from singer Michael Stipe, Rank and File and Dream Syndicate from drummer Bill Berry, the dB's and Love Tractor from bassist Mike Mills and the Replacements and Husker Dü from guitarist Peter Buck."

On another level, Stipe's lyrics, intelligible or otherwise, have always provoked listeners to think about the world they inhabit, and simultaneously provided a fantasy landscape where dreamers can roam free. Even a self-evident and commonplace juxtaposition of the two words 'Everybody Hurts' has provided comfort and solace for millions.

Back in the real world, R.E.M.'s record of participation in and practical support for humanitarian organizations and ecologically-motivated causes stands as a shining example of how rock'n'roll can change the world for the better. All of these achievements are on a planetary scale, but one of the things that seems to make R.E.M. happiest is having helped the town where they began. Right in the middle of town is The Grit, a much-loved vegetarian hangout with an 1800s shopfront. Owned and restored by Stipe, it's just one of several buildings bought and saved from destruction by R.E.M. and, like them, it plays its part in the community.

When Stipe summed up the state of the band at the time of the hits album, he said, "Things haven't been this good for a long time." Anyone who knew anything about R.E.M. knew he wasn't talking about record sales or concert grosses. He was talking about their relationship to each other. Stipe and Mills still live in Athens. Berry farms the land nearby and, although no longer an R.E.M. member, he remains a beloved friend. Buck now lives in Seattle, which he obviously loves, but is still a frequent visitor to Athens. Since the days at St Mary's, they've faced obstacles that would have destroyed most bands, and come out the other end stronger for it.

"Right now, I'm thinking it could last for a while," said Buck at the start of 2004. "But I also sometimes wake up at four in the morning in a hotel and I can't sleep and I haven't seen my family in a couple of weeks and I just think, 'Ya know I could go home right now and be OK.'" Indeed he could – but, so far, he never has done.

"The word that has been synonymous with R.E.M. since the start is integrity," says Stipe. "And you can break it down as much as you like but we're bull-headed and stubborn and we won't do anything we don't want to do. We just won't compromise our ideas; that's always been a very basic tenet of R.E.M. It's not easy to be so uncompromising, to keep a band going for 19 years and sell records and produce work you're so proud of. It's a sterling combination of stubbornness and creativity."

INDEX
ACKNOWLEDGEMENTS

AUTHOR'S THANKS

Grateful thanks to all those who agreed to be interviewed for this book, including Michael Stipe, Peter Buck, Mike Mills, Bertis Downs, Stephen Hague, Kelly Pike, Kurt Munkacsi, Billy Bragg, Andy Gill, Ian Copeland, Robin Hitchcock, Jason Ringenberg, Stewart Cruikshank, and Chris Eckman. And a very special mention to Peter Case, for agreeing to be interviewed, even though I managed spectacularly to screw up our arrangements.

Great big huge thanks to John Morrish for editing and keeping me on track without shouting; and of course Tony Bacon for asking me to do this book. Thanks also to Nigel Osborne, Mark Brend and John Ryall at Backbeat. More thanks to Martin Aston, Rhiannon Brewer-Patrick, Paul Connolly, David Fricke, Clark Collis, Rick Cornell, Andy Cowan, Anthony De Curtis, Jim De Rogatis, David John Farinella, Eric Flaum, Andy Gill, Brendan Gilmartin, Caroline Gracey, Sid Griffin, John Harris, Robert Hilburn, Barney Hoskyns, Bruce Kirkland, Dorian Lynskey, Toby Manning, Marianne Meyer, Bret Milano, Parke Puterbaugh, Scott Rosen, Sandy Robertson, Jon Savage, Sylvie Simmons, Mat Snow, Denise Sullivan, Adam Sweeting.

AUTHOR'S SOURCES
BOOKS

The following books, each of which I heartily recommend, provided all kinds of insight, factual information and cross-check confirmation about R.E.M., without which this book would have been much less interesting.

Billboard Book Of No.1 Albums.
Dave Bowler & Bryan Dray *Documental* (Boxtree 1995).
Rodger Lyle Brown *Party Out Of Bounds* (Plume 1991).
David Buckley *Fiction* (Virgin 2003).
Marcus Gray *It Crawled From The South: An R.E.M. Companion* (4th Estate 1992).
Oliver Gray *Volume* (Sarsen 2000).
Jacob Hoye (editor) *MTV Uncensored* (Pocket Books 2001).
Rob Jovanovic & Tim Abbott *Adventures In Hi-Fi* (Orion 2001).
Eric Olsen, Paul Verna & Carlo Wolff *The Encyclopaedia of Record Producers* (Billboard 1999).
Craig Rosen *R.E.M. Inside Out* (Carlton 1997).
Denise Sullivan *Talk About The Passion* (Charles F. Miller 1994).
Virgin Year Book 1993-94.

PERIODICALS

Needless to say (but I'm delighted to say it anyway) I gleaned all kinds of useful info and double-checked facts by reference to a number of periodicals, including: *Augusta Chronicle, Billboard, Blender, The Bob, Bucketful Of Brains, Chicago Sun-Times, Creem, Dazed & Confused, Details, Encore, Entertainment Weekly, Georgia Magazine, Goldmine, The Guardian, Guitar Player, Guitarist, Hot Press, The Independent Magazine, The Los Angeles Times, Melody Maker, Mix, Mojo, Music Monitor, Music Week, New Musical Express, Newsweek, New York Post, The*

Observer, Option, Premiere, Pulse, Q, Rock CD, Rolling Stone, Select, Sueddeutsche Zeitung, Shakin' Street, Song Talk, Sounds, Spin, The Sunday Times, The Toronto Sun, Trouser Press, Uncut, Varsity Review, Vox, The Washington Post.

WEBSITES

Websites too are another source of invaluable facts, and I visited all of the following addresses in the course of writing this book. As someone who trawls through rock-band websites on a daily basis, I'd like to make the point that R.E.M.-specific sites are, on the whole, astonishingly well done, with a great deal of care and attention that I don't see in every site I visit.

www.remtimeline.com

www.rem-fan.com

www3.murmurs.com

www.remrock.com

www.Rem4u.com.ar

www.geocities.com/SoHo/Studios/4608/asinfo/eponymous.html

http://home.netcom.com/~dperle/music/r-e-m.html

http://users.pandora.be/grand_royal/REM/

http://farmerboybill.tripod.com/unofficialbillberrysite/id7.html

wnw.daylightonline.com/financial/REM.htm

www.stud.ntnu.no/~turidbro/date.html

www.geocities.com/SunsetStrip/Stage/9208/

http://news.shopeasier.com/files/shopeasier_Michael_Stipe.html

www.geocities.com/mattrking/quicklist.html

http://headlines.wlrw.com/nmc/artists/rem/news.html

http://home.online.no/~smogols/remshowshtm/1983rems.htm

www.thei.aust.com/music2/remnantsdex.html

www.remison.com/main/index.php

www.onr.com/user/julie/rem/links.html

http://members.lycos.co.uk/undertow/manchester.html

www.kolumbus.fi/timo.klimoff/remnews.html

www.gamusichall.com/athens.htm

www.angelfire.com/80s/mikemills/mainout.html

www.onlineathens.com

www.40watt.com

http://indyweek.com

www.hybridmagazine.com

www.mitchworldusa.com

www.praxisrecordings.com

http://charlotte.creativeloafing.com

www.nyrock.com

www.hereinmyhead.com/musicians/stipe.html

www.bbc.co.uk

www.nme.com

www.cnn.com

www.bayarea.net/~teelk/velvet/awards.htm

www.neumu.net/inquisitive/rem/inquisitive-rem_06.html

PICTURE CREDITS

The photographs reproduced came from the following sources, listed here by location or page number. Jacket front: Mick Hutson/Redferns; jacket rear: Ebet Roberts/Redferns; 2/3 Rex Features; 7 Ebet Roberts/Redferns; 17 Ebet Roberts/Redferns; 28/29 Terry Allen; 42/43 Terry Allen; 54/55 Terry Allen; 68/69 Rex Features; 82/83 Ebet Roberts/Redferns; 96/97 Pictorial Press; 109 Rex Features; 121 Ebet Roberts/Redferns; 133 Graham Tucker/Redferns; 144/145 Rex Features; 159 Pictorial Press; 170/171 Michel Linssen/Redferns; 184/185 Michel Linssen/Redferns; 199 Paul Bergen/Redferns; 213 Rex Features; 227 Ebet Roberts/Redferns; 241 Paul Bergen/Redferns; 253 Paul Bergen/Redferns.

"The beauty of music is that it's so open to the interpretation of the listener. The intent of the writer is so much less important than the interpretation of the listener."
MICHAEL STIPE